2—

Gambling

The Complete Illustrated Guide to
Gambling

Alan Wykes

Doubleday & Company Inc.
Garden City, New York

Library of Congress Catalog Card No. 64-18632
The author wishes to express his gratitude
to everyone who assisted him to gather the
factual information contained in this book
and in particular to
Dave Billington; Willie Brandon; Lt. Col.
P. R. Butler; Dennis Castle; Watt
Fenton; Charles M. Glover; Alexander
H. Howard; The Hon. Lady Hulton; John
Kings; the late Benno Moiseiwitsch, C.B.E.;
Matthew Norgate; Reginald Pound; Maurice
Richardson; John Russell; Dr. William
Sargant; Fritz Schneider; F.O. Taylor;
Mr. Tilley, Assistant Archivist of Thomas De
La Rue Ltd.; Arland Ussher; John Waters.

Acknowledgment is due to J. M. Dent & Sons
Ltd., London, for permission to quote from
Joseph Conrad's "The End of the Tether."

Printed in Jugoslavia

Contents

1 The gambler and his motives

Gambling is a way of buying hope on credit. We are all the bonded slaves of the management that issues the credit cards. To realize the completeness of our bondage we have only to remember that each of us owes his existence to the chancy collaboration of two small fertile organisms; while an apparently chancy distribution of chromosomes, genes, and hormones influences our sex, coloring, and disposition. We press on through life toward a death whose manner and date depend entirely on chance. During our womb-to-tomb progress we never stop gambling, for we cannot know the outcome of each of the many decisions we have to make every day; we can only "hope for the best."

Even a man who sets out deliberately to free himself from the grip of chance is going to have a thin time. He can stop smoking because of the risk of lung cancer; he can give up alcohol for fear of damaging his liver; he can stay indoors to avoid the hazards of travel; he can keep his money in an old sock to avoid the risk of losing it. But if he carries his apprehensions to logical conclusions he will atrophy in bed, while his risk-taking nephew grabs the sock, spends the money on riotous living, and dies happily at the age of 94. With chance, as with many things, there is little justice.

Sensible people don't expect justice from chance. If they did, they would give up breeding children in a world that can't support them; they would not drink before driving or speed when sober; they would choose selfless leaders instead

of maniacs. As it is, they propagate *ad libitum,* have a last drink for the road, and risk everything on the leadership of a Genghis Khan or a Hitler.

In 1949—to press home my point about the injustice of chance—a man was haranguing the multitude at England's Ascot racecourse. His purpose was sincere: to discourage the gamblers. He had set up an iron-railed podium under a sheltering tree and had attracted an amused crowd. While he ranted away with many an apocalyptic gesture, black clouds gathered and heavy rain began. He turned the storm to his advantage. "The wrath of God is made manifest," he boomed. "The heavens are displeased by the evil of gambling." Perhaps, however, the heavens were more displeased by the lecturer's presumption. As the storm built up and the audience scattered to shelter, lightning struck the tree and the iron rail of the podium and gave the anti-gambler severe shock and burns.

Statesmen are for the most part thought of as cautious people. But every international conference is hedged about with the risks of crackpot challenges and diplomatic bluffs. And it would have been impossible to advance even to our present state of world relations without political leaders chancing their arms. Guillaume Dubois, a court favorite during the reign of Louis XIV, sought England's help in shoring up the crumbling morale of his decadent country. In doing so he risked his own somewhat pockmarked career and the future of France. But his gamble led to the first *entente cordiale* among England, France, and Holland, and eventually gained him an archbishopric, a cardinal's red hat, and appointment as prime minister. Today, statesmen hold the destruction of the world at arm's length by risky diplomatic maneuvers that offer odds that few steady gamblers would accept.

Inevitably, then, we ourselves gamble, and we entrust our future to the hands of gamblers. But in this book I am not especially concerned with our unavoidable daily risks as we cross a busy street or cast a vote. I *am* concerned with one of the most persistent—and perhaps forgivable—of human failings: The

Dedicated gamblers can always find something to gamble on. In these scenes from the French film *The Sheep Has Five Legs* (1954), gamblers turn from cards and dice to a more off-beat gamble—betting on which of two cubes of sugar a fly will land on first. Far left, the gamblers' excitement as the fly hovers between the cubes (left) before finally settling on one of them (right).

pleasure that so many of us take in placing bets, however small or large, on the uncertain outcome of events.

The paraphernalia of the gambler is varied and extensive. Cards, dice, mahjongg tablets, rings, and many another cryptic shape or design; animals of every kind (from insects to primates) in competitive events; men and women in every manifestation of human conflict; pawnbrokers' tickets in squalid back-street shops or ticker-tape machines in Wall Street; airplanes, motorcars, and water craft; electric hares, computing machines, newspapers, and telephones; wheels to spin and drums to mix lottery tickets; firearms, slot machines, matchsticks. One could go on interminably. The point is that all this apparatus merely offers variety of interest and a chance to develop skill. None of it is strictly necessary.

Determined gamblers will bet on which of two raindrops will first reach the bottom of a window pane, or on the number of hairs growing on a hirsute mole. Nor need the stakes necessarily be financial or even useful. The 16th-century English historian Stow reports that one Sir Miles Partridge played at dice with King Henry VIII for the bells of St. Paul's Church, and won them. The annals of the town of Chester le Street, in the north of England, record that in 1735, "a child of James and Elizabeth Leesh was played for at cards by Henry and John Trotter, Robert Thomson and Thomas Ellison, won by the latter pair and delivered to them accordingly." From China in the fourth century B.C. comes a poem telling the story of two gamblers who, having nothing else to stake, bet their ears on which side of a birch leaf would lie uppermost after its fall from the tree; the loser honorably severed the lobes of his ears and presented them on the leaf to the winner.

The annals of gambling are full of such anecdotes—some spectacular, some not. All of them substantiate the fact that there must be complex motives behind such compulsive urges to lose (which is what those of us who gamble a great deal inevitably do in the long run).

Left, desert Arabs using stones as pieces, and depressions in the sand as a board, in a form of *dara*—a gambling game (resembling ticktacktoe) popular throughout Africa. Right, a baccarat table in France's Deauville casino. Though the setting is far removed from desert stones and sand, the fascination of a game of chance remains the same.

Incidentally, there is no evidence to suggest that gambling is a natural instinct. The games of very young children are purely competitive and carry no reward but triumph and, occasionally, token "prizes." The competitive spirit apparently is born with the baby; but fascination with the elements of risk and the chance of gain develops later in the child's life, and therefore seems to be an extra provided by experience. In other words, gambling, in the sense of placing bets, is apparently part of a cultural pattern (though an exceedingly ancient one).

Why, then, do people gamble? What is it that makes the placing of a bet and the awaiting of its outcome so very exciting to most of us? It isn't easy to answer these questions. You won't find the answers by trying to observe your own reactions to the turning wheel at Monte Carlo; you'll soon be far too busy observing the *wheel*. But change the ethnological scene, and watch a couple of Africans playing *mbao* (a game with board and pieces, like chess, and involving some skill); you will witness a scene of emotional intensity, the players' eyes rolling and limbs jerking as they prostrate themselves and make appeals to gods of fortune. (But in this case the stakes are likely to be higher than you'd play for—a favorite wife, perhaps, or a herd of goats.)

In neither Monte Carlo nor the African bush, though, will you discover exactly what lies behind the fascination exerted by the whimsical turns of fortune. Actually, it is more than mere fascination for the really confirmed gambler; it is a necessity. Those of us who think ourselves jaunty devils whenever we place

a small bet on a horse certainly feel excitement; we yell as loudly as anyone else when our horse makes a final spurt for the post. But such exhilaration isn't so demanding that we would fling our families into penury to repeat it.

In the long history of gambling, there are countless cases of people who have done just that. Dostoevski, for example. He was in the clutches of gambling mania from 1862 to 1872. It was impossible for him to resist roulette as long as he had a penny in his pocket. His life with his second wife, Anna Grigorievna Snitkina, was a limping progress from one moneylender to another. Sometimes the moneylenders were friends and publishers, sometimes perfect strangers or pawnbrokers. Whoever they were, the repayments (when made) kept the writer and his wife in continual poverty. Yet he fed like a leech on the masochistic pleasure gambling gave him.

In her diary, Anna describes a typical scene: "He returned, having of course lost everything, and said he wanted to talk to me. He took me on his knee and began to beseech me to give him another five louis. He said he knew that that would leave us only seven louis and that we should have nothing to live on; he knew everything, but what was to be done? In no other way could he calm himself; he said that if I did not give him the money he would go off his head. . . . He begged me not to deprive him of the possibility of reproaching himself for his insane weakness, begged my pardon for heaven knows what, said he was unworthy of me, that he was a knave and I an angel, and so forth. . . . I could scarcely quiet him."

Dostoevski is only one of thousands on record as having towed their loved ones through the mud of poverty to satisfy an irrepressible urge to lose money. But finding the motive behind such an urge is no easy task. Ask a chronic gambler why he gambles, and you'll get a frosty answer. Naturally he sees no reason why he should explain, even if there is an explanation at hand, which is in most cases improbable.

To test my shaky faith in gamblers' knowledge of their own motives, I recently singled out 128 inveterate (as opposed to occasional) gamblers—all known to me personally. To each I sent a questionnaire—perhaps it should have been called a suggestionnaire—that suggested eight possible reasons for excessive gambling and invited the recipients to indicate any that they felt might apply to others if not themselves (an invitation designed to relieve the exercise of its resemblance to a confessional). The reasons I suggested were:

1. The acquisition of unearned money—i.e., a form of greed.
2. Social cachet—or, more bleakly, snobbery.
3. Sexual compensation.
4. Masochism.
5. Boredom: the refuge of an empty mind.
6. Intellectual exercise.
7. The desire to prove one's superiority to the forces of chance.
8. Inexplicable excitement.

This portrait of Fëdor Dostoevski was painted by the Russian artist V. G. Perov in 1872, when the novelist was 51. In a letter written four years later (right), Dostoevski thanked his friend and contemporary, the author Ivan Turgenev, for lending him 50 taler (about $36). This was one loan that Dostoevski, an inveterate gambler, paid back: At the foot of the letter is a note from Turgenev acknowledging repayment.

A quick riffling through the replies to the suggestionnaire confirmed my suspicion that only reasons 6 and 8 would be seen by the recipients as applicable to themselves. Reasons 1 (greed) and 2 (snobbery) were attributed to gamblers other than the recipients. Reasons 3 (sexual compensation) and 4 (masochism) got me nothing but some unprintably ribald comments. And only a very few respondents even bothered to consider 5 (boredom) or 7 (the desire to prove one's superiority to the forces of chance).

So much for my own probing (though I shall be returning to it later, to prove how seriously based its premises were). One might as well ask a pyromaniac why he finds so much joy in fire. An objective investigation is needed, based on a knowledge of the human mind. Inevitably, one turns to the psychologist and the psychiatrist.

In the early part of the 19th century, a Swedish doctor, Erik Kröger, set up what he called a "study spa" in Zürich and began collecting drunks and compulsive gamblers. A report on his observations, which he sent to a medical colleague, is enlightening (I have straightened out the doctor's somewhat difficult English):

"I now have my inebriates separated from my gamblers. Each room has a spyhole so that I can watch them unobserved. . . . I found my gamblers in Wiesbaden, where they had been thrown out of various gambling houses for unpaid debts and quarrelsome natures. One of them is greedy (he plays only

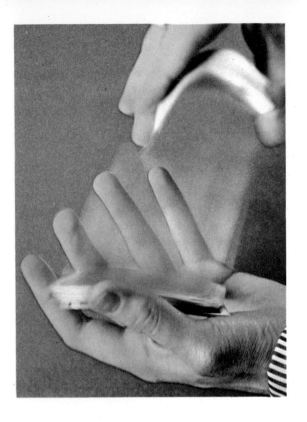

for small stakes and snatches his winnings impatiently); another clever and conceited, for he plays only games in which he can prove his own intellectual supcriority; another so empty-headed that he can give his mind to nothing but cards and can't understand even the simplest book; and yet another crazy with superstition, making him amusing to watch as he performs his ceremonies of mumbo-jumbo, rising from his chair and encircling it, bowing and whispering to his cards and dice, and working out complex formulae to control his luck. There are also two who display symptoms of great emotion—tearing their hair, grinding their teeth, and shrieking out in passion whether they win or lose. They will continue in this manner sometimes for 48 hours before falling into an exhausted sleep."

Unfortunately, Dr Kröger's studies petered out when the law gripped him for confining people against their wills. But, given the chance, he might have got in ahead of Freud with a study of one particular kind of behavior. In any case, he apparently uncovered at least three of the motives I suggested to my gambling friends—greed, boredom, and the desire to prove oneself superior to the forces of chance.

Freud, when he came along, suggested that sexual compensation was very much at the back of the gambler's urges. "The fluttering movements of a card dealer's hands," he wrote, "the thrust and withdrawal motions of the croupier's rake, and the shaking of the dice box can all be identified with sublimations of copulation or masturbation."

Freud saw sublimations of sexual acts in many typical gambling movements and gestures: in cupped hands riffling cards or throwing dice, and even in the croupier's rake reaching out for chips on a roulette table.

As we all know, Freud had an unsettling tendency to find sexual symbols in almost everything. But his idea has been supported by evidence from a good many later psychiatrists. Three whom I have questioned produced among them seven case histories involving marriages that had gone adrift—all of them featuring husbands who were heavy and insistent gamblers, five of them arraigned by their wives for sexual frigidity. One psychiatrist told me: "Of course I'm not saying that gambling is a consciously selected alternative to sexual activity; but it can be an outlet for sexual activity that has been frustrated—for any of a dozen reasons—in its normal form. Compulsive gamblers *do* exhaust themselves emotionally, and evidence sifted from a good many case histories suggests that they also incline to sexual frigidity."

Dostoevski wrote to his wife that he actually experienced orgasm on losing (not winning, please note) a large sum at roulette one night. And the American psychologist Robert M. Lindner has written a paper on "The Psychodynamics of Gambling" in which he cites the case of one of his own patients whose symptoms almost exactly paralleled Dostoevski's, and whose motive, Lindner found upon analysis, was simply a more satisfying alternative to masturbation caused by childhood frustrations. Chronic gamblers, Lindner states, "seem all to be strongly aggressive persons with huge reservoirs of unconscious hostility and resentment. . . ." Another psychiatrist, Ralph Greenson, says: "The gambler masochistically enjoys his fear of losing and continues it as long as possible, because when he leaves the table or racecourse to take up his ordinary life some

An 18th-century English gambling house, as depicted in William Hogarth's *The Rake's Progress*. The artist stresses the sordidness —the drinking and brawling, the gamblers gloating over wins, or (like the rake himself in the foreground) bewailing losses.

really intolerable fear awaits him; the smaller fear of losing his money is by comparison a pleasure. The mock struggle is a sublimation of a real struggle."

Difficult though it is to find people who would care to admit to such motives, even supposing they were aware of them, one occasionally glimpses dark streaks of self-revelation that bear out the analysts' findings. As, for instance, in an odd document by one Richard Minster, a 17th-century upper-class English felon who was beheaded for a long series of crimes and who records, in part, in his confession:

"One night during Epiphany I suffered my most grievous loss of money in the whole of my damned life, and was forced to return to the world which I am now to be quit of by my own damnation.

"During that sennight I had lost and recouped and lost again, and was much of an evenness in my reckoning. My harlot's jewels that she valued were gone, but in a flux of generosity I had bought her more and lain with her and ravished her in my joy and her lewdness. But ever the craze was upon me like a grumbling illness and perforce I went forth again on the Saturday minded to lose all I possessed. Lose! I say—for in my recollections there lurked the feeling of a beast, a fornicator suffering a virgin to take his whim, at each toss of the dice that lost me a fortune; a mounting turmoil within me, retarded each time by a winning throw . . . .

"I played with Mountgarde and Hilbery and gained ninety guineas from them in an hour, taking their notes because they were penniless. . . . My winnings sullened me, and in despair I raised my stake. Still I won. And so in the main it went on through the night. At one moment I had upward of fifty thousand guineas owed me, and still I went on, throwing scarce a losing die in all that time.

"The room was in a hubbub of calls of Deuce! Trey! and the like. All of us had taken off our greatcoats and laid up our swords and the room was heady with the wine fumes and tallow. It was a wild scene of depravity and in its midst I stood surrounded for my fortune, some of the players touching me and rushing back to their own tables to see how their luck fared then. I felt as though marching at some great triumph against fortune. But in my heart I was despairing, for I was winning a battle I sought to lose.

"But at last, toward morning (so I think; the notion of time was not with me) I gathered up my winnings—notes, gold, jewels, perukes, and all that the losers had been able to summon to their aid in their losses and cried to them to hear my last stake.

"I lost on the throw and can scarce describe the feeling of relief that overcame me. It was like a solvent to the harsh world to which I must now return."

It can hardly be denied, then, that gambling often gratifies a basic emotional or sexual urge. I am convinced that this type of satisfaction is more often sought (whether consciously or unconsciously) by the dedicated gambler than is material gain. For him, the winnings are a bonus added to the excitement of the gamble itself. Indeed, his *losses* may be equally a bonus. I believe that in the gamblers' world only the professional cheats and swindlers (such as Arnold Rothstein, who has a forthcoming appearance in this book) are motivated by avarice.

Of course, one occasionally comes across a really grasping character in gambling as elsewhere—the man who, having won a hundred thousand in a lottery, will sell his story to a newspaper for a few hundred more, even though the publicity can only bring beggars in droves to his door; or the skilled poker player who will ruthlessly take your last penny, not because he enjoys the game but because he enjoys counting his winnings. But these are not true gamblers. The true gambler is notoriously open-handed. It is certainly hard to see how such addicts as Dostoevski and Richard Minster could be motivated by greed, when they kept hammering away at the excitement that they invariably gained by *losing* money.

A wish for social cachet—keeping up with the Joneses—can be a motive in some forms of gambling (though, I suspect, a very minor motive). Football pools (forecasting the results of a number of matches) have been fashionable in northern Europe since 1933 and in Australia since 1940; and in many places *bingo* (a numbers game based on the lottery idea) is now edging up to the football pool in popularity. This may be at least partly because of the social advantages of doing what one's neighbors do. For instance:

A London carpenter named Francis Connolly, who won about £13,000 from a football pool in 1961, told reporters: "My wife and I don't care much about money, but it will probably come in useful in the future. We have no intention of moving. Neighbors are the most important thing in the world, and I reckon I've got the best I'll ever find. Anyway, I only did the pools because they did."

To move on to motive 5 in my suggested list: Because every kind of risk-taking is exciting in some degree, there is a strong probability that a good many of us do gamble as a refuge from boredom. One respondent to my suggestion-naire wrote: "It was certainly boredom in the first place that sent me to the poker table. While I was in the army, I suppose I had a completely empty mind, and when I saw a game going I joined in. I'd never even played cards before, except kids' games, and I'd certainly never gambled beyond an office sweep ticket. But after that I never looked back. Boredom certainly started it with me, and I sometimes think I go on because I'm still bored with life in general." But though boredom may drive some people to gamble in the first place, they would probably drop it quickly if they didn't eventually find more positive satisfactions in it.

Intellectual exercise, for instance. Surely such a splendid game as poker (which involves, among other skills, a knowledge of psychology) provides a man with plenty of brain-tingling activity. Or a woman, for that matter.

Incidentally, lots of women have been—and still are—more than a match for men at the gaming tables. The Greek biographer Plutarch mentions Parysatis, queen of Persia, who diced for the life of a slave and, after winning him, had him tortured to death. The English novelist and playwright Oliver Goldsmith writes of an old lady who on her deathbed played cards with the curate and, having won all his money, went on to play him for the costs of her own funeral. Her continued winnings gained her a much grander burial than she would otherwise have been able to afford. Between these two extremes, women abound in the field of gambling as thick as leaves in Vallombrosa. But save for one possibility, there doesn't seem to be any strong case for thinking they might be motivated differently from men.

That possibility is my suggested gambling motive number 7: the desire to prove one's superiority to the forces of chance. In this motivation I think women may have the edge on men. Capricious creatures themselves, they may well be fascinated by the so-called caprices of fortune, and may enjoy some close in-fighting with them. (Not for nothing is fortune supposed to be a god*dess*.) Of course, some women ignore the fact that the laws of probability take no heed of the sex of the gambler. They have their illogical fancies and may often

Not only rich prizes entice crowds into mass gambling like bingo (above). The fact that "everybody's doing it" is an added attraction, especially for bored housewives.

Women, of course, were gambling long before bingo appeared. Below, a fourth-century B.C. mirror case depicts the Greek goddess of love dicing with the god Pan.

be found backing a horse for the color of its jockey's shirt or a boxer for the color of his eyes. A hunch that pays off reinforces the women's belief in their own intuition; one that fails tends to be taken as a personal affront from another woman, and they gird themselves up for battle accordingly. On the other hand, a considerable number of women gamblers take a strictly "professional" approach. Ignoring "intuition," they attack with expertise; if their game is horse racing, they are vastly knowledgeable about horses' and jockeys' past records. Others may "play the percentages" in casinos; as an American friend once told me, "the hardest eyes and the coolest brows around a Las Vegas craps table belong to the women."

The gambler's motives are only a part of the psychological story. His superstitions and passions bear looking into as well.

All superstitions are derived from attempts to placate supernatural forces, and most of them are hangovers from days when man was a sight more credulous than he is now. Salt, it says in the Bible (2 Chronicles XIII:5), is a covenant, a bond of union between two people; the spilling of it therefore is unlucky. To primitive societies, the life-giving force of the sun wasn't inexhaustible, and therefore too many demands should not be made upon it. Hence, in Africa and Asia umbrellas achieved importance in diminishing those demands; because of their relation to the divine sun, they must never be raised in so earthly a place as a dwelling.

In several ancient civilizations ladders were believed to assist the souls of the dead up to the sky; to pass beneath one might hinder the spirit's progress. Mirrors were supposed to contain the soul of the reflected person; to break one would be to make the breaker soulless. The sanctity of certain numbers (especially 3, 7, 13, and 70) derives in the main from fertility and other rites connected with seasonal changes, the moon's phases, and other natural phenomena.

Since gamblers are continuously at the mercy of fortune (which some people can't help regarding as a supernatural force), they tend to be liberal with their observance of superstitious ritual, though usually without knowing the original significance of a particular routine. At cards or dice, you may carefully rise and walk around your chair to change your luck, but do you know that in effect you're describing a magic circle to fence out evil spirits? And when you blow on the cards or dice—as who doesn't—you are trying, essentially, to blow the breath of life back into a failing corporeality. The charms or tokens many gamblers wear or carry are precisely the same in purpose as the amulets of the Egyptians: They have precious qualities because they're made of a rare substance or are in the form of revered creatures.

Most of us prop up our frail resistance to misfortune by wishful thinking, "hoping for the best." But the dedicated gambler needs to be triply sure. In games in which skill is involved he can increase his skill and minimize his losses; but in games of pure chance he can do nothing but work out a scientific

Many gamblers wear lucky charms, but they can be as useless as the figurine in the hatband of this racetrack loser (from a 19th-century British drawing).

"system" designed to beat the laws of probability. Or he can ease himself over difficult bumps in his luck by distributing his faith among various words, actions, or tokens that were associated with success in the past, even if it was someone else's success (just as all the players in the room rushed over to touch Richard Minster when he was winning, presumably to draw off some of his luck like an electric charge).

Apart from the magic circle round the chair, and blowing on cards and dice, there are no superstitions especially associated with gambling. Each of us naturally tries to achieve his own personal harbinger of luck. One eccentric character named Blanchard won a big coup at Monte Carlo after a passing pigeon had soiled his hat. After that he went every season and strolled around waiting for another pigeon. One eventually came, too, and he won even more. But after that, nothing. So he never entered the casino again. All he left was a tradition that birds' droppings on one's clothes are lucky.

Some people won't play if they see a black cat on their way to a game; others won't play if they don't. (Cats are variously sacred and diabolical—sacred because of their associations with Egypt and China, where they were godlike beings guarding the granaries, and diabolical because of their links with witches, whose *alter egos* they were once supposed to be.) Crazes for mascots afflict places like Las Vegas and Monte Carlo from time to time, and any player who has been fortunate while owning a mascot isn't likely to let it out of his sight.

As for passions: The fearful uncertainties of the gambler's pursuit, plus the excitement and strain generated during play, are great revealers of temperament. There are gamblers who remain apparently unmoved while winning or losing vast sums, but the likelihood is that the deadpan mask conceals turmoil within—because the turmoil *is* gambling.

Often the turmoil breaks the surface of reasonable behavior. Henry I of England gambled on a game of chess with Louis I of France when both were in their princeling days, and because Louis was losing heavily he rose in passion and called Henry the son of a bastard, adding injury to insult by flinging the board in his face. Henry then cracked Louis over the head, splitting the scalp open, and would have finished the French heir off completely if some of the onlookers hadn't intervened. This unprincely fracas started a chain of events and exchanges that led to war.

Also among top people who have started wars by passionate insults at the gaming table were the dukes of Lorraine and Orléans. Lorraine slapped Orléans' face during a game of cards, and the direct result of this quarrel was one of those long, mad wars that rumbled through the provinces of France during the 15th century. When the duke of Orléans eventually came to the throne of France as Louis XII, he was recorded as saying, "A king of France does not avenge insults offered to a duke of Orléans"—a remark he intended to be loftily insulting rather than forgiving.

The French newspaper *Gazette de Deux-Ponts,* which seems to have had a roving reporter in Naples, reported in 1772 the case of a Neapolitan card player who, maddened by his losses, "suddenly lowered his head to the table and sank his teeth deep into the edge of the wood. The table was overturned, the pinioned madman with it, and his neck broken during the fall. Sobriety suddenly falling on the gaming house after this incident, the justices' men and the priest were summoned and gave verdict that the gambler's soul must have been invaded by the devil to have been aroused to such passion, and therefore he died in no state of grace. The priest refused to give the corpse the rites of burial, and it was taken to the sea by scavengers and flung in."

Spain, which has a long history of devoted gambling and a national temperament that is passionate in all things, naturally has a considerable number of recorded gambling quarrels and imprecatory outbursts. Even its quietly desperate losers make absorbing reading. There is the true story from the 18th century, for example, of the man who, together with his partner, had been steadily losing a fortune all evening. The partner had been cursing and raging at his losses and couldn't understand why his friend had suffered similar losses with silent fortitude.

"You must be bloodless," he yelled, "to let fortune go uncursed!"

"No," said the quiet one. And with that he undid his coat and shirt and

Tempers have always frayed easily in the gamblers' world—especially the tempers of losers. In this late 19th-century drawing, a furious loser takes his frustration out on a keno table in an American club. Keno is a forerunner of bingo ; players bet on combinations of numbered balls drawn by the operator (left).

In a street in Malaga (Spain), children and
adults together play roulette for sweets.
Though it is natural for children to play,
the gambling "instinct" is probably
acquired from imitation of adults.

revealed that, with every loss, he had furtively lacerated his chest with his dagger until it was a criss-cross design of bloody gashes.

One way or another, rage seems to hit gamblers hard. They have been recorded as stamping on dice, tearing up cards, putting burning candles into their mouths, swallowing billiard balls, and wrecking the furniture. Furniture wrecking seems to have been a favorite pastime among gamblers in the saloons of the American shanty towns soon after the Civil War. No game of draw poker appears to have been completed without the banging off of the newly invented Colt .45 and the destruction of every chair and table in the place. Henry Chafetz's history of American gambling, *Play the Devil,* gives a picture even more lurid than that of the Greek satirist Lucian, who in his *Saturnalia* also has much to say about gamblers breaking up the furniture.

But if rage, either suppressed or demonstrative, is so much in evidence as part of the gambler's make-up, you may well ask how this factor connects up with the secret enjoyment in his losses referred to by Ralph Greenson and other psychologists. The answer is that rage may become an *enjoyable* emotion when it releases tension. Anyhow, although the gamblers' stage is littered with the wreckage of berserk fury and the corpses of suicides and murdered men, one knows from experience that most reactions are far less spectacular. Like happy marriages, the undramatic gamblers attract little attention but are everywhere in the majority.

To generalize summarily :

The word "gambling" derives from the Anglo-Saxon *gamenian* (to sport or play), and of course there were contests of skill and strength before there was any betting on them. But as soon as the delectable hazards of chance were revealed to men, they saw rich new opportunities for battle. A whole new world offered itself for exploration, complete with richer rewards than any childish game could promise, and requiring less effort.

"If you climb that wall, Son, the chances are that you'll fall in the sea and drown."

"No, I shan't," says Son, climbing the wall. "I shall see the sea."

Which of course he does. He has won his first round against the laws of probability. Who but Son can gauge the egocentric pleasure of knowing that it's important that he doesn't tumble into the deep? And who but he can sense the excitement that pleasure may bring him in further bouts with chance—in daily life or at the gaming tables?

This, then, is the bedrock of the psychological side of gambling. Egocentricity plus hope (which is as instinctive as egocentricity in human nature) equals the necessity *all* of us have to take risks. Egocentricity plus hope, plus any one of eight or more motives as an individual compulsion, equals the psychological equipment of the serious gambler—the man who knowingly knots himself up with chance more tightly than he need.

2 Gambling through the ages

It would be pleasing to be able to state with conviction when gambling began. Pleasing but impossible. Gambling is a mental phenomenon as fire is a physical one, and there is no possibility of establishing precisely when man stumbled on either of them.

The first known man arrived on the scene during the Lower Pleistocene era, about half a million years ago. Since he was primarily concerned with food, this early Stone Age fellow may have stumbled upon the idea of chance in relation to his hunting activities: Although he could set up a trap before bedding down for the night, it was by no means certain that an animal would enter his neck of the woods before morning. Sooner or later he would appreciate that the odds against his getting a meal would be smaller if he left less to chance; and having realized there was such a thing as chance, he was on the road to grasping the notion of a bet.

There are six racial groups of mankind—archaic white, caucasoid, australoid, mongoloid, amerindian, and negroid—and there is evidence of games and gambling in the earliest records of all of them. It is reasonable to suppose, then, that when man segregated into races he took the notions of games and gambling with him. (The anthropologically minded will recall the opposing theory that ideas occurred independently to different races and were not disseminated before segregation. That theory in no way changes the fact that as soon as

A prehistoric painting from a cave wall at Lascaux, France. The cave dwellers believed that drawing a spiked trap (center) over the figure of an animal would help them to trap the animal. This "sympathetic magic" was perhaps the earliest way in which man tried to offset chance.

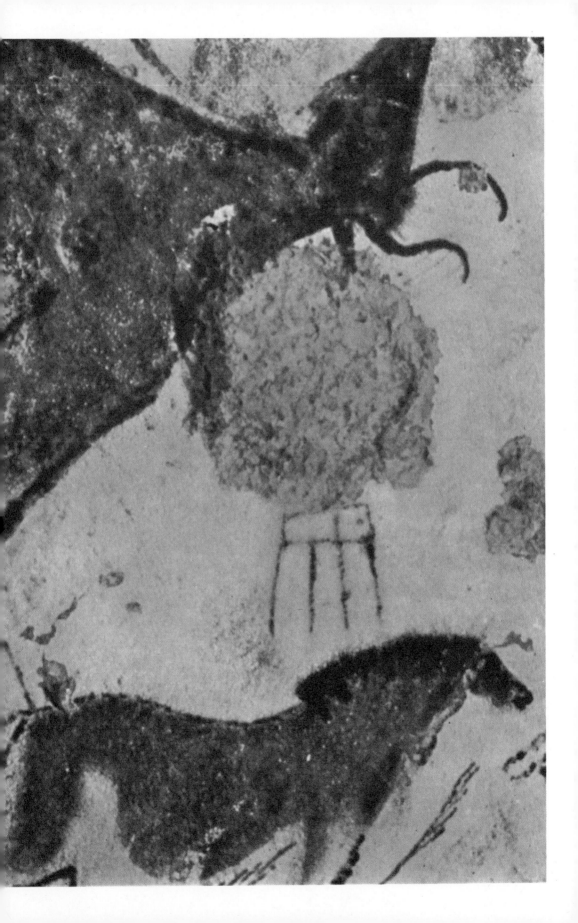

people could record their ideas in speech, pictures, or hieroglyphics they made references to games and chance.)

Most games are contests of one sort or another, and almost certainly the first kind of game to be played was a contest of strength, in which one man could prove his physical superiority over his opponent. Contests of skill—such as games in which targets are involved—presumably came later. And this is where the idea of chance as a game in itself is most likely to have entered the mind of man. Unskilled players probably developed games that simulated games of skill, but in which luck rather than ability decided the winner. Instead of aiming a stone or spear at a target, the early gamesters might have flung the stone —or shell or bone—into the air, so that chance could decide its position on reaching the ground. Dice would be a logical development from stones, shells, or bones. (The earliest known die is in fact the ankle bone of a sheep.)

Contests of speed, or races, probably appeared at the same time as contests of strength; and the simulation of racing brought about such games as *backgammon,* in which a course is reproduced in miniature and the players move their representative pieces along it, every step being decided by the throw of dice or their equivalent. Backgammon is the oldest known game of chance simulating racing; variations of it crop up in every known civilization.

Such a sketchy résumé of man's gambling activities during the long dawn of history must necessarily be mostly conjectural. But plenty of recorded facts are available after dawn stretched into daylight. For instance, in the Pyramid of Cheops at Gizeh near Cairo there is a tablet recording a mythical explanation of the origin (through a gamble) of our present calendar:

Nut, the goddess of the sky, had secretly married her twin brother, Geb, and had thereby angered Ra, the god of creation, who as a punishment decreed that the two were to be separated and that Nut should not bear a child on any day of the year. But Thoth, the kindly god of night, interceded on Nut's behalf by gambling "at tables" (probably dice) with the moon—the stakes being one seventy-second part of the moon's light. As a result of Nut's magical influence on the game, Thoth won, and he presented his winnings to her in the form of five new days to be added to the Egyptian calendar of 360 days. Because these five days were outside the scope of Ra's jurisdiction, Nut used them to produce her five children—Isis, Osiris, Horus, Set, and Nepthys.

From this narrative it is clear that gambling had been going on long before 3000 B.C., which is about the time the Gizeh pyramid was built. Other evidence of gambling among the ancient Egyptians includes ivory dice found at Thebes, dating from 1573 B.C. and now resting in a museum in Berlin; a mural (in the British Museum) showing two Egyptians playing *atep,* a game of pure chance in which one player bet on the number of fingers his opponent extended while the two players stood back to back and a referee kept the score; and the draught board (or checker board, if you prefer the term) of Queen Hatasu (1600 B.C),

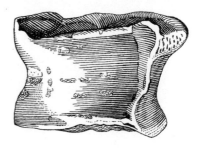
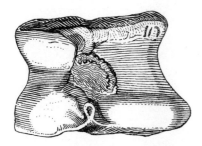

A drawing of the four faces of an astragal (the ankle-bone of a sheep or other cloven-footed animal), used in the earliest dice games. Each side has a specified value: Top left is six, right is four; bottom left is three, and right is one.

also in the British Museum. The Cairo museum has several copper bowls used in a game called *hab-em-hau,* in which players had to throw disks into the bowl in a special sequence; and various collections of Egyptology have papyri recording the fact that convicted gamesters among the populace were sent to work in the quarries—a harsh punishment, but one that suggests how deeply the gambling bug had bitten into the first civilization.

In China, which was very close behind Egypt in establishing a civilization, there are few written records of gambling until 300 B.C. But then, in the Confucian classics *Shih-ching* and *Shu-ching,* comes a reference to the invention of *wei-ch'i,* an elaborate game with hundreds of pieces that are used to simulate the moves in a highly complicated strategy of war; it may be a precursor of chess. The reference in the scroll implies that the game was invented by the Emperor Yao (about 2300 B.C.) so that his son could brighten his dull mind. *Wei-ch'i* is as nearly as possible a game of pure skill, but spectators bet on the outcome, and there are several references in Chinese literature to games played to decide which of two eligible candidates should be awarded provincial governorships.

There are also several references in *The Book of Songs* (second millennium B.C.) to agricultural workers finishing their day's grind at the harrow and rushing off home to indulge their fancy for "the drawing of wood"—a phrase that in context seems to mean the drawing of lots. At all events, the inveterate predisposition of the Chinese toward gambling seems to have been established well before the sun was over history's horizon.

Gambling plays a part in many legends of ancient India, like the tale (possibly fourth century B.C.) of Nala, a king with a fondness for dice. Above, an 18th-century painting of a scene from the legend shows Nala (top right) in a dice game (holding non-cubical dice). On the far left (seated) is his queen, Damayanti. The legend states that several gods had sought Damayanti's hand, but she had preferred Nala. To avenge the insult, a demon charms Nala's dice. Nala cannot stop gambling, and eventually loses his kingdom and all his possessions. He and Damayanti flee, penniless and half naked. In another painting (left) Damayanti seeks shelter in a neighboring kingdom. According to the legend, Nala finally overcomes the demon and wins back his kingdom with fair dice.

Right, Chinese pottery figures from the Han dynasty (206 B.C. to A.D. 220). The standing figure is watching the two seated figures playing *liu-po*, an ancient dice game (played with notched four-sided sticks as well as cubical dice) that was also used for divination.

In India, where there was a highly advanced civilization centered on the Indus River as early as 2500 B.C., there are no historical records until the time of the Vedas—the hymns composed by the priests and bards in honor of the deities. But the Vedic hymns, which reveal a good deal about the social history of the Indo-Aryans in the second millennium before Christ, leave no doubt that the chief amusements of the people were chariot racing—on the results of which great herds of cattle were staked—and dicing. So apparently by 1500 B.C. gambling was very much a going concern.

Cheating was a going concern too—which raises the eyebrows a bit, considering the holiness of these people. Loaded dice, trick dice boxes, and sleight-of-hand on the caster's part are frequently referred to. Loaded dice, in fact, played a big part in an epic gambling match between two families—the Pandavas and the Kauravas—for the possession of a kingdom.

The cause of the match was the envy of the Kauravas for the Pandavas' fortunes, which were then at their peak. Duryodhana, the instigator of the Kauravas' challenge, had an uncle, Sakuni, who could be relied on to win every game with the aid of loaded dice. And Yudihishthira, who represented the

Pandavas, was a poor player anyway; but he couldn't refuse the challenge, because it came from an equal (a raja) and a refusal would have stirred up even more acrimony than existed between the two families already.

Yudihishthira lost every game and gambled away all his possessions, including a hundred thousand slaves, a hundred thousand slave girls adorned from head to foot, and eventually his entire kingdom. But he foolishly persisted and staked his brothers' riches, then his brothers themselves, and finally himself. On a last fatal throw, the cheating Sakuni offered Yudihishthira the return of all his losses against the additional loss of Draupadi, his wife. And Sakuni again won with his crooked dice. The final scene of the tragedy describes the bitter exile of the Pandavas, and Draupadi's vengeful threat as she pulled her long black hair over her face and cried out, "My hair shall remain disheveled from this day until my people shall have slain the Kauravas."

This seems to be the first case on record of a man's staking his wife after losing everything else he owned. But if it ever came to the ears of later gamblers, its scarifying outcome didn't deter them. The staking of wives is a common occurrence in the gambling history of most nations. And not only wives: Mistresses, courtesans, and maidens have also gone with the winds of fortune. The writer Athenaeus (second century B.C.) mentions that Hegesilochus, one of the rulers of Rhodes, used to play at dice for the best bedfellows to be found among the Greek maidens—the catch being that the loser had the task of capturing and bringing the girl to the winner, after she had been selected by lot.

Lotteries as we think of them today—that is, as an organized gamble in which prizes are distributed to lucky ticket holders—didn't burst into the news until Roman times, which is a little ahead of my story. But in the sortilegious sense this form of gambling is of immeasurable antiquity. The choosing of a person in relation to some particular task or ceremony has been decided by lot since the earliest civilizations. Some aborigines determine who among them may be causing unrest by throwing a bone into the middle of a circle around which the tribe is gathered. The one to whom the bone points gets the sorcerer's attentions and dies within a few days. Even the bushmen of the Kalahari, of whom only a few thousand survive (still living in their own enduring corner of the Stone Age), decide the tribe's daily huntsman by casting a stone. And in the Aztec civilization in Mexico, the lottery method was often used to decide which of a number of prisoners of war should be taken as the day's sacrifice to the sun god.

As for gambling in ancient Greece—well, the Greeks gambled, for sure. Otherwise they would never have been able to include in their mythology the legend that, after defeating the Titans, Zeus and his brothers Poseidon and Hades became lords of the universe and cast lots to determine how it should be divided. (Zeus won the heavens, Poseidon the sea, Hades the underworld.) The die they used to decide this important division of power would have been an astragal—the hucklebone or ankle joint of any cloven-footed animal.

An astragal is oblong in shape, like two cube dice stuck together, with domed ends. The four flat surfaces were of course marked with figures or symbols when used as dice, and a cup or vase was used for throwing. Cups made for the purpose were shaped like the astragal itself, with one rounded end weighted, so that they stood upright on the table like tumblers.

The Greeks actually had a legend to account for the origin of gambling itself. According to this narrative, Tyche, the goddess of fortune, was wandering one day in the shady groves of Olympus when Zeus (then young and a bit of a seducer) corrupted her. The union resulted in the birth of an offbeat daughter whose only pleasures lay in inventing games of chance, gloating over the quarrels they caused, and encouraging depressed losers to suicide. Tyche endowed her with houses that had everlasting lamps at their doors to attract passers-by.

The Greeks' determination to account for everything, from the creation of the universe to the existence of gambling taverns, as the work of the gods didn't affect their strong moral sense. Gambling was frowned on by most of the law-givers as detrimental to the structure of the state, and it was punishable with terms of servitude, regardless of the social standing of the offender. Still, aside from the myths and laws, there isn't much evidence that the Greeks were given to gambling to the same extent as the Oriental races or, later, the Romans and Teutons.

Nor, in the formative days of their nation, were the Jews addicted to gambling. There is a good deal of lot-casting for one thing and another in the Bible, so we can safely assume that it was an acceptable thing to appeal to chance; and indeed no direct injunction against gambling appears anywhere in the Scriptures. All the same, the ancient Hebrews seem to have resisted most of its incitements until they ran up against the Romans. After that, Jewish law makers found it necessary to exclude gamesters from the courts of justice on grounds of unreliability and avarice.

The founding of the city of Rome by the legendary Romulus in 753 B.C. offered a fine assembly point for the extension of Etruscan influences—among them the Etruscans' feverish love of gambling. They brought with them the cubic die; the notion of the lottery as a free-for-all prize distribution to assist any celebration; backgammon; the seduction of children into gambling by means of a game played with nutshells; and coin tossing. (The Greeks had a tossing game called *night-and-day,* which they played with a flat shell that was black on one side and white on the other. The Roman version was called *ship-and-head,* because the coin had the prow of a galley on one side and the head of Janus on the other.)

While embracing the pleasures of gambling, the Romans at the same time denounced it in law. The noun *aleator* (gamester) was a pejorative one, and its utterance was taken as an insult; and the laws forbidding gambling promised little but loss, since the winners couldn't legally claim their winnings, but losers could recover their losses. Case law, however, was very different from statute

A 14th-century Persian miniature depicting a chess game played between a Hindu envoy and a Persian noble in the court of the 10th-century Persian King Khusrau I (center). Chess was played in Persia as early as the fifth century B.C.

law. By the time a few emperors had come and gone, gambling was an established feature of Roman social life. It was legal during the December feast of Saturnalia, and was encouraged by the example of such rulers as Augustus, Domitian, Heliogabalus, Caligula, Claudius, and Nero.

The Department of Archaeology in the University of Rome has on exhibition many an excavated fragment testifying to the Roman love of chance. These include a sign from the doorway of a tavern in a praetorian camp, telling the customers that food and gaming tables were always available; some loaded dice from beneath the lava of Pompeii; a triptych depicting two men in a tavern playing backgammon, quarreling over the game, and being thrown into the street by the landlord; gaming tables engraved with the 36 squares of a form of *checkers* (or *draughts*); and slabs of paving stones and columns that have had gaming scores and bets scratched on them by itinerant *aleators* pausing for a quick throw of the dice.

One game the ancient Romans (or the ancient Greeks, for that matter) didn't know about was *chess*. And no one seems to know very certainly about its origin. A Sanskrit manuscript dating from 800 B.C. mentions four-handed

Above, an ivory gaming box from about
1200 B.C. found in Cyprus. The box's
top is a board for *senat*, an Egyptian game
that was a forerunner of backgammon.
The pieces were kept inside the box
when not in use.

Below, a terra-cotta figurine (from about
300 B.C.) of two Greek girls playing
pollax (which was like the modern
children's game of jacks or five-stones),
by tossing astragals in the air and
catching them.

chaturanga—which means, literally, "four parts"—in which the moves of elephants, horses, chariots, and men are decided by throws of dice. But the closest forerunner of chess as we know it was a game called *shah-mat,* played in Persia in the fifth century B.C.

In the modern version of chess—which is at least a thousand years old and has 169,518,829,100,544,000,000,000,000,000 possible ways of playing the 10 opening moves—the only time the element of chance takes over is in the casting of a lot to decide who will play White and thereby gain the advantage of opening. All else is mathematics, logic, and psychology. But like every other event of which the outcome is uncertain, stakes can be laid on the result and frequently have been—not least by such colorful gamblers as Ivan the Terrible of Russia, who on his deathbed in 1584 played Boris Godunov at chess for the entire contents of his treasury.

But the history of chess doesn't really belong to my story. Most of the major developments in gambling (as distinct from just games) appeared in the thousands of years before the birth of Christ. Games of skill that included some element of chance (wei-ch'i and its derivatives), games of pure chance that simulated contests of skill (dice and its variants) or speed (backgammon and similar games)—all those had been evolved. Lotteries—also unequivocal appeals to chance—had made their appearance in simple forms.

Everything to come would be an elaboration of the basic themes. Card games, which would have to wait more than a millennium to appear more or less in their present form, are contests that combine both chance and skill. Roulette and similar forms of gambling are, like lotteries, entirely games of chance.

It could hardly be suggested that Rome declined and fell because of the Romans' weakness for gambling. The weakness was there, all right, and was recognized by the stern rectitude of the law; but there were other contributory causes of the fall—notably, the amorality of the emperors and the continual invasive prodding into Italy by the Goths and Teutons.

These same Goths and Teutons undoubtedly failed to make their European conquests wider and more complete because so many of them gambled themselves into slavery. In A.D. 250 one of their patrols fought and defeated a Roman patrol but couldn't resist risking a reversal of the battle on the toss of a coin. The Romans won, and the Goths allowed themselves to be taken prisoner. A Roman soldier who fought the Huns in Batavia (the ancient name for the Netherlands) reports: "They are quick to anger, but easily appeased with a game of dice or a stake upon a race of chariots. Not one of them, as in Italy is so often the case, was ever known to cut off his thumbs to avoid the service of Mars; but they have tumbled themselves into our very prison camps for the sake of the wily Fortuna."

At about the same time (between the first and fifth centuries A.D.), sailors from Phoenicia and Arabia were being flung by monsoons toward the eastern

Some ancient Greek and Roman dice.
1. A bone die, spotted like a modern die.
2. A strip of bone marked *malest* (bad luck)
on one side. 3. A six-sided bronze figurine.
4. A crystal die. 5. A strip of ivory marked
"winner" on one side. 6. A stone with
14 facets, marked with Roman numerals.
7. A marble die.

seaboard of Africa, probably onto the islands of Zanzibar and Kilwa Kisiwani. Both Phoenicians and Arabs record that they found the natives playing "a game of stones of uneven shape, which are moved about a number of marked depressions in the sand toward a 'castle' in the middle, which represents the prize put up by the challenging player." (This sounds very much like a precursor of mbao, which was mentioned in Chapter 1.)

About A.D. 1000 the Nordic explorer Leif Ericson took an expedition to the coast of Labrador and tried to establish a colony in Nova Scotia. But he and his compatriots were driven out by natives and forced to return home to Greenland, taking with them the idea of a crude game they had found the American Indians playing. There is no record of what precisely this game was, but it seems unlikely that it was very different from the game that had become well known in Greenland by the time the first Christian bishop established his see there in 1126. The bishop reports with some dismay that "in Estribygd the men use holy time to play at the game Leif Ericson brought from his travels, and would God he had not. For it is of evil chance. They spin a stick upon an axis, and to the man it points at when it rests go all the coins that each have contributed."

Other primitive societies sometimes gambled for greater stakes than money. Human sacrifices were often chosen by lot. And a criminal who had been condemned to death might be allowed to gamble, if not for his life, at least for the nature or time of his execution. In some South American Indian tribes, for instance, the fated man was allowed to "choose" the day of his own death by shooting an arrow at a palisade of trees—the trees being marked with a series of dates on the sides he couldn't see. And aboriginal societies in Central

Africa, Malaya, the West Indies, and Polynesia all had—and for that matter still have—various methods of trial by ordeal in which chance (as we should interpret it) plays a big part in deciding the guilt of the accused.

In one Congo tribe, for instance, a wife accused of adultery must plunge her hands into one of a series of bowls, and her guilt is proved if she chooses the one that has been filled by the witch doctor with a caustic solution instead of water. It seems a little hard that an innocent woman might by chance lose both her reputation and the skin off her hands. But all trials by ordeal are in essence a shrugging off of the guilt felt by the accusers; and what better to shrug it onto but the intangible persona of chance?

At the time of the Roman conquest of Britain by Claudius in A.D. 43, there were no trials by ordeal, but both Cymbeline and Boadicea (tribal rulers of Britain) are mentioned in the annals of Roman history as practiced dice players. Presumably dice had been brought in by the earlier Celtic invaders. And a much later historian, Ordenicus Vitalis, gloomily says in his 11th-century chronicle (if I may paraphrase him slightly for 20th-century readers): "Since the beginning, the spread of Christianity has been hampered by the devilish practices of the bishops in encouraging gaming among the clergy."

By this time, with Britain invaded in turn by Celts, Romans, Anglo-Saxons, Norsemen, and Normans (all the heaviest gamblers of Europe), gambling must have got a strenuous grip on the precious little spare time the populace had. In

In many primitive societies a suspected criminal's fate depends on chance in a trial by ordeal. Left, a witch doctor of the Digo tribe in Kenya applies a white-hot piece of metal to a suspect's hand. Presumably the metal caused a burn, proving the man guilty; right, he is banished from the tribe.

1190 those crusading kings Richard of England and Philip of France found it necessary to have a law drawn up settling just who could and who could not gamble, and for how much. The two kings naturally exempted themselves from the law. But apart from them, only noblemen, from princes down the scale to knights, could play games for money. And they were limited in their stakes to 20 shillings in any consecutive 24 hours. If they staked more, they had to forfeit all their stake money, plus another 100 shillings, to the church, and as a further punishment they were stripped naked and whipped.

Two reigns later, King Henry III instructed his clergy that henceforth they were to concentrate on spiritual matters and "leave diceing and chesseing undone on pain of durance vile." Possibly his edict was advisory rather than commanding, for when he gambled with his barons he invariably lost to them. In fact, a sizable portion of Henry's intended personal contribution to the building of Westminster Abbey disappeared into the pockets of the barons.

Shortly thereafter (as if "diceing and chesseing" weren't enough for the lawgivers to deal with), a notable development occurred in the history of gambling: Playing cards made their appearance in Europe. "Made their appearance" is a necessarily vague phrase, because there is no evidence to show whether they were invented or imported. But whatever their origin, cards whisked through Europe quickly, considering the difficulties of communication in those days.

The ledgers of the French Chambre des Comptes (the treasury) contain an

entry from 1392 debiting "three louis for painting three packs of cards in gold and different colors, for the king." (The king at that time was the mad Charles VI; but the tale that cards were invented to amuse him is clearly apocryphal.) In 1394 the duke of Saxony played a game of cards with the duke of Letzburg "for an unenclosed portion of the forest of Ardennes." And by 1423 card playing had become so popular that St. Bernard of Siena felt called upon to declare in a sermon that cards were invented by the devil himself, and that if people continued playing they would find themselves playing in hell pretty soon.

He might as well have saved his breath. Hell apparently held no terror for card players. England, the innumerable duchies and principalities of Germany, Scandinavia, and the Slav countries—all had playing cards by 1425. The likeliest bet is that so far as Europe is concerned they were first used (in Italy) about 1350. And there were a good many people besides testy St. Bernard who clamped down on their use among the masses. Magistrates and priests were always holding forth about them; and in Paris, Rome, and Bruges there were public card burnings in the city squares.

Lotteries, on the other hand, met with little condemnation. One reason, undoubtedly, was that the lottery became, for both churches and governments, a favorite means of raising quick funds. For example, the early settlers in Virginia were financed by a lottery held in 1612; London's first water supply, in 1631, flowed down a covered aqueduct paid for out of the proceeds of another; a thousand slaves were ransomed from Turkish galleys by another; the long European scuffle known as the War of the League of Augsburg was, toward its end, partly financed by over a million pounds raised by another; and the 18th-century reign of Queen Anne in Britain was peppered with lotteries, all hopefully (but often uselessly) designed to raise money to lessen the national debt, pay arrears of civil list salaries and pensions, and repair London Bridge, which kept falling down.

But Queen Anne's lotteries were the mildest form of gambling to flourish at this time. According to G. M. Trevelyan, in his *English Social History,* "both sexes gambled freely, the fine ladies and gentlemen even more than the country squires. . . . The expenses of gambling . . . burdened estates with mortgages which proved a heavy clog on agricultural improvement and domestic happiness. Immense sums of money changed hands over cards and dice."

And Sir Richard Steele, the moralizing British essayist, wrote in 1713: "It is so ordered that almost everything which corrupts the Soul, decays the Body. The Beauties of the Face and Mind are generally destroyed by the same means. . . . There is nothing that wears out a fine Face like the Vigils of the Card Table, and those Passions which naturally attend them. Hollow Eyes, Laggard

An early playing card, part of a Tarot pack from 15th-century Italy. Though the Tarot cards were originally used for fortune telling, by Renaissance times the basic pack had been altered greatly and was often used for gambling. Many Tarot cards bore representations of symbolic or mythological characters: Calliope was the Greek muse of epic poetry.

·D· CALIOPE XI ·II·

43

Looks, and pale Complexions, are the natural Indications of a Female Gamester. . . . But there is still another case in which the Body is more endangered than in the former. All Play Debts must be paid in Specie, or by an equivalent. The Man who pays beyond his Income, pawns his Estate; the Woman must find out something else to Mortgage when her Pin Money is gone. The Husband has his Lands to dispose of, the Wife, her Person."

Steele was by no means exaggerating. Ladies of quality were not only paying gambling debts with their bodies, but were also offering, when necessary, a debt-paying scale graded by sexual deviations. It was not altogether surprising that gambling and licentiousness came to be closely teamed in the 18th century.

In Virginia, the non-Puritans among the colonists who had settled there (on the proceeds of England's 1612 lottery) were spicing up the natives' natural gaming tendencies. The Iroquois, Narragansett, and Onondaga Indians had been eager gamblers for centuries; but they had always played with primitive roulette wheels or dice made of peach and plum stones, and their guessing and numbers games involved simple sticks and rushes. The colonists supplied cards, square dice, bearbaiting, cockfighting, gander pulling, and horse racing. And the Indians gambled their money and families away with reckless abandon.

In Europe at about the same time, a peripatetic Lutheran preacher called Pieter de Brinkheusen said that wherever he went in Holland, Germany, Belgium, France, Luxembourg, and Switzerland, he came upon "thousands of workmen, servants, clerks, and apprentices stealing their masters' time in the pursuit of lotteries and gaming; and thousands of masters and mistresses likewise wasting the hours in earning and losing the money to pay the servants who

Left, the 18th-century English M.P. Sir John Moreshead (second from left) oversees the felling of his trees to pay gaming debts (in a painting by Thomas Rowlandson). Many estates were lost in the gambling frenzy of the period. A detail from another Rowlandson painting, right, depicts "high society" gambling at dice in the home of an 18th-century duchess.

rob them in order to become gambling adventurers; all of whom see none of the tragedy that ensueth, nor the commerce in lust that in the very street corners is enacted in discharge of game debt, nor the money lenders' shops filled with the clothes and furniture of the benighted who have starved and diseased themselves for the adventures of dice and lot."

You will have noticed by now that much of the evidence for the existence of gambling in the past occurs in the form of strictures against it. After the 18th century more and more people (like Brinkheusen) began to associate gambling with all kinds of sin and depravity, and to turn the full force of their righteousness toward halting its spread.

Most modern opponents of gambling, of course, base their attacks on religious or moral grounds. But this was not always true. The ancient civilizations of Egypt, Greece, and Rome, for instance, made laws against gambling chiefly because their social structures were based on privilege. Gambling is a sensual pleasure; it was therefore felt that the lower orders ought not to have too much of it. Otherwise, the upper orders would have had to suffer the consequences of a general undermining of moral standards. Ethics did not enter into the matter at all—not as they did in, say, Jewish or Moslem law.

The Sanhedrin (the Jewish court of justice) excluded gamblers from both the magistracy and witness box, on the theory that the avarice motivating the gambler might make him accept bribes and twist the course of justice. (If the lawyers were thinking of professional and cheating gamblers, they may have been right. But avarice, as I have shown, is only one of several possible motives, and an unlikely one at that.) Furthermore, the law stated that all gambling winnings were rapine and theft, which must be punished by double restitution of the money won. However, winnings became rapine and theft only when they were won from another Jew. If a Jew won from a Gentile, he faced only the comparatively minor charge of having used his mind for a useless end.

The Koran bleakly forbids Moslems to play any games at all except chess, again on the principle that games are time-wasting. "Satan seeketh to sow dissension and hatred among you by means of wine and lots," says Chapter V, "and to divert you from remembering God and prayer . . . therefore abstain from them."

All the great religions, in fact, have denounced gambling. But societies have sometimes enacted laws prohibiting it for practical as well as ethical purposes. Medieval England, for example, clamped down on dicing for a simple economic reason: It was becoming more popular than archery and other games, and the fletchers, bowyers, and arrow makers were grumbling about loss of business.

In free societies, laws designed to control gambling for ethical reasons are usually based on the principle that legislation should repress vices that tend to produce poverty, inefficiency, and misery. In other words, the chief harm we can do our neighbors by gambling is by winning money from them and leaving them the poorer.

But, though *nearly* all gambling is done for money or commodities of intrinsic value, not *quite* all is. What about the Chinese gambler who staked his ears? Or the Teutons who staked their liberty? Or the man who won St. Paul's church bells from King Henry VIII? Or the Chester le Street card players who played for a child? It remains true that, whatever the purpose of anti-gambling laws, men who love to gamble do not depend on money for their adventures.

One might hold forth interminably on all the slings and arrows that have been hurled—by churchmen and laymen alike—at gambling in recent years. And not only for ethical reasons; gambling (like alcohol) has always included among its enemies a number of wild-eyed, unreasoning fanatics. The Ascot zealot I mentioned in Chapter 1 was a mild example compared with someone like a certain Russian madman called Ivan Kuzmitchov.

Kuzmitchov operated in and around his home town, Kamyshin, about the time of the Russo-Japanese war of 1904. There he ranted and raved through the waterfront taverns, trying to turn the Volga sailors' minds away from *faro* and *crown-and-anchor*. His father had lost a fortune gambling, and understandably this had soured Ivan's mind. But his prophecies of doom and disaster had little effect on the sailors, whom he merely annoyed.

One night he entered an inn from which he had been barred earlier in the same week. According to one report, the innkeeper produced a belaying pin with which he threatened to knock Ivan senseless if he didn't get out. "Everyone's had more than enough of you," he said. "I'm going to apply to the mayor to have you arrested as a dangerous nuisance."

A woodcut by the 16th-century Swiss
artist Urs Graf, teaching a moral lesson.
The woman is giving her husband's money
to her lover (right); the gambling
equipment (backgammon and cards) adds
to the scene's immorality. The motto
below says: "Think of the end, that is
my advice: for everything ends in death."

Seemingly, this had the desired effect. Ivan went off ("with his wild hair flying," the report says) and didn't come back. Two days later, he was found dead in his bed with his wrists slashed and, and as a final accusation, "Gambling kills" written on the wall in his own blood. Nearby were the mug he had drained his arteries into, and the toothbrush he had emblazoned the words with.

An anti-gambling museum opened by an Australian called Jed McCade was somewhat less grim, but just as fanatical. McCade had established a mid-sized fortune during the Australian gold rush of the 1850s and had watched a good many others do the same. And he had often seen those fortunes get redistributed in the gambling saloons—with, as he said, "an awful poverty resultant."

But the "poverty resultant" seems to have been only a warm front masking McCade's cold hatred for playing cards. He had got it into his head that they had been imported into Australia on a disease-ridden ship (disease unspecified) and that every pack of cards printed had inherited some awful contamination (possibly not the original one) that was deadly to all players. McCade was shrewd enough to realize that there were flaws in this theory, and that he would only get into trouble if he tried disseminating it among the prospectors. So he printed pamphlets containing an ordinary attack on the sinfulness of gambling and ending with the bleak invitation, in black-letter type, "Come To The Museum Of Death."

The museum was an irresistible attraction—though for more risible reasons than McCade had intended. It displayed, among other lurid exhibits, a door panel from an outback shack, inscribed "Rube Martin died here of the cupid's

itch [syphilis] caught from cards 18.7.79"; an embalmed hand bearing an affidavit from a Melbourne doctor stating that "this is the hand of John Singest, stricken with palsy while playing three-card monte"; numerous playing cards apparently infected with bacilli visible under magnifying glasses; and the skeleton of a man supposedly killed by some aboriginal poison that impregnated the cards dealt by his murderous opponents in a faro game.

Among similar fanatics who attempted to weaken the grip of gambling on San Francisco during the 1849 gold rush was a self-appointed vigilante, Curtis Greeves. He offered to cure habitual gamblers by plunging their hands into a bucket of red-hot coals that he toted from saloon to saloon. Astonishingly, he got one taker for this fierce cure—a miner named Henry Grimsdyke, who painfully lost the use of his right hand in consequence and then sued Greeves for $10,000 compensation (a suit that failed even to get to court, because of the prior incarceration of Greeves in an asylum as a dangerous mountebank).

Although it is unlikely that such eccentrics as McCade and Greeves made many gamblers' hair curl with their unbalanced ravings, there were occasional converts made. There is even a hint, in the newspaper report of Ivan Kuzmitchov's suicide, that a man who had won a thousand roubles at faro in one of the waterfront taverns Ivan had visited refused to pick up his winnings because he was scared of the warning in the suicide's bloody graffito.

All in all, though, the crackbrains have done no more than color the gamblers' pursuit with a laugh or two. Over-earnestness is invariably fatal in moral issues. The Puritans who levied fines for breaches of their rigid code ("Profanation of

Left, a 19th-century drawing from the American magazine *The Illustrated Police News*. Early opponents of gambling (who were often clergymen) sometimes met with counter-attacks from the gamblers. But not all forms of gambling have been opposed by the church. Right, a bingo game in progress (to raise money for the parish school) at a Roman Catholic church in Jersey City, U.S.A. Many churches today operate small lotteries, bingo games, and so on for charitable purposes.

Lord's Day 3s., Playing cards 2s. 6d., Makyng Tumultuous noises 1s. 6d.") were concerned with a problem of ethics. But the Victorian pseudo-moralists who screamed in tracts and pamphlets of the dangers of drink and gambling were for the most part unthinking pleasure-stiflers, who found a welcome for melodrama wherever they turned.

Obviously, it is impossible for anti-gambling legislation to keep an effective rein on an activity that, in many of its manifestations, can so easily be followed in private. In most countries the attempts at a reasonable compromise (to allow the people freedom to follow their own way of life and at the same time to prevent widespread poverty and misery) have resulted in a great overcrowding of lawyers' bookshelves. And every time attempts are made to untangle some of the absurdities that show up in the legal machinery, more shelf space is filled.

Under the common law of England, for example, betting and gaming of all kinds are legal, but the "aleatory contract" that a wager of any kind involves (which recalls the disapproving Roman term *aleator*) is not enforceable at law. England's Gaming Act of 1845 makes it impossible to recover gambling debts by legal action, and this basic rule hasn't been altered yet.

If your bookmaker welshes, you can try charging him with larceny, and if you get taken in by the operators of the find-the-lady (*three-card monte*) games on the London-Paris express, you can haul them up on a charge of false pretenses. But welshing bookies and other confidence tricksters are likely to have ugly organizations behind them, and you probably won't recover anything but trouble. At a different social level, and with a switch in the viewpoint, if you renege on your gambling debts in a respectable club, you'll find the resulting ostracism far more painful than any legal action could be. The phrase "debt of honor" has been most useful in circumventing the law.

America has no federal laws controlling gambling. The states make their individual arrangements, and at the time of writing organized gambling is legal only in Nevada. At various times in the past, New Mexico, California, Arizona, and Louisiana all tried attracting tourists with legalized gambling, but they ended up with a crop of gangster crimes that killed the tourist trade—and occasionally the tourists.

Nevada had legal gambling in the first decade of this century, then abandoned it because of wholesale corruption. Later, at the time of the Great Depression, when the mineral mines that are the state's basic industry became economically inoperable, the state legislators saw a way of attracting tourists with extremely liberal gambling laws. Las Vegas has become the center of gambling in Nevada; and the legalization (with some adjustments to cope with gang influences) has worked extremely well there so far as state income is concerned. Of that income, 20 per cent now comes from the $50 monthly fee each gambling house has to pay to the Nevada Tax Commission, and from the monthly $10 that is transferred from every slot machine to the same treasury.

Whether the arrangement has worked so well from the tourist-gambler's point of view is arguable. Within the two square miles that pin Las Vegas to the middle of the Nevada desert he can take his pick of 17,000 gambles. But if he has any sense, he will have discovered that Nevada is compelled to maintain a bigger police force than any other state of comparable size, and that a special inspectorate visits every casino and gambling club at irregular intervals to look for swindles.

The ambiguity of the moral and legal attitudes in both England and America is exemplary of the difficulty everyone meets when trying to cope with gambling as a social problem. Many nations (France and Italy among them) arrive at the compromise of forbidding private gambling but permitting such state-operated public gambles as lotteries. There are remarkably few countries that go to the extreme of forbidding all gambling; there are apparently none that go to the other extreme and allow all. Thus a round-up of legal and moral attitudes to gambling throughout the world would naturally reveal various shades of tolerance, intolerance, or ambiguity. But I have yet to discover a country where there is no gambling to legislate or moralize on.

Crowds in Las Vegas, the City of Gamblers, respond to neon invitations from some of the city's 300 casinos. The huge, beckoning cowboy is "Vegas Vic," the official trademark of the Las Vegas Chamber of Commerce.

3 The games people play

Among the profusion of activities invented by man to amuse himself, there are undoubtedly some games that are not gambles—games like athletics, in which chance plays little or no part. Just as surely, there are some gambles that are not usually thought of as games. But, as I have said before, life itself is a gamble; and it has often enough been called a game. So no one should mind if I begin this chapter with a look at some accepted features of modern life in which chance operates as much as it does in many actual games.

Speculation, for instance. Playing the market in stocks and shares may not seem to be a gambling activity, for it is necessary in all capitalist economies. And gambling is best defined as "an *un*necessary conflict with chance, symbolized by the placing of a wager on the outcome of an uncertain event." But speculation is still gambling, in spite of its economic necessity—for speculators engage in it by their own choice. They may define speculation as self-sacrifice in the cause of the national economy, but this won't prevent them from being classed as gamblers. Even a millionaire who evades the routine of actually playing the market cannot plead that his successes are engineered for him by his agents solely for the economic good of his country. Not without raising a few eyebrows.

In this businesslike game, not all the players are successful—and (as with most forms of gambling) not all are honest. Ivar Kreuger, the Swedish match king, was an unhappy example of dishonesty and failure. He was also a glaring

Children at Play, a painting by the 16th-century Flemish artist Pieter Brueghel. Many children's games (like many adult gambles) demand both skill and luck. Note the two kinds of bowling games near the wall, and the chancy game (center) in which a boy must strike a metal pot without being struck in turn by his blindfolded opponent.

AMMINISTRAZIONE AUTONOMA
DEI
MONOPOLI DI STATO

6%   SIX PERCENT   6%

Treasury Bill due 15 August 1935

£ 500.000.—

Fivehundred thousand Pounds Sterling

Interest payable 15 February and 15 August
every year first time 15 August 1931 against
stamping of this certificate. Principal and interest
payable at Barclays Bank Ltd London

Rome 15 August 1930

General Director

Guaranted as to principal and
interest by the Kingdom of Italy

Minister of Finance

Left, one of $39,200,000 worth of Italian treasury bills forged by Ivar Kreuger in 1931. The signatures were proved false by handwriting experts about a month after Kreuger's suicide in 1932. Right, Kreuger as he appeared at the height of his career.

example of the gambler whose masochistic compulsion to lose is as strong as the death-wish in a moth. In fact, Kreuger's compulsion itself could be called a death-wish.

Kreuger's gambles with money began in a big way in 1917, when he bought devalued American dollars with Swedish kronor, waited till postwar prosperity restored the value of the dollars, then sold them for more than twice what he had paid for them. With that profit (it was about $3,000,000) he began to build his industrial empire, through maneuvers that were based on lending money to war-impoverished nations in exchange for match-manufacturing monopolies. His control became world-wide and he was renowned for paying fabulous dividends. Statesmen and bankers of the highest integrity deferred to his financial genius, and after his death *The Times* of London included in his obituary the well-intentioned but somewhat innocent statement that his dealings had always been beyond reproach.

Not so. He was a swindler and a forger, and he mercilessly cheated millions of people all over the world. (In America alone, investors parted with over a quarter of a billion dollars.) By cooking the books of his own companies, forging bonds with the signatures of heads of state on them, and not only inventing assets but inventing nonexistent banks to keep them in, he managed to keep going an organization whose balance sheets (drawn up by himself) were under the constant surveillance of incorruptible examiners. And he kept it going for nearly 25 years.

The investigations following the collapse of the Kreuger empire (after his death) revealed that playing the stock market was apparently too simple a gamble for him. A solitary, secretive man, Kreuger needed greater risks than straightforward speculation, plus embezzlement to recoup his losses, to satisfy his compulsion toward disaster. Gambling against discovery of his colossal defalcations and embezzlements offered just such a risk. He increased it by employing a number of undercover agents to operate some of his swindles (thereby laying himself open to blackmail, on which he spent a fortune), and by giving out just as much information as his accountants and directors needed to support his fictions without seeing through them.

As the risks piled up, and more collateral was invented to secure more loans from increasingly suspicious banks, Kreuger must have felt the fulfillment of his compulsion approaching. At one time, when he was virtually held prisoner in New York while some preliminary investigations into his operations were going on, he appeared to have gone quite insane. He neither slept nor ate, and displayed all the symptoms of the gambler working up to his payoff.

The payoff came in Paris. In his flat at 5 Avenue Victor Emmanuel III, on March 12, 1932, Kreuger shot himself through the heart. His last gamble, a pathetic attempt to get New York to believe that some bonds supposed to be in a Berlin bank were actually there, had failed. He had no more tricks left to play. He apparently shot himself with composure, as if his 52 years of life had pleased him.

And undoubtedly they had. Kreuger had always played his impeccable appearance and his marvelously accurate memory (indispensable for instantly

visualizing falsified books) against the faith in printed figures that the speculative gambler must show. An innocent question (raised by one of his own company directors) about an item in a balance sheet had kicked the cornerstone away from his house of cards. "I have made such a mess of things," he said in his conventional suicide note, "that I believe that this is the best solution for all concerned." It was a bland disclaimer. Far from being a mess, his life's work displayed an intricate genius. He had twisted the laws of probability far longer than most gamblers do, and he had no reason (except a moral one) to be ashamed of his enterprise, even though it failed. Until then, his system had proved to be as nearly invincible as any system can ever be against the armory of chance.

Another profession that might be called a gambling activity is, perhaps surprisingly, law. For instance, an element of chance is very closely involved in the process of trial by jury. The verdict is the prize for which lawyers compete, armed with their knowledge of the facts of the case and their belief in the innocence or guilt of the accused. But their competition becomes a gamble because the final outcome (i.e., the verdict) is influenced by an unknown quantity: the collective mind of the jury.

A direct appeal to the emotions may antagonize a jury that is intellectually on the alert against such appeals; but with a predominantly simple-minded jury, it may gain the accused a favorable verdict. Clever and experienced lawyers often seem able to choose the right approach to sway a jury—but not infallibly. And the judge can do little more than attempt to clarify the evidence and the

Left, an Aztec drawing depicting a ritual ball game (resembling basketball; the two center circles represent hoops attached to the walls). The Aztecs played this game for serious purposes as well as for fun. In the early 16th century the chief Nezahualpilli predicted that Mexico would soon be ruled by strangers. Another chief, Montezuma, was skeptical, so Nezahualpilli bet his kingdom against three turkeys that a ball game would verify the prediction. Nezahualpilli won, upholding his reputation as a diviner— which was doubly upheld in 1519 when Cortés landed and overran Mexico (as in the drawing, right, of a Spanish attack on an Aztec temple).

arguments, and to enforce the rules of the game (in this case, legal procedure). Thus any trial by jury depends on the judgment of 12 people, selected by chance, whose knowledge or ignorance, personal emotions, and prejudices are totally unknown and unpredictable.

In other legal systems than ours, chance may play an even bigger and more direct part. The Andaman Islanders, for instance, try a suspected criminal by a kind of human roulette. Secured by guards, the accused stands in the middle of a circle of whirling dancers that includes the accuser and injured party. The rhythm and direction of the dance are controlled by a blindfolded drummer. If the dancers are halted with the accuser facing the back of the accused three times in succession, guilt is proved. As you may imagine, this doesn't often happen. The Andaman Islanders are happy people, much given to conversing in song, and have very little crime. So they can afford to be relaxed about their legal system and, when one of their infrequent trials becomes necessary, can play it very much as a game.

Also a game, but a terrifying one, is the setup depicted by the American writer Shirley Jackson in her realistic horror story "The Lottery." The story begins with the people of a mythical American village (population 300) assembling at the end of June for the purpose of choosing a "scapegoat"—a villager who will symbolically expiate the sins of the others for the preceding year. Every villager draws a slip of paper from the lottery box; one person draws the single marked slip. Then he and all the members of his family return their slips to the box for the second draw, to decide which individual member of the family will be the scapegoat. Whoever holds the marked slip this time is set upon by everyone else and stoned to death.

The grim practice of the choice of a scapegoat exists in fact as well as fantasy. It is closely tied up with primitive rites hopefully performed to ensure fertile crops. (One of the characters in "The Lottery" quotes a fictitious proverb: "Lottery in June, corn be heavy soon.") But the practice has been perpetuated through a great many civilized societies. In Judaism, for example, Mosaic law commands that a lot is to be cast on the Day of Atonement to decide which of two goats will be slain as a sacrifice. Then the rabbi, by confession, transfers the sins of himself and the congregation to the other goat, which is turned loose "into the wilderness." It escapes (or "scapes") death, which in this case is an honorable sacrifice to God; but it suffers the punishment of being dishonored by sin—symbolically an intolerable burden.

It may seem that activities involving punishment, cruelty, and death are too grim to be considered as games. But there's no doubt that, human nature being what it is, every willing participant in such activities gains a lot of excitement. And it is pitched in the same key as the excitement of gaming in the more accepted sense; for part of that excitement has to do with the hurt that the gambler feels as the result of his own losses, or that he inflicts on an opponent who is losing to him.

But these grim considerations are only peripheral to my subject, which is the games people play—when they are not playing cards, dice, or roulette, or betting on races, or drawing lottery tickets. (Each of these major categories of gambling will get a separate chapter to itself later.) In the survey of games to follow, I intend to show diversity by sampling. Any omissions will probably be either obscure variations on more familiar themes or else games played by so few people that they do not warrant inclusion. In other words, the survey will cover gambling games that are reasonably well known throughout the world—the games of pure chance, and the games that require some skill.

Games of pure chance are for the most part simply guessing games. They are universally played, and they will be found even where no other form of gambling exists. For instance, the Arctic explorer Knud Rasmussen noted the enthusiasm of the Eskimos for their primitive form of roulette (the "spinning game" that Leif Ericson brought to Greenland). And the anthropologist Störvildt records that the Eskimos "sometimes decide, by the indication of the pointer after coming to rest, the area of their next hunting trip." Presumably, in an area like the Arctic, one direction is as likely to be fruitful as another. Störvildt also mentions, by the way, that the Eskimos' marriage customs permit interchange of wives among husbands, and that wives are often staked in the spinning game. "I learned of one case," he says, "where a young hunter, preparing for a long journey to replenish the larder, played at spinning the wheel the night before setting out and won all 17 wives of his fellow players. With dire results; for to refuse to accept them would have been socially insulting, and to accept them, which he did, meant that he had to support them while their husbands were away—no mean task for a lone hunter."

Guessing games probably got their start during those ancient days when a man couldn't count on his future stretching much past the next full moon. People in those days went in for a lot of divination. It comforted them. Gloomy forebodings or happy auguries were attributed to sticks, straws, spears, and stones flung into the air and directed by the winds of fortune to land in certain positions.

One of these objects might have become a special totem or talisman—perhaps an unusual stone, thin and flat, light on one side and dark on the other. It would have been tossed into the air to let the side that landed uppermost decide important questions—such as where the best hunting would be found. Then someone might have perceived the advantages that could be gained by correctly guessing the result of throwing the talisman. And this might have led to competition between guessers. In time the stone would probably have lost its magical qualities, coming to represent simply two opposing chances that could be sided with. From there it would have been a simple step (adding excitement to the prophesying) to let some material possession be the prize for a correct guess. Man would have placed his first bet.

All this is pure conjecture. But if anything like it ever did happen, it is easy to see how coin tossing (as soon as there were coins) became a gamble. It is the

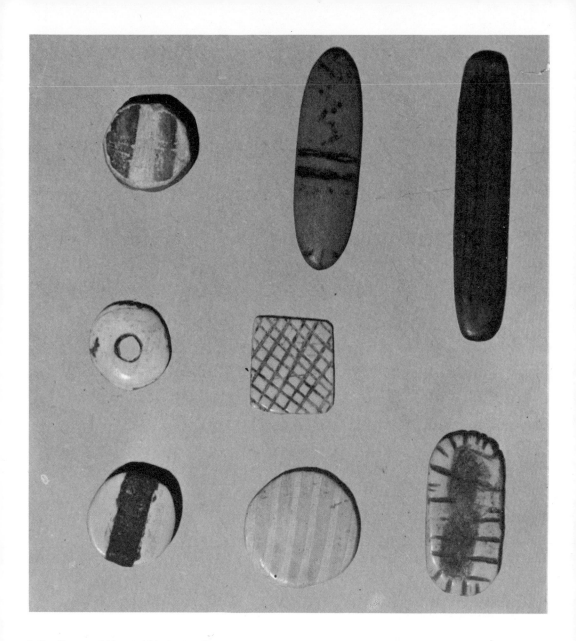

Left, a Transvaal (South Africa) witch doctor examines the "wise stones" that he casts to foretell his tribe's future and to guide him in his important decisions. Dice probably evolved from stones like these, and from sticks like the carved divining sticks (right) also used in the Transvaal. Above, some primitive dice used by Indians in southwest America about A.D. 900. Top row : a bone die and two wooden dice (perhaps belonging to a medicine man). Center row : a bone die that once had a turquoise inlay, and a bone die with cross-hatched cuts. Bottom row : a bone die with a central groove filled with pitch ; a striped shell die ; and a clay die.

simplest of all games of chance. The coin itself can, of course, be the prize; but it is more usual to have other material gains or losses at stake, and to use the coin merely as the deciding instrument.

By its very nature, coin tossing has always been suitable for a private gamble between a few people, rather than as a game that can be built into a professional gambling enterprise. But the private gamble can often develop into a full-scale coin-tossing match. For instance, the Arabian caliph Abdul-Malik (about A.D. 700) once lined up the officers of his army in the palace courtyard and had them toss coins to decide which of them should share in a distribution of some of the wealth of Syria.

The Australian game of *two-up* (which originated from the older British game of *pitch-and-toss*) is a more modern kind of private coin-tossing match. In this game, two pennies are placed on a flat stick (called the "kip") and are thrown into the air by the "spinner." The bettors place their money on whether the coins will land as two heads or two tails; a head and a tail is a "no-throw." In spite of its illegality (and therefore in spite of police raids), two-up remains and flourishes as almost an Australian national game.

The original connection between divination of the future and coin tossing has never quite died away. For instance, by throwing three coins six times and noting the arrangement of heads and tails, you can find the place in the *I Ching* (the ancient Chinese oracle book) that refers to your future. And many Malayans and Koreans will toss a coin in the morning to decide which side to get out of the bed, thus pointing the whole of that day in a direction approved by fortune (and, incidentally, shirking responsibility for its outcome).

The Koreans also have a proverb: "Who continues the world must continue at *fan-tan*." It alludes to the belief that a husband can copulate productively only after winning three successive fan-tan games in the interval between two of his wife's menstrual periods. In fan-tan, an unknown number of beans, coins, or other small objects is concealed under a cup, and the four players bet in advance on whether one, two, three, or no beans will be left after the remainder have been taken away in groups of four. The proverb thus seems to jeopardize the future population of Korea somewhat more than the actual population figures indicate.

Fan-tan is widely played throughout the East, and has also been exported to Portugal (along with other games using jackstraws or elongated wooden dice with notched edges instead of spots) from Macao, the Portuguese colony in China. Of course, practically any kind of gamble is widespread in oriental countries—except Borneo and Thailand. But both the Borneans and the Thailanders play more games with tops than with cards, dice, or anything else. The tops are identical with the "teetotum" used in India—that is, a pentagonal wood block carved to a point at one end and with a short wooden stem projecting from the other for spinning it with. The five angles are notched with from one to five notches, and in the basic game the players bet on their scores with each spin.

Above, children play a coin-tossing game that imitates the adult game of two-up (a widely popular gamble, especially in Britain and Australia). Two coins are tossed from a flat stick (below) and players bet on either heads or tails.

The Western world's game of *put-and-take* (rarely encountered since the 1930s) uses an octagonal top marked P1, T1, P3, T3, P4, T4, P-all, and T-all. A player puts or takes from a central pool according to the side that lands uppermost. I suspect that the reason for the virtual disappearance of put-and-take from the English and American gambling scene is that too many loaded tops were being used. In other words, there was a great deal too much putting by novices and taking by cheats.

Cheats, of course, can turn almost any game to their advantage. In coin tossing, for instance, there is the standard routine of the coin with the same figuration on both sides. And there are several other more complicated gimmicks. A coin with a tiny nick in its edge on one side, when spun like a top on a wooden surface, makes a slightly different sound when landing on the nicked side from the sound it makes when landing on the other side. A practiced trickster can identify that sound and will bet that, blindfolded, he can guess which side up the coin will fall. And a coin with a slightly rounded edge on one side will always fall on that side when spun. Also, a practiced cheat can identify by

In fan-tan, an unknown number of beans is placed under a bowl, while bets are laid (on numbered corners). The bowl is lifted and the beans taken away four at a time. Bets are on how many will be in the last batch.

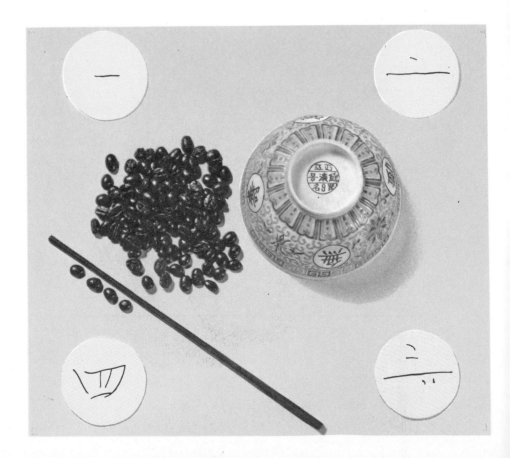

touch the underside of a coin as he catches it after a toss, and can turn it over by sleight-of-hand before displaying it.

There are a number of games that are never played fairly. Many of them involve mechanical contrivances found in fairgrounds or pin-table saloons, and the chances of winning anything (other than a token "bait" prize) are nil. The oldest of all these games, however, is not mechanical but depends on sleight-of-hand. In Chapter 2 I mentioned one of its manifestations—*three-card monte* (also called *find-the-lady* or the *three-card trick*), in which the victim bets on which of the three cards is a queen, after the three have been put face down on a flat surface and shuffled around by the quick-fingered operator. This widely known cardsharp's trick derives from a game variously called *thimblerig, cups-and-balls,* or *three sea shells.*

Three sea shells (also called the *shell game*) is the oldest form. It is referred to in a Chinese story of the third century B.C. and in a letter written in the second century A.D. by the Greek rhetorician Alciphron, who describes a peasant being inveigled into a game during one of the many festivals in honor of the

In three-card monte, bettors must pick the queen after the operator has re-arranged the cards. Even skilled gamblers can be defeated by the speed at which the operator moves the cards (or palms the queen).

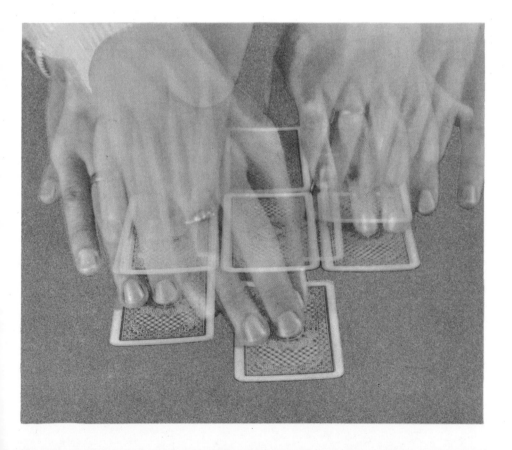

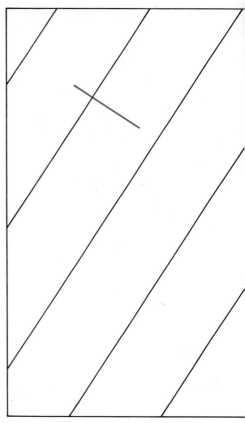

One of the oldest carnival gambles, the "wheel of fortune." The wheel is spun, and players bet that it will come to rest with the pointer at a specific number.

Bettors in the needle game must drop an inch-long needle between lines an inch apart. Odds are 3.14 to 2 that the needle will touch a line.

gods. In the shell game, three hollow shells are put on a flat surface and a small pebble is concealed under one of them. The victim watches the operator push the shells around and tries to guess which shell is concealing the pebble at the end of the maneuver. The pebble is then extracted by sleight-of-hand, so that whichever shell the victim bets on, he loses. After he has made his bet, the pebble is cunningly replaced under one of the two shells he hasn't bet on. Or, alternatively, the shells can be moved around with such speed that it is impossible to keep sight of the important one. (This is usually the method used in the three-card version of the trick.) Often the operator has a partner pretending to be an ordinary bettor. He is allowed to win heavily, in order to attract (and reassure) other players.

The elaboration of the shell game called cups-and-balls came into being in Europe in the 12th century A.D. It was probably a side-issue of the game of *bilboquet* played by children, in which a cup on the end of a stick is used to catch a ball attached to it by a string. The cups (inverted on a table) can, of

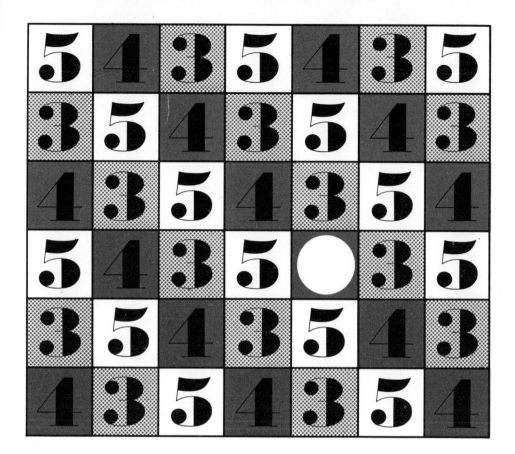

The penny pitch looks easier than it is. To win, the player must throw a coin so that it lands entirely within one of the squares on a smooth board, without overlapping.

course, be used in exactly the same way as shells. The elaboration came with the use of three cups and two colored balls. The balls could be made to seem to move from one cup to another by false pockets in the cups (as in the egg-bag trick used by modern conjurers).

Later still, thimbles and a pea were used, and the cheat working the game came to be known as a "thimble-cove" or "thimble-rigger." *Villainy Unmask'd*, an anonymous book published in London in 1752, warns its readers especially against the dangers of betting on which of the thimbles the pea will be under: "It is under none of them." But, as the British sociological journalist Henry Mayhew noted in *London Labour and the London Poor* (1851), the warning apparently wasn't taken; for by then "the thimble trick" had assumed the status of an open street game.

During the 19th century, American confidence men on Mississippi river boats used walnut shells and a pea or ball of paper, varied with the three-card trick. The American historian John O'Connor says that the down-river passengers "allowed themselves to be fooled by any simplicity, but that on the journey back a greater degree of sophistry was needed." The river-boat swindlers also enticed the innocent travelers (according to O'Connor) into games of *chase-the-queen*, "setting up their trays in the best positions under the awnings and seeing to it that their partners set amongst the passengers were of good dress and mien."

A more modern version of the game is played today with bottle caps from beer or Coca Cola bottles. Wherever it's played, the innocent who believes that his eyes are sharp enough to follow the movements of the shell, bottle cap, or queen, or that because he has spotted a bent corner on the key card he has an advantage over the operator . . . well, he'll learn.

The innocent stands a better chance in the widely played *match game* (*mora* in Italy; and *atep*, still, in Egypt, even though matches are now used rather than fingers), for cheating is not an invariable feature of its operations. The match game is wholly a guessing game, but your chances of winning are proportionate to your mathematical and psychological abilities. Broadly, the object of the game is for one player to guess the total number of matches held in the right hands of all the other players. He bases his guess on the knowledge that each player has three matches and may conceal none, one, two, or all of them in his right hand. Any number can play.

Organized match games at Baden, Macao, Las Vegas, and other gambling

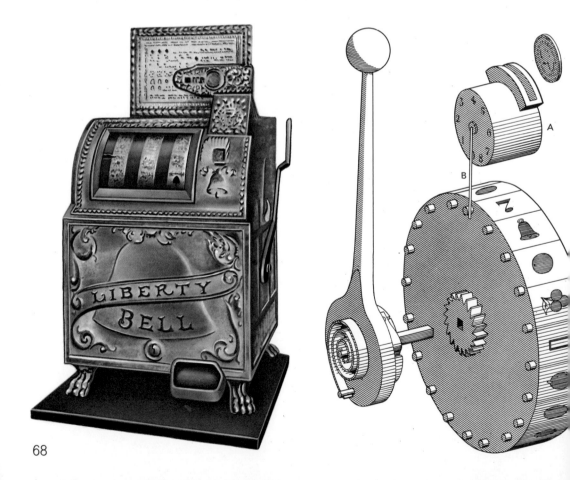

centers usually have six players and big stakes. But wherever the game is played, it is also played informally for small stakes such as rounds of drinks or bus fares. The rules are simple : Each player must have an opportunity to be last caller in a series of games (because the last player to call his guess has distinct mathematical and psychological advantages); and bluffing can be as important as it is in poker.

In all games of pure chance, for that matter, the rules of play are simple— which is why they attract such vast numbers of amateur (but determined) players. One of the simplest gambles, known all over the world, is the slot machine (called the "fruit machine" in Britain—and also, practically everywhere, called the "one-armed bandit").

As nearly everyone knows, the slot machine is a mechanical device that absorbs coins. Each coin inserted allows the player to pull a lever that sets three independent vertical reels spinning. The peripheries of the reels bear colored symbols (some of them representations of fruit), and if they come to rest with specified combinations of symbols running parallel to a "payoff line," the machine dispenses some of its coins to the player. The player backs nothing but the chance that his pull on the lever will bring the reels to rest at a favorable combination. The machines can be geared to pay back any percentage of the coins it absorbs—82 to 94 per cent being as fair as you can find. There are 20

Far left, a late 19th-century version of Charles Fey's first slot machine. Left, a simplified diagram of a slot machine's mechanism. The coin starts a timing device (A) that turns a rod (B) like a clock's hands. One device governs each of three reels ; pulling the handle spins the reels, and after a few seconds the rod stops them. Modern machines (like the one on the right) have been complicated by the addition of gadgets that vary the timing of the reels on each spin, control the payoffs, and prevent interference by would-be cheats.

| First Reel | Second Reel | Third Reel | | First Reel | Second Reel | Third Reel |

With 20 symbols on each reel of a slot machine (left), there are 8000 possible combinations. Twelve of these pay off—but some of the 12 can be made several ways. The combination of one cherry plus any two other symbols (top line above) can be made with either of two cherries on the first reel and anything *not* a cherry on the second and third reels. But three sevens can be made only one way.

symbols on each reel, which means that there are 8000 possible combinations of symbols. But only 12 of these will pay back any coins.

The inventor of this profitable contrivance was Charles Fey, an American mechanic who must have known as much about human nature as he did about machinery. In 1895 (when he was 29), he made the first one, called it the Liberty Bell, and hired it out to a San Francisco gambling saloon for a rental of 50 per cent of its profits. Fey may not himself have been a gambler, but he must have understood, consciously or subconsciously, some of the psychological motives (see Chapter 1) that cause people to enjoy their losses. For wherever a slot machine stands, there stands also for most of the time someone compulsively feeding it with coins.

One such compulsive player was a young Indian businessman who went to Tokyo on a sales-promotion visit for his firm. Eating in a café, he noticed a block of four slot machines that operated simultaneously. He fed them with four coins and received a payoff of eight coins. With these he began a gambling marathon that went on for six days and nights with only four three-hour intervals for food and sleep. During that time he pulled the handle 70,000 times, collected winnings amounting to the equivalent of $1500, and paid them all back into the machines together with $100 of his own money. Although his winnings had amounted to such a considerable sum over the period, there had never been a point after the first four-coin win at which he had been in pocket. During one stretch of play, he had put the equivalent of nearly $20 into the machines before collecting a jackpot of well under $10. He subsequently persuaded the directors of his firm to branch out from their business of exporting curry, mangoes, and powdered rhinoceros horn, to form a company to import slot machines from America. It flourished.

Although the ordinary straight slot machine brings its owner or hirer an unfailing profit, there have always been owners or hirers who have adjusted the mechanism of the machines to pay back only 20 per cent of their earnings. Nor have fixers on the playing side been rare. In the early days of the slot machine, crude attempts were made to fix continual payoffs. Players drilled holes in the outer casing and inserted wires through them to hook out the metal slide that traps the coins, or wedged open the payoff trap with a spatula. The manufacturers were not slow in defeating such attempts mechanically. But another method, called "reel timing," was not easy to track down, since there was no apparent interference with the mechanism.

The method was simple in principle but difficult in practice. First, the player had to determine the exact number of seconds that each reel spun before coming to rest after the handle was pulled. Secondly, he had to memorize the sequence of all 60 symbols on the three reels. Having established the timing of a particular machine, the player had to bring an even trickier talent into operation : He had to be able to count, with stop-watch accuracy, a certain number of seconds between the insertion of the coin and the pulling of the lever. By observing the line-up of symbols through the window before beginning the operation, and knowing from memory which symbols lay above and below the visible ones, the player could (if his counting was accurate) set the reels spinning at a particular second after insertion of the coin had started the clock mechanism, so that they came to rest at predetermined positions.

Surprisingly, a good many people managed to acquire this complex skill. Or perhaps not so surprisingly. People have always been as ready to adapt their ingenuity to the dubious as to the respectable enterprise. At all events, the takings of one firm of manufacturers suffered a gigantic drop during the period before the reel-timing method was discovered. Once discovered, of course, it was easily scotched by mechanical means. And to date, I know of no new method of cheating the slot machines. Nor, however, is there any diminution of the number of players who have convinced themselves that eventually they will find some new way to beat the reels.

Slot-machine gamblers need skill only to cheat; but in many games the gambler needs skill (as well as good luck) to win legitimately. Most card games belong in this category : Chance dictates what cards are drawn, ability governs what is done with them. But the same principle operates in many other kinds of game—for example, the complex Chinese game of *mah-jongg* (which somewhat resembles *rummy*, although played with tiles rather than cards).

Its proper name is *ma-tsiang* ("sparrows"); "mah-jongg" is just a manufacturer's trademark. But since it is better known than the other, I'll stick to it. The game has never satisfactorily translated itself from China, Korea, Japan, and Malaya to the West, but (as the middle-aged may recall) there was a short-lived American and European mah-jongg craze during the twenties.

The tiles used in mah-jongg are about the size of dominoes (but thicker), and are usually made of ivory backed with bamboo. They are divided into three suits (called bamboos, circles, and characters) and each suit has nine ranks. Additionally, there are four each of red, green, and white dragons, four winds, four flowers, and four seasons, making a total of 144 of these poetically named pieces. A game begins with a ceremonial arrangement of the tiles into a wall. Three of the four players then take 13 tiles and the remaining player 14. The object of the game is to achieve a winning hand by discarding and drawing tiles.

A winning hand is four sets of three and a pair, or seven pairs, or a run of 13 with a pair of any number in that run. When a player achieves such a hand, play stops and the winner is paid by the losers according to the scores they hold in their hands. The scoring is immensely complex because of cumulative doubling, which makes totals enormous (sometimes running into hundreds of thousands) and stakes difficult to fix. This may be one of the reasons why the game lost popularity; but it seems more likely that the exoticism that was a feature of the twenties (exemplified by mah-jongg, Russian boots, Spanish dancing, surrealism, Paraguayan *maté*, and gypsy bangles) faded with that decade into the grim shadows of American and European depression.

Games like mah-jongg (and like some card games or other "parlor" games) are of course played as much for pleasure as for gambling purposes. Nevertheless, betting can be and often is introduced into these games—usually in order to increase the pleasure. This is also the case with many games played with a board and pieces, as, for example, *Monopoly*.

In this game, too, chance and skill are both involved. According to moves decided by throwing dice, the players shift their representative pieces to places on the board that offer them opportunities to speculate with toy money and toy property. The winner, of course, is the player who acquires the most property. Monopoly had a great vogue in Europe and America during the years of depression in the early thirties—mainly because it offered opportunities for vicarious speculation with money and property (the very success anticipated for the game by its American inventor, Charles B. Darrow, who made a million dollars out of his foresight). The vogue died at the beginning of the war and was supplanted by the vogue for real speculation and takeover bids—except, apparently, in South Africa, where Monopoly has always been played at a serious level, with real money and real property. One wealthy South African has told me that, in his home in Bloemfontein, he and half a dozen other property owners would play a Monopoly game every Saturday night, "winning and losing half of Maitland Street and Hoffman Square" between them. He also told me, by the way (though there is no other evidence for this), that the site of Harvard University's observatory in Bloemfontein was won in 1847 by Major Wardle, the founder of the city, in a *baccarat* game.

Skill becomes increasingly dominant in many of the best known board-and-pieces games. In *checkers* and *chess,* for instance, chance determines only which player will have the opening move, and there are no opportunities for gambling except on the result of the game.

The origins of checkers are misty, and it is by no means certain whether it is a later or earlier game than chess (whose history was discussed in Chapter 2). It seems to be fairly well established that the checkerboard games played by the Egyptians and Greeks were more like *backgammon,* with pieces being moved according to the throws of dice. There are no reliable records of checkers (as we know the game today) being played before the 12th century, when a version

A mah-jongg game. The player on the right has won with a hand containing (top to bottom) two fives of the "characters" suit; three "red dragons" (one hidden); three fours of characters; four east winds; four ones of characters; and two seasons. Players draw from the tiles in the center. The counters represent points won.

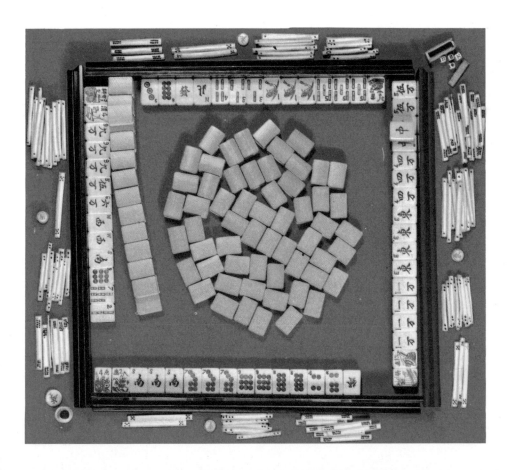

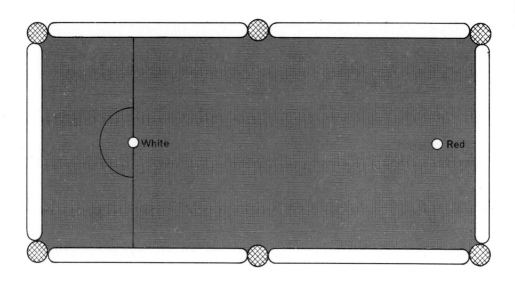

Above, a billiards table at the beginning of
play. The first player shoots the white ball
(his "cue ball") at the red ball, perhaps to
pocket the red or to pocket his cue ball after
hitting the red. When he misses, the second
player introduces his cue ball and begins.
(He can shoot at the other cue ball as well
as the red.) Below, the layout for a game of
snooker. The first player shoots the white
ball at the pyramid of red balls to scatter
them. To score, he must pocket a red ball
and then any colored ball—and can repeat
the sequence until he misses, when his
opponent begins (using the same cue ball).

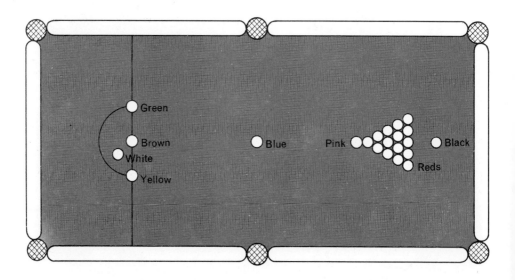

using a board with 100 squares was played by King Boleslav III of Poland, who divided the country among his three sons according to the strategical ingenuity shown by them in the game.

Billiards is another game in which chance plays virtually no part, but which (along with its many variations) is often connected with gambling. South Africans, for example, are as devoted to gambling on billiards as on Monopoly. Bets placed on this game by both players and non-participating gamblers account for one third of South Africa's entire gambling expenditure—which, it must be added, is not especially large. (In South Africa, billiards once figured in a drama that had nothing to do with gaming. When a disastrous storm hit Port Elizabeth in 1902, a billiards table was dragged out from a waterfront saloon and used as a raft to rescue survivors from the barque *Thekla*.)

Billiards is played with three ivory balls—two white, one red. Each white ball is the "cue ball" (i.e., the ball struck by the cue) of each opposing player. In the basic form of billiards, there are three ways of scoring: the "winning hazard," where the cue ball knocks one of the other (or "object") balls into a pocket; the "losing hazard," where the cue ball is pocketed after striking an object ball; and the "cannon" or carom shot, where the cue ball strikes both object balls in succession. A player continues at the table as long as he can keep scoring; when he misses, his opponent starts.

The word "billiards" derives from *billard*, the French word for cue; the pockets on billiards tables used to be called "hazards"—hence "winning" and "losing" hazards. The game seems most likely to be of 15th-century Italian origin, but was made fashionable in the 17th century by Louis XIV of France—allegedly because his doctors suggested exercise to relieve the troubles of his alimentary tract.

The game has undergone a good many changes in 500 years, both in equipment and rules. Tables have been bedded with oak, iron, marble, and slate. Cushions have been stuffed with sawdust, feathers, flock, and rubber. Pockets were originally wooden, but nets came into use in the late 16th century. Ivory obstacles known as "port" and "king," which were placed on the table and affected scoring if touched by the balls, have disappeared. And cues have become longer and thinner.

Several different versions of billiards are played today. The French use a smaller table than the British, have abandoned pockets, and use only cannon shots. Americans often use four balls instead of three and sometimes use no pockets. Britons have remained conservatively attached to the 19th-century version of the game, though they have invented or introduced many other games that can be played on a billiards table. Of these only *snooker* is played extensively today.

Snooker is a development of "pyramids" (in which 15 red balls are arranged pyramidically and have to be struck and pocketed by one white ball). It was invented in 1875 by Lieutenant Sir Neville Chamberlain of the Devonshire

Regiment (stationed at Jubbulpore, India, at the time). He suggested adding a ball to the game of pyramids he was playing in. Gradually more and more balls of different colors and values were added until there were 22 (including the white cue ball).

In the usual version of the game, a player must first pocket any red ball (for which he gains one point). He then can try to pocket any one of the other colored balls, which are yellow, green, brown, blue, pink, and black, and for which he gains (respectively) two, three, four, five, six, or seven points. The red balls stay down, but a pocketed colored ball is returned to the table. When all the red balls are gone, the players start trying for each of the colored balls, in the above order; and the game ends when the black is pocketed.

The word "snooker" derives from *neux*, the French word for a freshman at a military academy. It came to be applied to the game because Sir Neville reproachfully called a player who had missed an easy shot a snooker. When the player took umbrage, his feelings were calmed by Sir Neville with the words, "We're all snookers at this game."

In America, snooker ousted billiards early in this century as the most popular ball-and-cue game, though Americans also favor a simpler game called *pool* (which is played with 15 balls numbered from 1 to 15 that must be pocketed in consecutive order). The word "pool," however, is often used as a general term for many different versions of ball-and-cue games (including snooker). In America, it has inevitably been associated with gambling—and not only gambling on the game itself. Because most forms of gambling were illegal, the neighborhood "pool hall" came to be a good place for a back-room game of cards or dice, or to place a bet on a horse. And it attracted a collection of small-time criminals, bookies, toughs, confidence men, and every kind of "hustler." Thus snooker pool is still (in the minds of many self-righteous pillars of society) unfortunately connected with vice and depravity.

Dominoes, the last game of chance and skill to be dealt with here, today has its greatest popularity in Ireland. During a recent visit to the Isle of Man (which British Crown Colony, incidentally, passed a law in April 1962 permitting gambling casinos), I witnessed a dominoes tournament between Dublin and Connemara players. Ramsey, the northern port of the island, had been chosen as the venue because it was neutral ground, or so the captains of the teams told me. When I suggested, with stolid Anglo-Saxon logic, that surely any place between Dublin and the Connemara Mountains would have been neutral ground, one of the captains said, "Sure, but how the devil, then, would we ever get out of Ireland?"

Three ways a billiards player can control the direction of his cueball. Striking it low (top picture) makes it stop short or roll backward after hitting the object ball. Striking it on one side (center picture) makes it curve to that side after hitting the object ball. Striking it on a sharp downward angle (bottom picture) makes it jump—a useful trick if another ball lies between the cueball and the object ball.

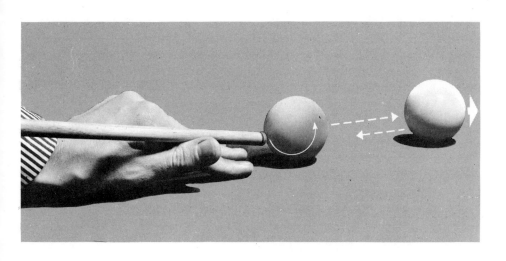

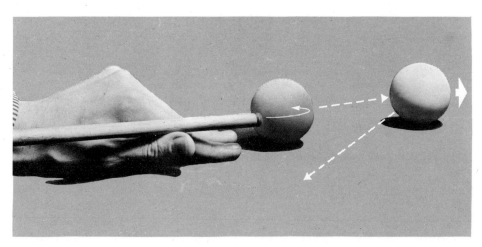

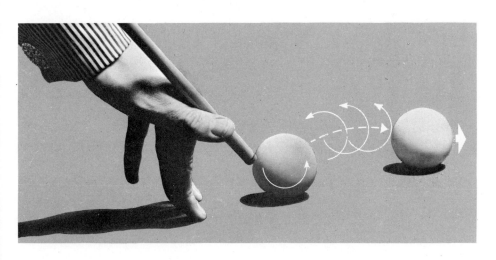

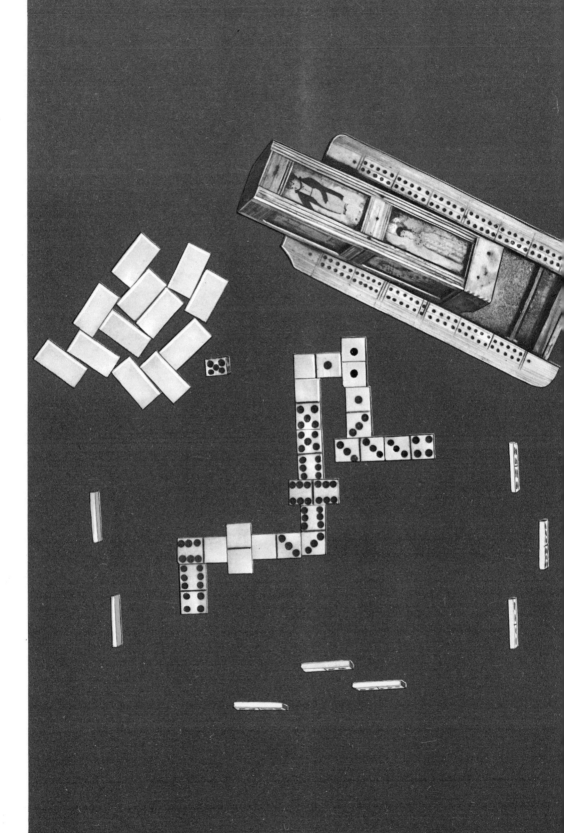

The tournament was conducted with the fierceness of tribal warfare. All the players remained in a purdah of sobriety—which, since the matches went on for six days, showed a real spirit of dedication. But the supporters got wildly drunk, beat each other up, and laid extravagant bets at every opportunity. Once the Mountains of Mourne were staked against Galway Bay, and the referee told me that in Irish tournaments "a certain amount of poetic license" was always to be expected.

Tournaments of this size crop up only when some challenge is slowly passed along from hamlet to village to town to city to county to district. But all over Ireland people play dominoes at least as much as cards, and bet on it nearly as often as they bet on football or horse racing; though of course the transactions are mostly small, occurring mainly in pubs and houses, and rarely involving the services of a bookmaker.

Dominoes—that is, the pieces themselves—are chummily called "stones," "bones," or "cards." The games played with them today are Spanish and Italian in origin and first appeared not much earlier than the 17th century. In the two main games, *block* and *draw*, each player matches numbers endwise as the pieces are laid down; but in *matador, all fives,* and *all threes* the object is to make the end pieces total seven, five, or three. The much earlier and far more complex Chinese games are closely associated with dice games, and will be discussed in Chapter 6.

As a game for betting on, the popularity of dominoes seems to have taken a tumble during the present century. Apart from Ireland and China (where practically anything and everything is played that can carry a bet), few countries take much serious interest, though habitués of British pubs play dominoes for drinks—as they play *darts, shove ha'penny,* and *skittles,* which are all games involving far more skill than chance. The only element of chance in dominoes lies in the dealing of the pieces, but that is enough to add excitement to a game of slow tempo.

It is presumably the temperament of the day that has ousted the game from its 18th- and 19th-century popularity. In fact, the temperament (and tempo) of the modern world is probably responsible for many changes in man's gambling habits, among which might be included the tendency toward "credit betting" with bookmakers by telephone, rather than personal placing of the bet. This has been called the age of the "armchair athlete"; it is just as much the age of the "armchair gambler," who bets regularly on games that he does not or cannot play, that he watches from a grandstand or on television—games like the big-time, professional, "spectator" sports.

A domino set thought to have been made by French prisoners in England during the Napoleonic Wars. A three-handed game is in progress. The next player must put down a domino with a four (or a double four) to match the ends of the line. The player on the left is winning, for he has only two dominoes (on edge in front of him) to play. Top left, the bank from which a player can draw extra pieces if he needs them.

4 The games people watch

Watching other people play games has been one of man's favorite leisure-time occupations for a long while. For one thing, we all enjoy the thrills of battle and conquest; but most of us would prefer to get this kind of enjoyment vicariously rather than by facing a fighting bull in a Spanish bull ring or a heavyweight champion in a boxing ring. Also, of course, any kind of athletic contest offers many an opportunity for gambling. The spectator has no control over the game (unless he has "fixed" it by, say, bribing the players). So from his point of view the game's outcome can depend almost as much on chance as on the players' ability.

Horse racing, of course, is the undisputed favorite of gamblers who prefer the onlooker's omnipotent view to the participant's role. And Chapter 8 will show just how big a gambling "industry" the race track is. My concern in this chapter is with some of the principal sports aside from racing that attract gamblers' money—and with a few well-known sports that, for reasons that will emerge, don't. As an indication of the importance of sports events in the gambling world, it has been estimated by one authority that Americans gamble more than $10,000,000,000 annually on sports other than racing.

One reason for the wide popularity of gambling on sports events is that the process is so uncomplicated. You don't need to learn a number of complex rules of play or betting procedures, as you do in most casino games or in card

The crowded grandstand at Forest Hills, New York, during a tennis tournament. Millions of people enjoy watching sport; and for many spectators, gambling on the outcome adds an extra edge to the excitement.

and dice games. Your basic need is only the address or telephone number of a bookmaker, some cash to put in his hand, and the knowledge of what athletes or teams are competing. It might help you to know something about the nature of the game, but it isn't necessary in order to bet. If the bookmakers' whereabouts are unknown to you (as might be the case in countries where the law says that bookies are criminals), you can always have a friendly bet with a fellow spectator.

In fact, this is undoubtedly the way most betting on spectator sports is done. Sports fans, who may never have seen a casino and who may not know poker from mah-jongg, will often demonstrate their faith in the athlete or team of their choice by betting with the opposition's followers. The bet itself may be small, perhaps for only a drink; but temporarily the fan is a gambler.

Fighting is probably the oldest spectator sport (aside from racing); and of the various kinds of fighting that still draw audiences today, *wrestling* is undoubtedly the oldest. There are both Egyptian and ancient Chinese pictorial records of wrestling from about 2000 B.C., which show that the sport must have been as graceful a form of mayhem as could be found. Many elements of grace survive in the kind of wrestling called *sumo*, which could be called the modern Japanese national sport. But the grace that has survived can often be obscured by the bulk that has been created—surprisingly in a people of small physical stature—by generations of marriage between the sons and daughters of different families of sumo wrestlers, which has resulted in the evolution of increasingly powerful physiques.

The ancient scribes of the Far East make frequent references to wrestling. In the first century B.C., for example, a Korean wrestler named Kehaya boasted that no man could match him and appealed to the emperor to put his strength to the test. In those days, of course, a wrestler who issued such a challenge was gambling not only with his prestige but with his life. Another wrestler, Shikune by name, accepted the challenge and defeated Kehaya, following up his triumph by kicking the vanquished man in the ribs and breaking the bones in his body one by one until he died. Upon which Shikune was promoted to high office.

In the year A.D. 858 the throne of Japan was staked on the outcome of a wrestling match. The Emperor Buntoka had two sons, Koreshito and Koretaka, both of whom aspired to the throne. Their claims were decided in a wrestling match fought for them by two professional wrestlers, Yoshira (for Koreshito) and Natora (for Koretaka). Yoshira was the victor, so Koreshito ascended the throne.

From the time of ancient Greece (where wrestlers fought naked, their bodies smeared with oil as an anti-perspirant and sprinkled with sand to afford a good gripping surface for the opponent) until early in this century, wrestling was a respected sport. But its recent history has been a history of decline. In the professional wrestling ring today, enormous men perform well-rehearsed and often comic antics for the entertainment of spectators who are mostly at home in front of their television sets rather than at the ringside. These contests are no more than elephantine acrobatics, with the "winner" allegedly scheduled as such long before the start. Few people are foolish enough to bet on these matches; nor would any bookmaker accept such a bet.

Amateurs have to some extent maintained the classical style of wrestling as a sport under the sponsorship of the International Amateur Wrestling Federation. But while you could readily *see* an amateur match in, say, France, Britain, or Germany, you would find it difficult to place a bet on it (except with a friend). Bookmakers, it seems, just aren't very interested.

Nor are they particularly interested in *judo*, a special form of wrestling developed in Japan during the last years of the 19th century. But in this case the absence of gambling isn't due to a decline in the integrity of the sport. Quite the contrary: So much honor is attached to the practice of judo—which is claimed to be a philosophy fostering moral qualities like respect, kindness, self-control, and sincerity, as well as an art—that gambling is never mentioned in the same breath. Anyway, not by the international array of judo enthusiasts. Sports reporters will tell you that some private betting does occur at judo matches in Europe and in Japan, but not enough to make the bookies interested in studying the sport, working out odds, and so on. It seems that bookmakers have a better chance of making a profit in the big sports that attract large followings and therefore more gambling money—sports like *boxing*.

The word "boxing" applies to "scientific" fist fighting (in which gloves are worn and other definite rules are obeyed) rather than to uncontrolled brawling. The Greeks, who accounted for their invention of boxing by saying that it was inspired by the gods, used light gloves and wore belts to indicate the demarcation

Two Japanese Sumo wrestlers come to grips at the beginning of a bout. Even today, after centuries as the traditional sport of Japan, Sumo's popularity remains unchallenged.

Above, an Egyptian copy of a Roman statue of two wrestlers. In antiquity, wrestling had a high reputation as a sport; today, a professional match (left) is usually a rehearsed entertainment, and most bookmakers will refuse to accept bets on the outcome.

Professional boxing matches are occasionally "fixed"—as was the 1909 fight for the world heavyweight championship between America's Jack Johnson and Steve Ketchel (pictures, above right). Johnson agreed to allow Ketchel to last the full 20 rounds; but in the 12th round Ketchel double crossed Johnson and began fighting in earnest, taking Johnson by surprise (top right). Johnson recovered, and retaliated by knocking Ketchel out (bottom pictures).

line for foul blows. The Romans added blood and sadism to the sport by adopting the spiked and weighted glove they called the *cestus*. Fist fighting virtually disappeared as a popular spectator sport until about the 17th century, when it was revived in the form of the bare-knuckle blood bath that was called "pugilism" and that tended more to the Romans' idea of a good fight than the Greeks': In 18th-century Britain, the fourth Duke of Queensberry is recorded as having bet 1000 guineas to 500 guineas that, if the fight he was watching continued for another 10 rounds, nobody would be able to put a sovereign on the floor without its being smeared with blood.

The Queensberry Rules (which helped to transform pugilism into modern boxing) were not the invention of the fourth duke, but of the eighth marquis, who drew them up in 1867. They were revised in 1890 and again in 1923. Today the basic rules call for the use of padded gloves, a "ring" between 12 and 24 feet square, and "rounds" of from two to three minutes duration with rests of 30 seconds or one minute, and they forbid wrestling, holding, or foul blows (which include those with the open glove and with the shoulder or elbow as well as those below the belt). There are variations in the rules in many countries: In America a slightly bigger ring than the European one is used, and in France the sport shows the influence of the old French fighting game *savate*, in which kicking as well as hitting is allowed. But most of the major fights (for

European or world championships) are fought under an agreed set of rules based on Queensberry's.

A championship fight, especially in the heavyweight division, is an event that reverberates (literally, in these days of radio and television commentaries) far beyond the world of sport. As with the Derby, people who otherwise never bet in their lives will have a gamble on a heavyweight championship. Nor is it difficult to find someone to take a bet, in spite of the fact that gambling on boxing (as on most spectator sports, for that matter) is illegal in a great many parts of the world.

In the 18th century a would-be bettor would simply have asked the fighters' seconds, who acted as distributors for bookmakers' pamphlets specifying the odds and the limit on bets. In England today a bettor could lay his bet with a bookmaker in a betting shop; but in, say, France or America he would have to search out a bookmaker's agent—a member of a profession that in these countries is necessarily on the fringe of the underworld. Bars, barber shops, or newsstands might be good places for the inexperienced gambler to begin his search; but the ringside itself is still the best place to find the bookies and get your money down (though, at all times, discreetly).

Illegality or no, the bookmakers must on the average do pretty well. Gambling on boxing is big business. For example, when Italy's Primo Carnera defeated America's Jack Sharkey in 1933 for the heavyweight title, Mussolini complained that the money bet on Carnera in America alone was worth the equivalent of a year's export crop of Italian peaches. And in 1946 (a year when, among other things, the great American Negro champion Joe Louis successfully defended his heavyweight crown twice, against Billy Conn and T. Mauriello) the year's betting in America on *all* boxing totaled $500,000,000.

I quote these figures from some years ago because recently (though the bookmakers have by no means been put out of business) gambling on boxing has experienced something of a decline. More up-to-date figures are less impressive: Since 1960, for instance, the yearly betting total on American boxing has been less than $20,000,000. The boxing pundits believe that the influence of television has contributed to this decline. People apparently prefer to stay home and watch the fights, and thus miss the opportunity for ringside betting. Some commentators suggest that more fixing of fights goes on than is admitted, and that this form of cheating is one of the causes of the decreased interest in boxing as an opportunity for gambling. But only a few fixes come to light, as far as the general public is concerned, and then usually long after the event. In recent times, for instance, the French champion Georges Carpentier admitted in his autobiography that his ignominious defeat by Siki in 1922 was fixed. Carpentier was paid the equivalent of about $4000 to "carry" Siki (i.e., to hold back so that Siki would seem to be putting up a good fight) before taking the victory. But Carpentier carried his opponent too far; Siki unexpectedly floored him and took the title.

Ernest Hemingway's famous short story "Fifty Grand" describes in fictional form a case of fixing that is unlikely to be as fictional as it pretends. It is the story of a boxer called Jack Brennan, a miser by nature, who deliberately backs his opponent, Jimmy Walcott, with $50,000 to win. It is not so easy, however, for Brennan to want to lose and at the same time to pretend to strive for success. Walcott is informed of the plan by a couple of double-crossers and tries a similar plan himself. In the fight, Walcott delivers a foul blow that would give Brennan the victory; but Brennan refuses to acknowledge the blow as foul, battles on in agony, and himself delivers a foul blow that loses him the fight. "It's funny how fast you can think when it means that much money," is his comment as he lies in his dressing room.

Gambling spectators are always attracted to fights between animals—and, it seems, the stranger the animal the better. The Siamese, for instance, gamble on battles between male fighting fish (gorgeously colored relatives of the Paradise fish), which have been specially bred for pugnacity and endurance and will battle for periods of several hours. They also gamble on aggressive crickets contained in glass jars and goaded into fighting by the skilful application of small wooden lances. And Arabs bet on matched scorpions that will fight to the death on a battlefield formed by a plate or saucer.

But the most popular kinds of fighting that involve animals also involve humans. Spain is a great card-playing country, but between April and November the gambling expenditure of the country shifts markedly onto *bullfighting* and *cockfighting*. (Recently Franco's government accused the people of spending over a tenth of their total income on gambling—illegally—at the bull rings and cockpits.) Bullfighting is nowadays almost exclusively confined to Spain and Mexico; but it is first recorded as a popular pastime in the frescoes of Knossos painted about 1500 B.C. Some of these frescoes show girls as well as men battling with bulls; in others, depicting crowd scenes, you can spot money changing hands—though this may be money for entrance to the amphitheatre rather than wagers. Both the Minoan Cretans of Knossos and the Thessalonians were ardent supporters of bullfighting; later, the Romans imported the sport and the upper crust gambled hugely on popular bulls and bullfighting.

Today, almost every town in Spain has its *plaza de toros*. The *corrida*, which is usually a series of six bullfights (the number may vary at times of special festivals), begins with a procession around the arena, after which the first bull is freed and engaged by the picadors, who are mounted on blindfolded horses. The picadors take the brunt of the bull's first charge and rouse its fighting fury by gouging it in the neck with short pikes. They are followed by the *banderilleros,* who enrage the bull even more by sticking beribboned darts into its neck. The payoff comes when the matador, the star of the afternoon, battles the bull with flowing cape and finally kills it with a single sword thrust. Unless, of course, the bull kills him first.

Left, three stages in a Spanish bullfight : First, a mounted picador rouses the bull's anger by thrusts with a lance ; then (above) the bull is further enraged by wounds from *banderillas;* finally, the matador (after lengthy and graceful "play" of the bull with his cape) braves the horns to plunge a sword into the bull's heart.

Cockfighting (right) is another often gory contest involving animals. Below right, a diagram shows the layout of a Cuban cockpit. The cocks are weighed and spurred before their fight to the death.

Betting goes on at bullfights without much attempt at concealment. Program attendants and soft-drink vendors often act as bookmakers' agents, calling the odds and taking bets. Bets are usually placed on which of the afternoon's six matadors will be judged (by appointed referees or, occasionally, by a visiting dignitary) to have dispatched the bull with the greatest subtlety of technique.

Cockfighting appears to have been established in ancient Greece by the soldier Themistocles, who, leading his men into battle against Xerxes of Persia in 480 B.C., saw a couple of cocks fighting and made a stirring battle speech about them : "These animals fight neither for the gods of their country nor for the monuments of their ancestors, nor for glory, nor for freedom, nor for their children, but for the sake of victory, and in order that one may yield to the other." After winning the battle, he instituted an annual cockfighting festival as a thanksgiving for the cocks' inspiration.

Subsequently, both cocks and quails, brass-spurred and force-fed on garlic to rouse their wrath, were pitted against each other in a sport that spread all over Europe. Greece and Spain seem to be the only countries that have kept in use the original cock battlefield—a table with raised edges to prevent the contestants from falling off. Elsewhere the birds fight in a fenced arena, or (more usually) in shallow pits.

Russia, Germany, Britain, and Italy have scarcely any cockfighting left (a little is still to be found in the north of England). But over practically the whole of the United States, Mexico, Latin America, the West Indies, the Philippines,

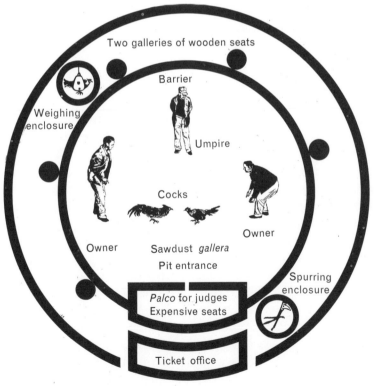

Two galleries of wooden seats

Barrier

Umpire

Weighing enclosure

Cocks

Owner

Owner

Sawdust *gallera*

Pit entrance

Spurring enclosure

Palco for judges
Expensive seats

Ticket office

Since Roman times, camel fighting has been popular in Turkey, where the animals are specially bred for pugnacity. The annual championship at Germancik attracts a crowd of eager fans—many of whom have private bets on the fight.

France, Belgium, India, Spain, and Greece tournaments go on endlessly. The sport is illegal in most of these places, though three of the United States (Florida, Kansas, and New Mexico) have given it license. Approval of the sport, of course, doesn't necessarily imply official approval of gambling on it. All the same, enthusiastic bettors are as irrepressible in cockfighting as in other spectator sports. *Time* reports that during a four-day tournament at the Orlando Game Club, Florida, the betting totaled $750,000, with gamblers coming from as far afield as Rhode Island, Texas, and Michigan.

Much of this betting was done privately, but there is no scarcity of bookmakers at most cockpits. Bettors standing around the pit shout the odds they want to lay and the bookmakers shout back if they are taking the bet. If the authorities are putting on the pressure, bets are laid in bars, cafés, etc.

Let me point now to some of the more popular team sports:

Baseball is of course America's national sport, and an enormous amount of gambling money changes hands annually during the season, when 154 games are played in the two major leagues. For example, a syndicate of bettors once

A newspaper cartoon of the 1870s (depicting baseball at the mercy of the hyena of gambling) reflects a period when crooked gambling threatened to destroy the sport. Today, of course, baseball is flourishing—and is a top draw for gamblers.

won $825,000 from a bookmaker with one bet on a World Series (the final play-off between the two top major league teams). Gamblers have tried to make their winnings certain by fixing games, as in the famous "White Sox" scandal of 1929 (to be discussed in Chapter 13). But today professional baseball doesn't fix very readily; the fans are among the most alert and knowledgeable sports fans in the world.

Aside from the $2,000,000,000 (according to one estimate) that is bet annually (through bookmakers) on individual teams in major-league baseball games, there is also a small following of gamblers who prefer to bet on baseball by means of pools. Many of the pools are arranged privately between friends or office workers, but others are more professional; they are set up in the major cities by bookmakers or other entrepreneurs, who sell one-dollar tickets that entitle the holders to forecast the five teams that will score the greatest number of runs in a week. The prize for the lucky prophet can often be around $25,000.

This extensive betting on baseball in a country where such gambling is illegal is facilitated by the telephone. A person who wants to bet on a baseball game (or any other sports event) has only to contact a bookmaker's agent (as usual, through a bar, newsstand, or similarly convenient meeting place), to have his bet handled, recorded, and passed on by telephone. These agents are known as "pickup men" or "writers"; they collect and pay out on behalf of the book-makers, who pay them 10 per cent of their net winnings—a tax-free untraceable income that bothers the federal authorities considerably, since it means a tax loss to the nation of about $5,000,000,000. In a 1962 report from a senate committee on gambling, a commissioner of the Department of Internal Revenue is reported as saying that large-scale gambling requires "the widespread use of telephones. Regular customers phone in daily wagers to bookmakers, and bets are accepted by telephone from out of town gamblers."

Football (the highly complicated helmet-and-shoulder-pad American kind) is the second highest moneyspinner in American spectator gambles. College and professional games attract around $1,750,000,000 in bets yearly. The main attraction in professional football is the National Football League; 14 teams played 98 games in 1962, and the crowds drawn amounted to about 4,000,000 people. There are lesser leagues, like the American Football League with eight teams, and the United Football League with six teams. And of course there is college football. The 600-odd college teams inspire a lot of alumni nostalgia: Over 21,000,000 people attended college games in 1962. Bets are usually laid privately between football fans, or with bookmakers through the same discreet procedure as in baseball.

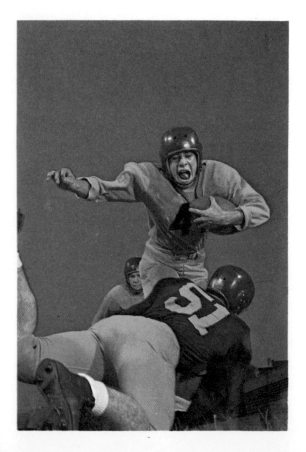

Left, an American football player is tackled by an opponent. Right, a diagram of a basic football play—"the forward pass." The red-shirted player on the left has run (along the yellow line) to take the ball thrown by his teammate on the right. (In striped shirts are the referee, linesmen, and umpire.) Below, a chart showing a typical "bookie's edge" in a football match. Since Army is the stronger team, bookies must try to offset heavy betting on Army by paying out on an Army win only when its score exceeds Navy's by more than nine and one-half points.

Army 9½ points over Navy

Lose **Army 39**	**Navy 39**
Lose **Army 6**	**Navy 21**
Lose **Army 21**	**Navy 12**
Win **Army 30**	**Navy 14**

But sometimes discretion is not enough. In 1963 there was a minor gambling scandal involving members of the Detroit Lions (a team in the professional National Football League). Five players had each bet $50 on another team to win the year's championship, and two other players were found to have been making occasional bets for several years. The N.F.L. Commission fined each of the five $2000, and the two others were indefinitely suspended from playing. There was no hint of crookedness in these bets; but, the Commission pointed out, players who gamble on their own sport run the risk of getting deep in debt and being tempted into fixing a game to recoup. Also, of course, gambling on football is illegal everywhere in America except Nevada.

Football is not free of the menace of fixing. The senate report on gambling mentioned before refers to a case in 1960 of a member of the University of Oregon team who was approached with a bribe of $5000 to "make mistakes" so that his team would lose a match against Michigan. The case was brought to light by the player himself, who rejected the fix and informed the police.

American *basketball* has been more notorious than football for its fixing scandals of the 1950s when college stars or whole teams were being bribed to throw games. The bookmakers lost a lot of money, and have naturally been suspicious of all basketball betting ever since. A gambler would be lucky to find even a big-time bookie who would accept a bet over $100—whereas the same bookie would be delighted to cover a baseball bet of several thousand dollars.

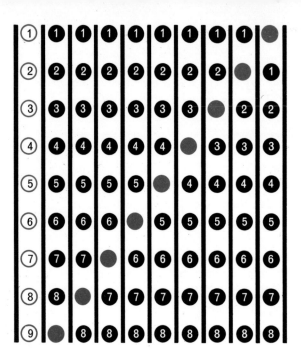

A soccer player (below) represents Europe's most popular spectator sport. Gambling on soccer is mainly handled by "football pools" organizations, who share out the amounts staked every week among those bettors with the correct forecast. Right, a Swedish pools coupon shows the results forecast for 12 matches : A cross indicates a draw ; 2, a win for the "away" side ; 1, a win for the "home" team. Sometimes a bettor may request a "permutation" of his forecast. Left, a table sets out the nine different ways in which a selection of, say, eight drawn games can result from a total of nine matches. This is the equivalent of nine different forecasts, and nine times the stake money can be won.

Adress | **Postadress**

23 sept. 1962 — STRYKTIPSKUPONG Nr 4622500

	1	X	2	1	X	2	1	X	2	1	X	2	1	X	2	1	X	2	1	X	2	1	X	2
Djurgården—Norrköping			2																					
Elfsborg—Degerfors		X																						
Högadal—Hälsingborg			2																					
IFK Malmö—Goteborg	1																							
Örgryte—Hammarby	1																							
Boden—IFK Luleå		X																						
Holmsund—Lycksele	1																							
Karlstads BIK—Sundbyb.		X																						
Sirius—Sandvikens AIK																								
Råå—Landskrona		X																						
Sleipner—Derby			2																					
Sifhälla—Norrby	1																							
		1			2			3			4			5			6			7			8	

Association football (soccer) is the main spectator attraction in practically every European country, as well as in South America, Russia, Africa, most of Australasia, and elsewhere. Betting on the game in most places is almost entirely concentrated in pools, a widely popular form of gambling for the amateur or small-time gamblers who occur in any country in big-time numbers. Football-pool gamblers in countries like Sweden, Britain, Switzerland, and Germany usually submit both the guess and the stake money by mail. Each week during the football season promoters send out printed coupons (to anyone who asks for them) that list all the league games to be played the following week. On his coupon the gambler attempts to forecast the results.

He can usually choose several kinds of forecast—for example, which teams will win games played on their home grounds, which teams will win away from home, and which games will be drawn. And he can vary his stake money to fit the number of chances he wants to buy. As with pari-mutuel race-track betting, all the stake money is pooled and shared out among the winners by a system of points. The promoters take a percentage for their operating costs and profit, and (in some countries) the state takes a percentage in tax. (The state also profits handsomely by the sale of postage stamps and money orders.)

In 1961, bettors in Scandinavia spent the equivalent of $150,000,000 on football pools, in Australia $240,000,000, and in Britain $333,000,000. The prize money is divided among the gamblers who forecast correct results; and in a week when thousands of people guess right, the dividend is naturally small. But for a single all-correct forecast it has been as much as $750,000.

The football pools are considered by many gamblers to be nothing more than lotteries, requiring no skill or special knowledge on the part of the bettors. And, indeed, investigations have shown that many big prizewinners not only know nothing about the teams they had bet on—they have never even seen a game. But this is undoubtedly true in practically every other sport as well. Even in racing, many bettors back horses that they have chosen at random; and in, say, England or parts of Europe where off-track credit betting is allowed, it is possible to bet on horse races for years without ever seeing a horse. So the lottery comparison is more than unfair to the countless football fans who never miss a game, who pride themselves on their deep knowledge of the different teams and players, and who try to put that knowledge to work for them by betting on the pools.

It is difficult to pinpoint the football pool's first appearance as a public gamble. In England, small groups of gamblers in offices and shops may well have been forecasting results and dividing the pooled stake money since the widespread formation of football clubs during the latter part of the 19th century. Many people remember privately run pools prior to the 1914 war. But the questionable legality of the enterprise got in the way, and it wasn't until 1924 that a man named John Moores promoted the world's first public *postal* pool with credit betting. The total staked on the first coupon was just under five pounds. In 1960, the latest year for which figures are available, John Moores's firm, Littlewoods Ltd., collected the equivalent of $145,600,000 in stake money and paid out $67,200,000 in prizes, $42,000,000 in tax, and $30,800,000 in expenses.

In Germany, Italy, Spain, France, and many other countries, football is the "national sport." In England it shares that honor with *cricket*, which is also a favorite among such British Commonwealth nations as Australia, New Zealand, India, and the West Indies. Cricket is an outdoor bat-and-ball game (derived from a 14th-century game called *club-ball* or *creag*) whose admirers view it as a sort of holy grail free of any taint of gambling. But true aficionados know differently. The 19th-century English writer Mary Russell Mitford, in her *English Life and Character*, expresses the cricket purist's sincere hatred for matches played "for money, hard money, between a certain number of gentlemen, and players, as they are called—people who make a trade of that noble sport, and degrade it into an affair of betting, and hedgings, and cheatings, it may be like boxing or horse-racing . . . ."

Miss Mitford would have been less than pleased to know that, according to one British authority, international matches today ("test" matches in cricket parlance) often load the bookmakers of all the countries concerned with up to a quarter of a million pounds in betting money yearly. Ordinary inter-county matches in Britain can also carry a sizable fortune in stakes; and there are lotteries based on the number of runs that individual batsmen make in each of the matches of the season. Further down the scale, "beer" matches are often played between opposing clubs if a scheduled match ends early, the stake being a barrel of beer.

Golf is a noble sport with a history going back to the days of the Romans, whose version was called *paganica* and was played with a crooked stick and a

Right, a late 18th-century British watercolor depicts players at the Marylebone cricket club. During the 19th century, cricket was popular only with the English upper classes; today, it is played and watched in most countries of the British Commonwealth.

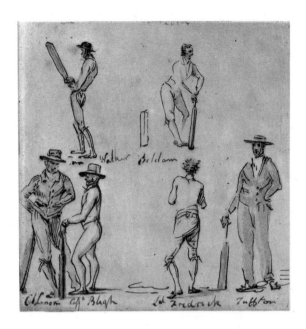

Below, a batsman of the West Indies team that won the "test" series against England in 1963. Large sums are always gambled on the outcome of both test matches and inter-county matches, and several British football pools promoters operate cricket pools during the summer season.

ball stuffed with feathers. Until recent years it has never attracted much of the gambler's money, partly because of its special appeal to top people (it was adopted as a pastime by James I of England in 1618) who can afford the relatively expensive equipment and club membership dues demanded of players, and partly because of the extensive perambulations that are required of spectators. But since the early part of the 19th century (until when the game was exclusive to Scotland) there has been a great spread of its popularity and a follow-up by the ever-increasing number of gamblers. England sometimes allows bookmakers (usually under protest from the Professional Golfers' Association) to carry on their business at tournaments, but they are requested to be soberly dressed, refuse cash bets, and refrain from shouting the odds.

In America things are somewhat different, and about $500,000,000 gets gambled annually on golf—mostly in ways particularly suited to the game. At many professional tournaments the bettors set up a kind of pool. The players are "auctioned"—that is, gamblers bid to "own" a player, and they may pay up to $25,000 for a top man. During play the "owners" can sell shares in their

Polo is largely a rich man's sport, which mainly attracts private gambling. In this diagram of a polo "play," one player hits the ball with his mallet toward the goal (left) while his teammates block opposing players.

man (and sometimes even make a profit). The money spent on "buying" the players goes into a pool that is shared out thus: 50 per cent to the owner of the winning player, 20 per cent to the owner of the second, 15 per cent to the third, 10 to the fourth, and 5 to the fifth. (The owner of the winner usually gives his golfer 10 per cent of the winnings.) In 1959, the total pool at the Las Vegas Annual Tournament of Champions was $285,000—a record at that time —and a Los Angeles man who backed the golfer Stan Leonard won $95,760. Sometimes, according to some commentators, golf pools can be rigged; some of the top pools have been discontinued for this reason. But smaller tournaments still often have such pools.

Many regions in America have developed their own special forms of golf-course gambling. At Westchester County, N.Y., the favorite gamble is called *bridge,* and has bidding associations with the card game. Each person in a four-some tries to predict his score (the "bid") for alternate holes; he wins one point for making his bid and one point for every stroke below it, at $1 a point. Brook Hollow, Dallas, Texas, specializes in *hammer*—a cry made by either of two players (playing for $1 a hole), when the other plays a bad shot. The hole must then be played out for an extra $25 as well as the original bet. *Wheel* is particularly associated with the East Potomac club in Washington; each player of five foursomes makes 19 separate bets (the "wheel") against his 19 opponents. *Pari-mutuel,* mainly a spectators' gamble, is popular at Orchard Lake, Detroit, where each foursome in a tournament is a "horse." The Tam o'Shanter club in Chicago fosters *bingle-bangle-bongo,* which depends more on luck than skill. On each hole the "bingle" is the first player whose ball reaches the green, the "bangle" is the player whose ball lies closest to the hole, and the "bongo" is the player who sinks the longest putt—each collecting a tribute that can vary from 50 cents to $50 apiece from the other members of the foursome.

Polo is an ancient game based on *savlajan,* a variant of horse racing popular in Persia in the sixth century. Today, because of the expense of buying and keeping polo ponies, polo is more of an upstage or specialist sport than, say, boxing or football, and the majority of gamblers pay correspondingly little attention to it. There was, however, regular gambling on polo at a British polo club in the early years of this century. The grounds were near a racecourse and spectators and bookmakers came over to watch polo after the races. Bets were small, but people would bet astonishingly quickly on the game as it ran (and it's a fast game)—i.e., on who would score the next goal, or whether the man with the ball would score, or who would score the most goals. In India there has always been some private betting among onlookers at polo games, but the law prevents it from amounting to a great deal. In Britain, in 1953, there was an unsuccessful attempt by the Polo Association to set up a totalizator, but a permit was not granted.

As for *tennis,* there is no doubt that many private bets are made on the results of championship matches in tennis-mad countries like Australia. Only a few bookmakers in most tennis-playing countries are interested enough to work out odds (which would be based on the proven abilities of the players). You might be able to place a bet in France (for instance, on matches at the Tennis Club de Paris) if you were a regular customer of a bookmaker. And Scandinavia permits bookies to set up shop in such places as Stockholm's King's Hall (though the bookies must stay outside if they want to shout the odds). The English Lawn Tennis Association, on the other hand, have never dreamed (anyway officially) of lowering the tone of the game by permitting public gambling. In fact in 1961 they sternly refused permission to a firm of bookmakers who wanted to set up shop at Wimbledon.

Ice hockey is the national game of the Canadians, who have adapted it from a British fen-country game called *bandy*. A sizable piece of Canada's gambling expenditure goes on the game, but the amount still isn't very big—$15,000,000 a year being the official figure. This may well be because there are only six teams in the main league (the National Hockey League) and the bookmakers must quote odds that are in their own favor if they are to stay in business. Four of the six teams are American, which attracts a few million dollars of American gambling money. The smaller leagues in Canada, and in the European and Scandinavian countries that play ice hockey, are usually ignored by bookmakers: Gambling on these games occurs mostly in the form of private betting among the spectators.

Private bets on most spectator sports are usually laid on which team will win, the size of the score, or other side issues. But in the annals of hockey there is a story of a more out-of-the-ordinary friendly bet, involving two Montreal physicists who were researching into the speed of propelled objects. One bet the other a dollar that during the course of a specified hockey match the puck would reach the speed of at least 100 miles an hour and at least one of the players would reach the skating speed of 40 mph. They made arrangements to have the use of the press box at a game between the Montreal and Detroit teams, took along their apparatus with all its complications of photoelectric cells and the like, and carried out the experiment. The fastest traveling puck they recorded was in a shot to goal of 87.35 miles an hour, and the fastest player's top speed reached 27 miles an hour. These two recorded speeds, however, established that ice hockey deserves its reputation for being "the fastest team game in the world."

Another incredibly fast game, *jai-alai* (pronounced "hi-li" and meaning, in Basque, "merry festival") is famous for its gambling. This game, which is sometimes called *pelota* (Spanish for "ball"), began its long term of popularity in Cuba at the beginning of this century: Today it is common in most of southern Europe, Latin America, and the U.S.A. It can be played by two or more players, using a ball slightly bigger, harder, and heavier than a golf ball. This is hit against the wall of an especially marked court and must bounce in a certain area. Florida legalized pari-mutuel betting on jai-alai in 1933, and a

The rules of pelota (or jai-alai) vary in different countries ; but wherever it is played, its fans gamble frenziedly. Above, a player wields the bat that is used in South America's version of the game. Right, a diagram of a play between two teams of three players (purple and green). Players A, B, and C have in turn hit the ball against the two walls (colored yellow) ; the orange spots indicate where the ball has bounced. Since the ball may bounce only once between each stroke, green has just lost a point.

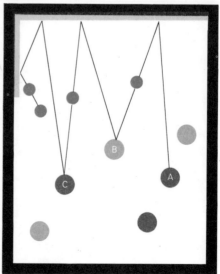

season at Miami can last over a hundred nights and attracts an average audience of 3,500. Each program usually features nine separate games, and the bettor places bets as for horse races—for "win" and "place"—on two players (or two teams) who must finish first and second in the night's play for him to win. The payoff on a $2 ticket may be anything up to $200.

As for *athletics,* or "track and field" sports, there are practically no places where public betting (in the sense of a "book" being opened for backers or athletes) flourishes to any extent. Anywhere games are held, of course, one can find someone who will offer odds against a particular athlete's winning an event. But, in general, bookmakers don't pay much attention to athletic assemblies, and the rules of the Olympic Games, which are certainly the greatest of such assemblies, forbid their presence. Anyone connected with the Olympics would be shocked at the insinuation that their fair athletics were being sullied by gambling. This attitude is most likely due to the mystique left over from classical times, when athletes competed for laurel wreaths and immortality.

All the same, human nature (in terms of gambling) reveals itself today as it probably did in classical times. According to a contributor to a book called *Olympic Odyssey* (1956), many athletes today bet on themselves. And newspaper sports reporters admit that they see a good deal of private gambling among the spectators (and perhaps among themselves). In the same book, an instance of this kind of gambling is given by Bobby Tisdall, creator of the then world's record for the 400 meters hurdles at the Games in Los Angeles in 1932:

"One day I had the honor of being routed out of my little hut in the Olympic village by Douglas Fairbanks (Senior) and Will Rogers. I think they were snooping around the 'paddock' for likely winners. Anyhow I heard later that Douglas won a thousand dollars on me."

Gambling, in fact, seems to be as indestructible as immortality.

Left, the Irish athlete Bobby Tisdall winning the 400-meter hurdle race at the Olympic Games held in Los Angeles in 1932. There is little organized gambling on athletics, and professional bookmakers are banned from the Olympic Games. But as in any contest, private betting cannot be prevented, and spectators (sometimes even competitors) often gamble on the outcome of the Games.

The finish of the 120-yard 1963 "Powderhall" race (so called after the village where it was originally held), which now takes place every New Year's Day at Newtongrange in Scotland as a main feature of an annual athletics meeting. Unlike the majority of other countries, Scotland permits open gambling on professional athletics. Evidence of this organized betting are the stands operated by bookmakers that can be seen in the background, behind the spectators. (Also identifiable—behind the runner numbered 5—is a "tic-tac" man, who is probably already taking bets on the next race.) Gambling on athletics is so common and so popular in Scotland that many of the sports pages of newspapers quote the odds offered by bookmakers on competitors in well-known events.

5 What are the odds?

Serious scientific investigation of the laws of chance (which came to be known as the Mathematical Theory of Probability) seems to have begun in Renaissance times, when so many other pioneering ventures in science were taking place. And some of the early investigations were made by the same great thinkers who were undermining age-old superstitions and paving the way for modern science —men like Johannes Kepler or Galileo Galilei.

Kepler, as an astronomer, was concerned with stars, not gambling; but when a bright new star appeared in 1604, he collected the views of some other star-gazers and approved the theory that the star had appeared because of the *chance* concurrence of atoms. Thereupon, he made a stab at some calculations in order to determine the time and the mathematical probability of another similar concurrence.

Galileo's contribution to the probability theory has a more direct relationship with gambling itself. He turned aside from his impressive work in other scientific fields to answer the trivial query of a gambling friend. The friend wanted to know why, with three dice, the number Ten is thrown more often than the number Nine. Galileo prepared an analysis of chances and showed that out of 216 possible cases, the number Ten has the advantage over the number Nine in the ratio of 27 cases to 25, because there are 27 combinations of dice forming the number Ten and only 25 forming Nine.

On an English racecourse white-gloved "tic-tac" men use a complex code of hand signs to signal the latest odds to bookies around the course. Racing odds are not mathematically fixed; they depend largely on a horse's past "form," and fluctuate as pre-race bets are made.

But the man who made the most extensive early examinations of probability was Gerolamo Cardano (1501-76), sometimes called Cardan. While a student at the University of Padua, Cardan began assembling notes for his *Liber de Ludo Aleae* (the *Book of Games of Chance*). He had plenty of opportunity for studying the subject, for his income was mainly derived from gambling until he achieved some fame as a physician, mathematician, philosopher, and inventor.

The *Book of Games of Chance* is a scrappy compilation; Cardan would frequently work out a solution to a problem, later discover that he was in error, and confusingly leave both the wrong and the right answers without any reference to the links between them. But it is comprehensive in subject matter, if not in treatment. Moral, historical, practical, and arithmetical aspects of gambling are all considered—though some of them not very deeply. Cardan warns his readers that, if they must gamble, they had better gamble for small stakes and that their opponents "should be of suitable station in life." He adds, however, that "in times of great anxiety and grief [gambling] is considered to be not only allowable, but even beneficial." There are instructions for playing *primero* (a card game similar to poker) and hints on watching for cheats who use soapy cards and mirrors in their finger rings to reflect the playing surfaces.

Aside from all this material, the book includes Cardan's notes on the principles of probability. He began his cogitations logically enough by considering that a die has six sides and that in a single cast of the die (since there is no skill or factor other than chance involved) any one of the sides is as likely to fall uppermost as any other. "Six equally likely cases" was Cardan's actual phrase. The probability of a particular side of the die falling uppermost he therefore expressed by the fraction $\frac{1}{6}$.

Thus, for determining the probability of an event that is governed by *pure chance*, the universal formula is $p = \frac{f}{c}$ (p being the probability, c being the total number of possible cases, and f the total number of favorable cases). Applied to the tossing of a coin, the fraction would be $\frac{1}{2}$, since there are two sides to the coin and one chance in a single toss that either the head or the tail will fall uppermost. To make this clear to the mind that is always dazed by formulae, here is the first Law of Probability in words:

The probability of an event is the number of cases favorable to that event compared with the total number of possible cases, so long as all the possible cases are equally likely to happen.

Cardan then went on to calculate the probabilities with two and three dice. He saw that with a single throw of two dice the total number of possible cases is 36, because any one of the six sides of one die can appear in combination with any one of the six sides of the other (6 x 6 = 36). And with a single throw of three dice, yet another six sides have to be taken into account, so that the sum would be 6 x 6 x 6 = 216 possible cases.

The calculation of possible cases is a simple matter of multiplication; but the calculation of *favorable* cases when two or more dice are being thrown is more

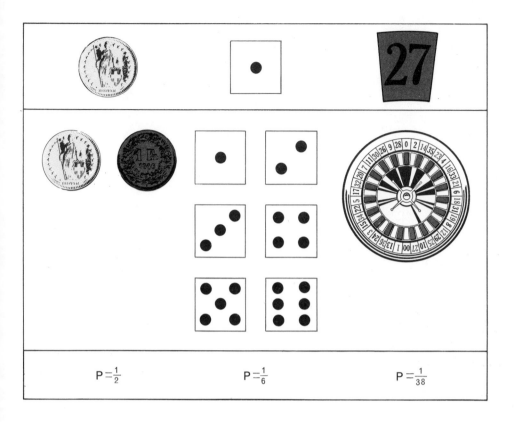

$$P = \frac{1}{2} \qquad P = \frac{1}{6} \qquad P = \frac{1}{38}$$

Above, Cardan's probability formula $(p = f/c)$ applied to coin tossing, dice, and roulette. Each side of a coin has a one in two chance of falling uppermost; each side of a six-sided die has a one in six chance; each roulette number (on an American wheel) has a one in 38 chance.

Below, a chart showing all the possible ways of throwing any number that two dice can produce. Seven comes out as the best bet with six possible combinations; thus the odds against it are 30 to 6. But the odds against throwing Two or Twelve (each can be made only one way) are 36 to 1.

2	3	4	5	6	7	8	9	10	11	12
1	2	3	4	5	6	5	4	3	2	1

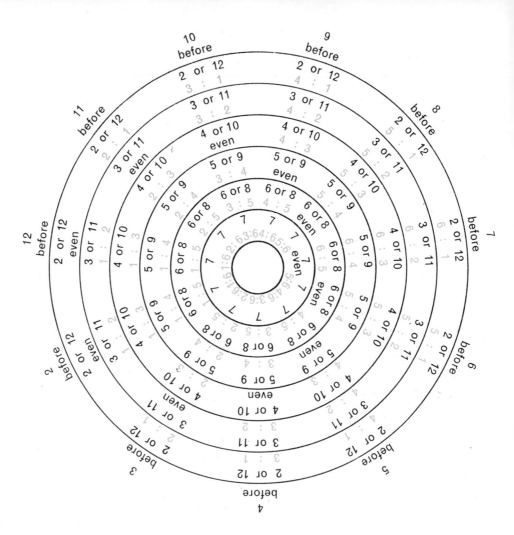

Above, a chart showing the odds against throwing any number before any other with two dice. The numbers that can be thrown are in black, the odds in blue. Reading in from the outer circle, the odds against throwing, say, a Nine before a Two or Twelve are 4 to 1 ; before a Three or Eleven, 4 to 2 ; before a Four or Ten, 4 to 3 ; and so on.

From the chart below, a craps player can gauge his chances of throwing a required number. A Seven or an Eleven made on the first throw wins ; a Two, Three, or Twelve loses. If a player throws a "point" he wins only if he duplicates that number *before* throwing a Seven. In casino craps, the dice can be backed either to win or lose.

Lose	Lose	Point	Point	Point	Win	Point	Point	Point	Win	Lose
2	3	4	5	6	7	8	9	10	11	12
					⚀⚅					
				⚀⚄	⚁⚄	⚁⚅				
			⚀⚃	⚁⚃	⚂⚃	⚂⚄	⚃⚄			
		⚀⚂	⚁⚂	⚁⚃	⚂⚃	⚃⚃	⚃⚄	⚄⚄		
	⚀⚁	⚁⚁	⚁⚂	⚂⚂	⚂⚃	⚃⚃	⚃⚄	⚄⚄	⚄⚅	
⚀⚀	⚁⚀	⚂⚀	⚃⚀	⚄⚀	⚅⚀	⚅⚁	⚅⚂	⚅⚃	⚅⚄	⚅⚅

difficult. Cardan first took considerable trouble to work out all the possible ways in which a dice player can throw a specific number. With this useful knowledge any player can work out his chances (or "favorable cases") of throwing a particular number in any single throw of, say, two dice. It becomes clear that though he has only one chance of throwing a Two or a Twelve, he has six chances of throwing a Seven. Fractionally expressed as favorable cases, these are $\frac{1}{36}$ and $\frac{6}{36}$ ($\frac{6}{36}$ is expressible also as $\frac{1}{6}$). Not only that. The dice player can now tell exactly what the odds are against his throwing any particular number, and from that knowledge can decide the amount of his bet—or whether he should bet at all.

The odds can be determined by simply comparing the unfavorable cases with the favorable ones. In throwing a single die, for instance, there are six possible cases—the six sides of the die. You therefore have a one in five chance of throwing a specific number in one throw. Or, to express it in the usual way, the odds are 5 to 1 against your throwing a specific number with one die in one throw. Similarly, with two dice there are 36 possible cases. A Twelve or a Two can each be thrown in only one way; so the odds against your throwing a Twelve or a Two in one throw of two dice are 35 to 1. The odds against scoring Eleven (or any other number that can be thrown in two ways) are 17 to 1 (i.e., 34 to 2). In tossing a coin, the odds are equal, for it is equally likely that heads or tails will fall uppermost. In drawing a card from a 52-card pack, the odds against its being the king of Clubs (or any other specified card) are 51 to 1. On a 38-number roulette wheel, the odds against any one number's coming up are 37 to 1.

With Cardan's information about the favorable chances of throwing a particular number, you can also work out the odds against throwing, say, a Six before a Seven. Such information will come in very handy if you play *craps,* a game (developed by American Negroes in the early 19th century) that is a simplification of a European dice game called *hazard.* Craps is played with two dice, and the rules are simple. The thrower of the dice wins if on his first try he throws a Seven or an Eleven (a "natural" or "pass"). He loses if he throws a Two, Three, or Twelve (a "crap" or "miss-out"), but he may continue to throw. If he throws a Four, Five, Six, Eight, Nine, or Ten (which is called the thrower's "point"), he neither wins nor loses but goes on throwing the dice until he either duplicates his point (also a pass or win) or throws a Seven (a miss-out or loss).

It is therefore an advantage for the craps player to know the probability of throwing, say, a Six before a Seven, for in casino play he may back the dice either to win or lose. Because there are five ways of throwing a Six, and six ways of throwing a Seven, the probability of throwing a Six before a Seven is $\frac{5}{11}$. Thus the odds are 6 to 5 against throwing a Six before a Seven. The probability of throwing a Four (or Ten) before a Seven is $\frac{3}{9}$ or 6 to 3 against (because there are only three ways of throwing either Four or Ten). In the same way, for a

Five or Nine the probability is $\frac{4}{10}$ or 6 to 4 against; and for Eight (as for Six) it is $\frac{5}{11}$.

Cardan's historic achievement was to crystallize a rule:

Events may be graded into three kinds: (a) the "impossible" (such as throwing a Seven with a single die); (b) the "certain" (such as the fact that one side of a thrown die must fall uppermost); (c) the "probable" (such as a Six falling uppermost on the first throw of a die). If (a) is expressed arithmetically as 0 and (b) is expressed as 1, then all the degrees of probability in between can be expressed as fractions.

The important thing to remember about this elementary rule is that it is applicable only in games of *pure chance* (like dice, roulette, or lotteries). It would be foolish to forget Cardan's phrase "equally likely cases" and attempt to apply the rule to, say, a race between six horses. One horse may be faster than another, or better ridden, or have more endurance, or may fall down, or turn and run the wrong way. Many factors (for instance, human and animal temperament, terrain, weather, or weight) can affect the result. The only reasonable certainties after the "off" are that six horses are running and that one (or possibly two) will get to the winning post before the others.

So to bet on the result of a race you must choose one of two courses: Either you can muster up all your knowledge of these particular horses and jockeys

During the running of the 1962 British Derby, the "favorite" was brought down in a pile-up involving six horses (left). The odds against the eventual winner were 22 to 1. Such unpredictable accidents show why Cardan's probability formula can be applied only to games of pure chance (like coin tossing or roulette) in which each possible case has an *equal* chance of winning.

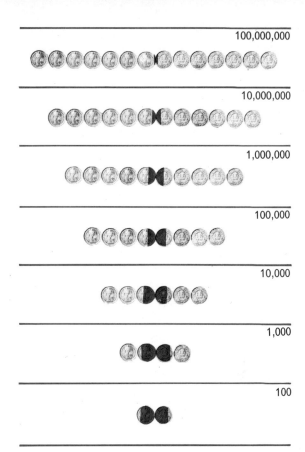

100,000,000

10,000,000

1,000,000

100,000

10,000

1,000

100

Right, a simplified diagram of the "law of large numbers" in terms of coin tossing. The difference between the number of heads and tails thrown tends to decrease as the number of tosses increases. When the number of tosses nears 100,000,000, the totals of heads and tails thrown may be expected to approach equality. With an infinite number of tosses, the totals (in theory) would even up.

and all the relevant factors (previous performance, ability of jockey, character of the track, odds offered, and so on); or you can place your bet blindly, making your choice for some arbitrary reason (a "hunch" or the color of the jockey's shirt). It is of course true that probabilities are worked out arithmetically and offered as odds on or against a particular horse's winning; but they are calculated by the bookmakers from experience and in accordance with the amount of money that is bet (see Chapter 8), not from the $p = \frac{f}{c}$ law.

One more observation is necessary about Cardan's basic law of probability. It concerns a very important characteristic of the law—and one that is very often forgotten or ignored by most people (who instead wryly substitute the altogether different element of "luck"): In a game of chance (where all the possible cases are equally likely and all the favorable cases are known, as in dice, coin tossing, or roulette) it may seem reasonable to assume that all the players have an equal chance of winning. And, according to the probability law, they have—*in the long run.*

"The long run" is a popular phrase used as a synonym for a general mathematical law called the Law of Large Numbers. To illustrate this law in simple terms: In, say, 10,000 tosses of a coin the proportion of heads will deviate by less than 1 per cent from the probable proportion of $\frac{1}{2}$. As the number of tosses increases, the deviation from equal proportions of heads and tails decreases.

That is, the proportions theoretically tend to even up as the number of tosses approaches infinity. So the long run isn't simply a stretch of coin tossing with a beginning and an end. It is an *interminability* of coin tossing, from an unspecified first toss somewhere in the past to a never-to-be-achieved last one in the future.

To understand the long run in relation to dice, imagine a circle representing the totality of dice games—past, present, and future—with all the players standing on the periphery throwing dice. If it were possible for all those players to stay permanently on that circle and throw that infinite number of throws, they would all have *precisely equal* chances of winning, just as the six equal sides of their dice would each fall uppermost an equal number of times. But since players constantly join, leave, and rejoin the circle, and since the number of games remains indeterminate (because the future hasn't happened yet), each player adding to this infinity of throws has to accept the specific *variation* in chance that happens to be current as he joins.

The variation may be working against him so far as financial success is concerned. But if you ignore all the stakes laid in all the games around the circle, you will see that "for" and "against" are meaningless terms where chance (a natural law) is concerned. Chance is heedless of artificial contrivances like dice or money or evaluations of "for" and "against." Chance brings about natural events like the distribution of geniuses among earthquake victims, or the incidence of black cats in gamblers' paths. It is man that decides whether these events are valuable ("for") or harmful ("against").

A player in a bridge game who is dealt a hand consisting of 13 Spades—the complete suit—may think the event remarkable. But the odds against his being dealt a complete run of a single suit are exactly the same as the odds against his being dealt any other *specified* combination of 13 cards (specifically, 635,013,559,599 to 1). And the card player who talks of "a run of bad luck" (when he picks up several consecutive hands of cards that are inconveniently useless as winning hands according to the rules of the game) must remember that chance is as heedless of the rules of bridge as of the existence of money. His chances of picking up winning hands are exactly the same as the other players' chances *in the long run*; but not necessarily in the same evening's games. It follows, then, that the longer he plays the better are his chances of evening up with his opponents in the drawing of winning hands.

Although the true long run is an infinite number of games, it is clearly impracticable to consider it as such. In practice a run can be considered only relatively long. But the principle remains valid. Professional gamblers who act as bookmakers or run casinos are in the position of playing against more or less unlimited time and wealth (represented by continual bets placed by innumerable people). They are therefore forced to give themselves an artificial advantage, either by charging a fee for each bet they accept, or by paying off their losses at less than the proper odds. I'll explain the workings of that advantage later. At

In the long run, seen here as dice throwing from before ancient Greece into the future, all combinations would occur an equal number of times. But because a gambler plays in a short run, his chances vary.

the moment I want to urge you to remember the importance of the long run.

After Cardan, many great minds applied their mathematical powers to the task of extending the theories of chance and probability, among them the 17th-century French mathematician and thinker Blaise Pascal. Several widely varying claims to fame are allowable to Pascal: his *Pensées*; the differential calculus (which he cleared the way to); the early blooming of his mathematical genius (his sister said that as a mere child he rediscovered the 32 theorems of geometry); the calculating machine (which he invented); his religious fervor; and his solutions to the gambling problems of a gamester called Antoine Gombaud, the Chevalier de Méré. De Méré had rightly deduced, or perhaps guessed, that the odds favored his throwing a Six at least once in four throws of a die. He had won himself a lot of money betting on that proposition. Multiplying his chances, he had wrongly deduced that with two dice the odds would favor his throwing at least one double Six in every 24 throws. Unaccountably this idea had worked against him, and he was going bankrupt. So he turned to Pascal for help.

Pascal discovered that the chevalier wasn't giving himself an even chance, let alone a favorable one. His mathematical procedure was fairly sophisticated (specifically, he multiplied the odds against winning by the colog of the hyperbolic log of two, i.e., 0.693, in this case 35 x 0.693 = 24.255); but the equation proved that to give himself an even chance, de Méré would have to throw the dice 24.255 times. Of course, you can't throw anything a fractional number of times. But had he bet on throwing a double Six once in every 25 throws, he would have had slightly better than an even chance of winning.

This slight edge is usually called a "favorable percentage." In the chevalier's case, the favorable percentage was 0.745 per cent (arrived at by subtracting 24.255 from 25). In other words, the odds *in favor* of his throwing a double Six in 25 throws were 0.745 per cent better than even.

Favorable percentages are extremely important to gamblers who operate a "house" (that is, who put themselves in the position of enduring a long run by accepting bets from all comers). They must give themselves a slightly favorable percentage in order to remain in business against virtually unlimited time and capital. For however big the house's capital is to begin with, and however long it remains continually in business, it can never match the aggregate time and capital available against it.

To illustrate how a gambling house adjusts its odds, here is a hypothetical case in terms of roulette :

Imagine a roulette wheel excluding the zero and the American double zero —that is, with only 36 spaces. And imagine that you have $36 to bet with, and that the house is paying the *true* odds of 35 to 1. You back the number of your choice with a dollar at every spin. Assume that you lose 35 times and that with your last dollar your number comes up. Because the odds are 35 to 1, you win $35 plus the dollar you bet with on that spin. You have in fact broken even and are back where you started with $36. But this would never do for a casino, which has to make a profit as well as stay in business. It cannot make a profit solely from losers, since in the long run the amount of money received from losers will tend to even up with the amount paid to winners. But if a gambling house pays out at *less than the true odds* to every winner, then it will gain an artificial advantage.

If the house odds in that imaginary roulette game were 30 to 1 instead of the true odds of 35 to 1, you would win only $30. With your dollar bet returned, you would still be $5 lighter in pocket than when you started. This is the margin of profit that keeps the house in business. If you were luckier, and your chosen number came up in the first spin of the wheel rather than the 36th, you would have $30 more than you started with. But the house would still be saving itself money ; it has in effect "charged" you $5 for gambling privileges (the extra $5 that you would have won if the odds were true). Although winners rarely realize it, it is they perhaps even more than the losers who make casinos (and bookmaking) such profitable businesses.

The percentage worked out by a gambling house in its own favor varies from house to house (and with different games). Some of them take very high percentages indeed; others, like the Monte Carlo casino, rub along on a maximum of $2\frac{26}{37}$ (2.7) per cent, which according to their calculations is the lowest possible figure that allows them to cover the expenses of running the place and to make a reasonable profit without driving gamblers away. And there is nothing fraudulent about these percentage rake-offs; most gambling centers make it clear what percentage they take, so the gamblers know (or should know) what odds are being offered before they place their bets.

In games combining skill and chance, like most card games, the most skilful player is in the same position as a casino. His extra skill is equivalent to the artificial advantage of a favorable percentage. The more skilled he is compared with the other players, the more quickly he will begin to win and keep his winning lead. Chance, of course, determines the cards each player is dealt, but unless the players are equally skilled (in which case they will in the long run all

Right, a 36-space roulette table (without the zeros). Imagine a player betting a dollar a spin (on, say, the 4) who loses 35 times but wins on the 36th spin. If the casino paid at *true* odds of 35 to 1, he would break even, winning $35 plus his last $1 bet. To stay in business, casinos must pay less than true odds. The chart below shows what would happen to that player if (with $60 capital) he played eight similar rounds—losing 35 bets and winning the 36th—at a casino paying 30 to 1. He would lose $35 and win $31 each round; after eight rounds he would have lost his entire capital.

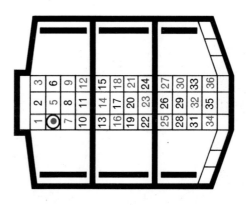

	Stake	Lose	Win	Capital
First round	35 $1	$35		$60-$35 = $25
(36 bets)	1 x $1		$1 + $30	$30 + $1 + $25 = $56
Second round	35 x $1	$35		$56-$35 = $21
	1 x $1		$1 + $30	$30 + $1 + $21 = $52
Third round	35 x $1	$35		$52-$35 = $17
	1 x $1		$1 + $30	$30 + $1 + $17 = $48
Fourth round	35 x $1	$35		$48-$35 = $13
	1 x $1		$1 + $30	$30 + $1 + $13 = $44
Fifth round	35 x $1	$35		$44-$35 = $9
	1 x $1		$1 + $30	$30 + $1 + $9 = $40
Sixth round	35 x $1	$35		$40-$35 = $5
	1 x $1		$1 + $30	$30 + $1 + $5 = $36
Seventh round	35 x $1	$35		$36-$35 = $1
	1 x $1		$1 + $30	$30 + $1 + $1 = $32
Eighth round	32 x $1	$32		$32-$32 = $0

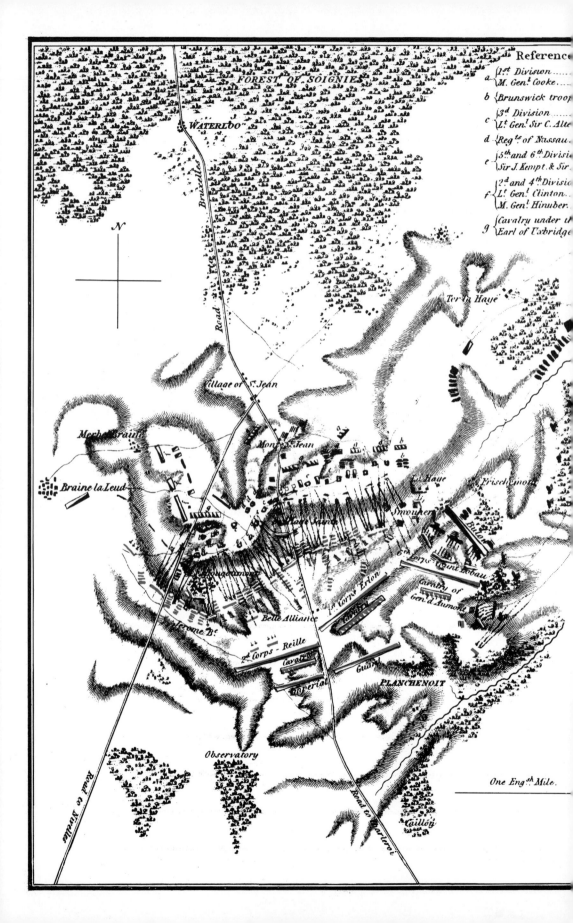

FOREST OF SOIGNIES

WATERLOO

N

Ter la Haye

Village of St Jean

Merbe Braine

Mont St Jean

Braine la Leud

La Haye

Frischemont

La Haye Sainte

Smouher

Plon

Village

Hougoumont

1er Corps d'Erlon

Cavalry of
Gen. d'Aumont

Corps Count Lobau

Jerome B.

Belle Alliance

2d Corps - Reille

Cavalry

Guard

PLANCHENOIT

Imperial

Observatory

One Engsh Mile.

Road to Nivelle

Road to Charleroi

Caillou

break even) chance is counteracted by skill, and the less skilful players are eventually certain to lose.

Innumerable fallacies have been perpetuated about chance and probability, many of which more or less echo Napoleon's remark that security is "the mathematical elimination of chance"—as silly a thing as has been said by him or anybody else, since it is impossible to eliminate a natural law. Perhaps his fallacious reasoning is responsible for the notion, staunchly clung to by soldiers, that it is *mathematically* impossible for two shells to fall on the same spot. The odds against a shell's falling on a designated spot on a battlefield are, of course, related to the aim of the gun and the size of the target area. But they are not increased by one jot after the fall of the first shell.

The soldier in a shellhole who thinks "I'm safe here because mathematics has eliminated the possibility of another shell's falling on the same spot" is perpetuating exactly the same fallacy as the casual gambler (call him Lucky Jim) at a roulette table who observes that red has come up for 10 consecutive spins, and who therefore puts his bet on black because he thinks it simply *must* come up on the 11th spin. The probability of black has not been increased in the slightest by the 10 preceding reds; for (this is a basic rule in any game of pure chance) every single cast of a die, toss of a coin, or spin of a roulette wheel is *completely unrelated* to every other cast, toss, or spin, whether before or after. In other words, the chances of Jim's winning on any particular spin of the wheel are not improved in the slightest by his knowledge of the results of the 10 (or 100, or 1000) previous spins.

At this point I had better deal with a possible objection to that statement. "Surely," some Lucky Jim might say, "black ought to come up on the 11th spin or soon afterward *by the law of averages!*" But the phrase "law of averages" is often wrongly used, and in this context is meaningless. What most people mean by the "law of averages" is the "law of large numbers," which (as we have seen) says that in the long run all the possible cases will happen an equal number of times. In terms of roulette, the law would say that, as the number of spins of the wheel approaches infinity, the number of blacks tends to even up with the number of reds.

But 11 spins of the wheel do not constitute a long run. So Lucky Jim, betting on black on the 11th spin, has no need to concern himself with the long run, or the law of large numbers, or with any mathematical law other than this one: The probability of black's coming up on any one spin remains the same no matter what were the results of preceding spins—a probability of $\frac{1}{2}$.

Lucky Jims are usually much more reasonable about their expectations in lottery gambles. Lotteries (and other forms of numbers gambles), though offering a prize distribution that is dependent on pure chance, are not participating

Napoleon maintained that he could mathematically eliminate chance from a battle by carefully calculating every move and countermove beforehand. But events proved that chance can't be eliminated. Left, a battle plan of Waterloo.

117

games from Jim's point of view. He merely buys a ticket, knowing that the single event of the drawing of the lottery will decide whether he wins or not. If there were 100 different lotteries, all being drawn at consecutive moments on the same day, and if he had a ticket in each of them, he would not expect the numbers of the first 99 tickets drawn to affect the number of the 100th ticket. Yet that is what he is expecting of the random whims of chance if he supposes that 10 consecutive reds in roulette can influence the result of the 11th spin of the wheel.

(One noteworthy fact about lotteries and other numbers games, though: Each time a ticket is drawn in a multiple-prize lottery or pool, the odds against the success of the remaining numbers are reduced. If there are a million tickets in the lottery, the odds against a specific number's being drawn first time are 999,999 to 1, and they are reduced by one each time a ticket is drawn. But in a million-ticket lottery this is scarcely an encouraging reduction in odds.)

It must not be assumed that the few basic elements of the theory of probability that I've discussed so far—odds, favorable percentages, the long run, etc.—are all there is to it. The theory had grown into quite a jungle of complicated mathematics even by Pascal's day; and, after him, extensions and revisions to the theory were made by, among others, Huygens, Jacques and Daniel Bernoulli, Newton, d'Alembert, and Gauss, while the French astronomer Pierre Laplace co-ordinated the findings of more than a dozen mathematicians over two centuries in his *Théorie Analytique des Probabilités,* and included his own application of the theory to the causes of phenomena and statistics.

Huygens, a 17th-century Dutchman, was an early statistician who paved the way for life insurance by working out tables relating to the probable expectation of life at various ages. The Bernoullis—a Swiss family of mathematicians who spread their achievements over the 17th and 18th centuries—popularized the newly discovered calculus of Newton and Leibnitz, worked out innumerable calculations concerning hydraulics and pneumatics, and systematically studied every known field of mathematics, including one very important to the theory of probability: the field of large numbers. This particular exploration has come to be known as the "Bernoullian Series of Bernoullian Numbers"; it plays a part in my brief look at statistics later. The German mathematician Gauss produced the Law of Errors, which stated that in repeated measurement of the same object or process, it must not be expected that the outcome of every observation will be the same. Newton's revelation of the differential calculus and d'Alembert's studies of the laws of dynamics both opened new possibilities for the development of the theory of probability; but these discoveries get far too complicated in their mathematics for summarization here.

All these towering scientists had been concerned with probability in the line of their studies as physicists, astronomers, geodesists, and mathematicians. But their work opened the way for the gambler, and also for the insurers, bankers,

Above, a bingo session in Britain. From a "cage" containing balls numbered from 1 to 90, an operator draws a ball; its number is announced by a "caller" and displayed in lights above the stage. Each player holds a card containing any 15 of the 90 numbers in any order. When a number tallying with a player's number is called, he covers it with a marker; the first player to cover a complete line, wins. Right, a simplified bingo card. Five of its numbers (in red) have been called. (Incidentally, in 90 numbers there are 43,949,268 possible sets of five *different* numbers.)

2	12	32	40	61
4	17	34	47	65
9	19	38	49	68

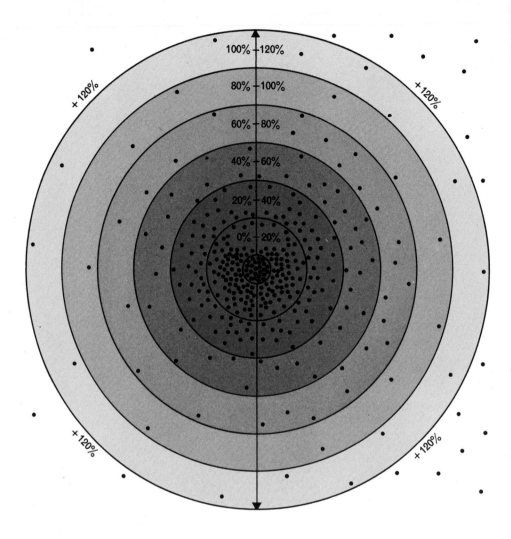

Above, a chart showing the results of predictions (based on extensive market research) made for the Japanese daily newspaper *Chubu Nippon Shimbun*— predictions of the probable number of readers who would see advertisements in particular positions on the front page. After the estimate was made, it was tested by showing a page to a large sampling of readers who were asked which advertisements they could remember. Each dot on this graph represents an estimate ; each section of the circle represents a certain percentage of accuracy. Estimates for an advertisement falling in the center were absolutely accurate ; those in the inner circle were up to 20 per cent out ; those in the outer circle were 100 to 120 per cent out. In this case the estimate of overall readership probability proved to be 84 per cent accurate—a good result for a probability estimate of this kind.

Ten years' planning, a quarter of a billion dollars, and two years' market research went into producing the Edsel motorcar (right), launched by Ford Motors in 1957. Research predictions indicated a high probability of success for this new car. But research cannot entirely eliminate risk : The Edsel didn't meet the expected response. It was withdrawn from production after two years.

advertising men, nuclear scientists, and doctors of today. The theory of probability is used in determining the behavior of atoms, in working out problems of genetics, in fixing life-insurance rates based on tables of mortality, in conducting opinion polls, in advertising detergents to the likeliest buyers, in establishing the life cycles of bacteria and political parties, and in predicting the success of all kinds of commercial enterprises. But it is used, in some of these cases, in a rather different way—i.e., in association with the science of statistics.

The observation that statistics can be made to prove anything is a euphemistic version of Disraeli's remark: "There are lies, damned lies, and statistics." As a generalization it isn't true, though it *is* true that a statistician can, if he wishes, forget or suppress important factors in statistical analyses and thereby create false impressions. However, giving such rogues no more than that brief mention, I'll turn now to the *proper* uses of the science (simplified to avoid the complex and esoteric mathematics that are involved).

Statistics are measurable facts recorded in figures and interpreted with some special object in mind. The objects may be extremely varied. I have mentioned opinion polls, insurance, advertising, medicine, physics, politics, and commerce as activities depending on, or at any rate using, statistics. But there are other more surprising uses for them. For example, they have several times been used to establish the disputed authorship of literary works.

A writer's style has certain measurable characteristics—specifically, the repetitive use of certain words and the length of his sentences. Quite recently (in 1962) two American professors of mathematics announced that they had used a computer to determine the authorship of a dozen 18th-century essays that had been the center of a major literary controversy for well over 100 years. The essays were undoubtedly written by either Alexander Hamilton or James Madison, but no one could be certain which. With the computer, a count was made of certain key words in the problematical essays and in the known works of Hamilton and

Statistics are not only a means of measuring an existing situation (like population figures); they also provide a means of estimating the probability of future occurrences. For instance, the chances of winning one of the many prizes in the Irish Sweepstakes are about one in 1000, calculated by dividing the number of prizes by the number of tickets sold (above left). The chances of being involved in a road accident in Britain— based on official accident figures for 1962—are about one in 156 (below left). So a British citizen is roughly six-and-one-half times more likely to be involved in a road accident than win a prize in the Sweepstakes.

Chances = $\dfrac{\text{Prizes}}{\text{Tickets sold}}$ = 1000:1

Chances = $\dfrac{\text{Accidents}}{\text{Population}}$ = 156:1

Madison. When these counts were compared, the statistical result added up to apparent proof that 11 of the essays were Madison's.

Some statistical measurements can be made with accuracy—like counting the population of a country or measuring the amount of land washed away from a coastline each year. But statistics are also used to assess probability—for instance, in commerce, to assess the probable welcome awaiting a new product. In the advertising industry (which would be called upon to make such an assessment for a manufacturer) the method is called "market research." But this term usually refers to investigations of the *actual* response of the public to various products. What I am concerned with here is the public reaction to a new product —a testing-of-the-odds process that is called "sampling." A manufacturing company that is concerned with launching a new product—say, a cake mix—will hire an advertising agency to handle the project. The agency's job will be the laborious business of collecting statistics. Obviously, they will need figures relating to the sales of existing cake mixes; to population densities in different areas; to the areas in which most home cooking is done; to the potential receptiveness of the public to the *idea* of bought cake mixes; and so on.

A thorough sampling will also take statistical account of the attitudes of husbands and children, as well as wives, to different kinds of cake; of the income groups in which cake is an acceptable food; of nutritional values; and of the composition and times of meals in general. And the agency may well explore some unusual notions. For instance, common sense may indicate that the cake-making market is exclusively formed of family units, but statistical research may reveal that thousands of young unmarried people are aching for just such an activity as cake making.

Some of these statistics—for instance, sales and population—will be readily available; others will have to be sought. They will be found by asking people questions. And the form the questionnaire takes will itself be the subject of intensive research, since statistics from some other sampling project may prove that direct and oblique questioning have different advantages.

The consensus among advertising agencies is that the best method of questioning is by knocking on doors and asking the people who open them the questions. The casual approach in the street and the postal inquiry are less effective. And it is at the stage of deciding which doors to knock on that the laws of probability first come into the sampling operation.

The ideal would be to get an unaffected answer to every question in the questionnaire from every interrogable person in the country. But by applying the laws of probability to certain known factors (like the number of interrogable people and their distribution among areas, income groups, and age groups) the agency may find that an effectively ideal result can be gained by asking, say, one person in 5000. The choice of the particular 5000 and the particular one person will also be made by referring to the laws of probability, which may provide some useful indications. They may reveal, for instance, that if three doors are to be knocked on in three different streets in the same town, they had better not all have the same street number; if three Number Ones are chosen, the answers may be affected by the fact that Number Ones are corner houses with a slight social edge on the rest of the street.

Summarily, then, the statistics of actual measurement and those involving the laws of probability will both be used to prepare the way for the sampling. And when the sampling is completed, both will again be used to analyze it and give the manufacturers the information they need in order to launch their gamble— for putting a new product on the market is always a gamble, as the Ford people learned when they tried to sell Edsels to the American public.

The statistics brought to light by the sampling will provide the agency with further statistics showing the kind of advertising campaign that will probably be most effective in promoting the sales of the cake mix. If, for instance, the sampling shows that young unmarried people are unexpectedly interested in cake mixes, it becomes important to spend a proportion of the advertising allotment on telling them about the new one. Telling them (and everybody else) involves, among other things, the statistics of magazine circulation. And magazine circulation is in itself a problem in which the laws of probability can be used again.

Suppose, for example, the makers of the cake mix decided to advertise in the two biggest-circulation home magazines in the country (to get at the big market) and also in a magazine bought mainly by young unmarried people (to get at the unexpected smaller market). The problem of duplicated circulation then arises, for it is likely that the young unmarried people will see the home magazines as well as their own. The laws of probability can tell the advertising agency the chances of any reader's seeing one, two, or all three of the advertisements. (Specifically, assuming that one reader in five sees the advertisement in any one magazine, the chances that the same reader will see it in two magazines are 13 in 125, and in three 1 in 125.)

As you can see even from this quick sweep of the statistical horizon beyond advertising and commerce (a sweep that has ignored the algebraic complexities), there are a great many ways in which the laws of probability can help manufacturers to reduce the risk (the *gamble*) when bringing out a new product.

Another high-powered modern industry—insurance—depends to a great extent on statistics and probability. The business of the modern life insurance actuary (the word derives from *actuarius*, the shorthand writer who recorded the decisions of the Roman magistrates) depends on the ability to compute premiums, which are the insured person's contributions to cover a specified risk. The insurance company is, in effect, gambling on the life expectancy of its customers. The amounts of premiums are determined in much the same way that bookmakers and other professional gamblers determine the odds or percentages that will give them a good chance of winning against a long run (that is, against the practically unlimited time and capital of all their customers). Both the bookie and the actuary use the laws of probability; but where the bookie uses his knowledge of horses, jockeys, etc., the actuary uses population statistics —or mortality tables.

These tables show recorded birth and death rates over a number of years, and from them the actuary can work out your chances of survival during a given future period. The amount of the premium is, of course, based on these chances; but added to it will be a further sum to cover the expenses of the insurance company, its profits, and contingencies arising from short runs of luck that work against the company. (I have purposely avoided any reference to "bad" luck; adjectives were invented by man, luck was around earlier.)

Even these runs of luck are predicted by the laws of probability. They manifest themselves (so far as life insurance is concerned) in unusual numbers of deaths due to such occurrences as war, famine, and pestilence. These are deviations from expectation. Similar deviations can be predicted for any event governed by chance. The American mathematician Arne Fisher, in his *The Mathematical Theory of Probabilities,* describes an experiment in which 10,000 drawings were made from a pack of cards. Since there are an equal number of red and black cards, the expectation was that each color would be drawn 5000 times. In fact 4933 black cards were drawn—a deviation of 67. The deviation predicted for 10,000 cases by Gauss's Law of Errors was 33.7, so apparently something went adrift with the experiment. But the Bernoullian Numbers

Above, employees at London Airport sell insurance to customers before a flight. Right, a diagram shows (in simplified form) how an insurance company calculates a premium i.e., what to charge a client. The amount of an individual payout is determined in accordance with such factors as accident statistics.

$$\text{Premium} = \frac{\text{Payout to one insured person}}{\text{Number of people insured}} + \text{profit margin}$$

Total with two cards	Possible combinations from 52 cards
21	64
20	136
19	80
18	86
17	96
16	86
15	96
14	102
13	118

Left, a chart for the blackjack player showing the number of ways (with two cards) of making each number between 13 and 21. (In blackjack, a player tries to obtain a higher total card count than the dealer without exceeding a total of 21.) Right, a chart for four three-card hands (which total—left to right—16, 15, 14, and 13) showing the chances of each hand's reaching a count of between 17 and 21 with any number of extra cards; exceeding 21 with any number of extra cards; and exceeding 21 with *one* extra card.

(Jacques Bernoulli's series of numbers that determine the frequency distribution of events) must also be used when calculating predictable errors; and the combination of these two laws, applied to the result of the experiment, proved that a deviation of about twice the normal is expected once in five and a half times.

All the possible applications of all the laws of probability cannot, of course, give reliable figures to insurance companies unless the mortality tables to which they are applied are themselves reliable. James Dodson, an 18th-century English pioneer actuary, worked out a table of premiums payable annually to ensure £100 on death at any age between 14 and 67; but the mortality tables of those days were so inaccurate that the premiums were fixed at too high a rate and Dodson's company accumulated huge reserves of money. (It was later returned in the form of bonuses.)

This situation would be unlikely to arise today. Even if there were no laws regulating profits, an insurance company whose premiums were too high would simply lose customers, as would a casino whose "favorable percentage" was too high. So the premium or the percentage must be of a size that will in the long run give the company or casino a profit but won't alienate potential customers. In gambling casinos, however, the players are not totally at the mercy of the house's favorable percentage. Many gamblers try to put the laws of probability to work on their side of the card table or roulette wheel by devising "systems" that are supposed to increase their chances of winning. As will be seen in later chapters, there are several things that can make the most cunningly devised system go awry. Not the least of these is the excitement of play itself, which can make a gambler throw his mathematics to the winds and plunge.

But some gambling systems have proved to be reasonably reliable. The ordinary player of the card game called *blackjack* (or *twenty-one*) may not be greatly helped by the basic knowledge that there are 1326 different ways in which two cards can total the numbers from two to 21 and that there are only 564 two-card combinations worth 16 or more. But he can do better than that, if his mathematics and memory are up to it, by using a system developed by Edward O. Thorp, an American mathematics professor.

Total with two or more cards	♠10 ♦2	♠4 ♣3	♠6 ♥6	♠Q ♥2	♣2 ♠7	♥3 ♠3
Total chances of reaching a count of 17 to 21	20 in 52		22 in 52	23 in 52		25 in 52
Total chances of exceeding 21	32 in 52		30 in 52	29 in 52		27 in 52
Chances of exceeding 21 with one card	32 in 52		28 in 52	24 in 52		20 in 52

Blackjack is a relatively simple game: Basically, the player must take cards from the dealer (or banker) that total 21 or less, and he wins if his total is higher than the dealer's. The ace counts one or 11; court cards count 10; other cards count their face value. In a two-handed game this is the usual procedure: The dealer gives his opponent and himself one card each, face down. Then he gives his opponent a card face up. The opponent can "stay" (i.e., refuse additional cards) or he can ask for more cards to increase his total. (If his total goes over 21 he loses automatically.) When the opponent stays, he makes his bet. Then the dealer gives himself a card or cards (face up), depending on what he needs to increase his total (but to stay under 21), and covers the bet.

Thorp based his system on the fact that the cards usually aren't shuffled after each hand of blackjack. Thus when certain combinations of cards have been used, the odds (or the "favorable percentages") favor the player rather than the dealer. For instance, when the fives are gone, the player has a favorable percentage of 3.3 per cent; but the dealer has an edge of 2.7 per cent when the aces are gone.

The player must keep track of all cards played; he must also be aware of the changes in advantage when different combinations of cards are gone. For this knowledge the player would have to follow Thorp's example and use a computer to work out all the various fluctuations possible, and the size of the percentage in each case. But armed with these facts, a player would be able to know whether or not he had an edge even after the first hand, and could judge his cards and bet accordingly.

It is doubtful if a more complex system has ever been devised. But Thorp's own experiences (he has promised a book on the subject) seem to indicate that few other systems have been so successful. Even when betting cautiously, Thorp was able to win $2000 in less than four hours in a Las Vegas club. And his success was capped when he was barred from several casinos in the same city—because he was winning too steadily. Most other gamblers' systems seem excellent in theory but prove imperfect in practice. Which perhaps is just as well— or all the excitement of gambling might be lost in a flood of mathematics.

6 Seven come eleven

The dice game played for Christ's raiment by the soldiers at the foot of the cross is probably the most famous reference to dice in Christian history. But dice are a lot older than Christianity. They probably go back even further than the Theban dice (1573 B.C.) mentioned on p. 30—back to the crude sticks, shells, or bones used for divination by primitive man. Crudity, however, is no indication of age: The astragals (ankle bones of sheep used as dice) in the British Museum and Pennsylvania University Museum are not all necessarily earlier than the accurately shaped ivory Thebans, or than some stone dice discovered at Naucratis in Egypt and dated 600 B.C. Astragals were still in popular use even in Roman times (the Latin word for astragal is *talus*).

Dice (with which I include for the moment astragals) seem to have appeared in Asia very early. But their first use there was most likely as motivators in games like *backgammon,* in which pieces are moved on a board in directions and distances prescribed by the throw of dice. Backgammon (in one form or another) is the precursor of practically every modern board-and-pieces game in which the moves are decided by dice—even parlor games like *snakes-and-ladders* or the more sophisticated *Monopoly.* Boards and pieces for a dice game that must have been very similar to modern backgammon have been found on sites of the early Mesopotamian civilizations, which were 3000 years before Rome. In fact, backgammon in some form is probably the oldest of all games combining skill and

The dice come out on a typical casino craps table. Craps, America's favorite game of chance, is now played extensively in gambling centers throughout the world.

chance—though the element of skill involved lies mainly in the use of one's knowledge of the possible combinations that can be thrown with a pair of dice. Evidence of its presence (though none of its invention) has been found among the relics of most old civilizations—including the Chinese, Indian, Aztec, American Indian, Celtic, and Saxon.

Backgammon is essentially a race game for two players. Each player tries to get all his pieces off the board before his opponent, and the dice determine how often and to what extent the pieces are hindered or advanced. Each player's side of the board is divided in half by a bar. On one side of the bar is the player's "inner" table (containing six points); on the other side is the "outer" table (also with six points). There are 15 white pieces and 15 black. The pieces are moved the number of points corresponding to the dice (the number thrown may be shared by two pieces). White moves his pieces from Black's inner table to Black's outer, then to his own outer and finally to his own inner. Black moves in the opposite direction.

Arrival at a point already occupied means that the occupying player must return his piece to the bar, from which it may be allowed to move again only when the player throws a number coinciding with an unoccupied point. When a player has got all his men to his inner table he must try for a number that will allow him to release his pieces from the board; if he can achieve this before his opponent, he is the winner.

There are three degrees of victory: a single win (or "hit"), which is achieved if the opponent has already begun to take his pieces from the board; a double

Left, a Greek vase painting (from 550-525 B.C.) depicting Achilles and Ajax dicing during the Trojan War. They are probably playing some form of backgammon, which is one of the oldest of board-and-pieces games using dice as a motivator.

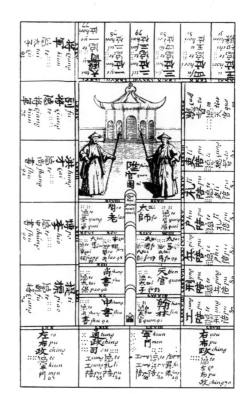

Right, the chart used for the popular Chinese game "promotions." The chart (made of paper or silk) is divided into different headings, with various civil services appointments listed beneath. Colored counters are moved upward or downward ("promoting" or "demoting" the players) in accordance with the throw of four dice.

win (or "gammon"), meaning that the opponent has not yet taken any of his pieces away; and a triple win (or "backgammon"), in which the opponent merely has a piece in his own inner table. The winner of two of three games is the final victor. Betting by players and backers is usually on a straight ultimate victory, but it may also involve side bets on the different degrees of victory in individual games.

Simplification and elaborations of backgammon exist in profusion all over the world. All through the many versions, from the Indian *pacisi* (which is played on a cruciform board) to the nursery game *ludo* and the countless commercial variants with topical slants that are marketed from time to time (with names like *Totoplay, Motogo,* and *Grand National*) the idea of race simulation is maintained. Backgammon itself is played to some extent in Europe and America and is very popular in the Middle East and Asia. In France it's called *tric-trac,* in Italy *favola reale,* and in Germany *trich-trach* or *puffspiel.* But in the Western world it is by no means as popular as cards or as dice games involving no more than the dice themselves. In many European cities it is difficult even to find a shop selling the equipment.

The Chinese have a version of backgammon called *coan ki* ("the game of the vases"). This game is played on a rectangular board divided laterally into eight parts along which small (and often beautifully carved) ivory "vases" are moved in accordance with the throws of two dice, from one end to the other and back again. The first player to get home wins, provided he has a majority holding of vases.

131

Above, a modern backgammon board. Essentially a "race" game for two players, backgammon is the forerunner of most modern board-and-pieces games played with dice. To win, a player must get all his pieces off the board before his opponent. The throw of two dice determines the advance of the pieces. Left (from a 17th-century Turkish manuscript), a backgammon game in progress at a feast. Backgammon, in one form or another, is played practically everywhere in the world—but especially in the East. In terms of dice gambles, the Western world generally prefers those using dice alone.

Shing kun t'o, "The Game of the Promotion of Mandarins," another Chinese game, is popular today almost everywhere in the world where there is an Oriental population. It is played on a big rectangular paper or silk chart divided along one long edge into eight headings beneath which are listed various civil service appointments. The players move colored counters, in accordance with the throws of four dice, upward or downward through the grades of promotion.

There are several Japanese versions of this game, which are known generally as *sugoroku* (a word meaning "double sixes" that is applied to any game in which a player's success depends on his throwing a higher number than his opponent). These versions are played variously on paper charts, wooden boards, or boxes with compartments; the stages of progress through which players move their pieces are sometimes symbolic (from night to day, across rivers of time, and through obstacles represented by black and white watching "eyes"), sometimes professional (as in the Chinese game), sometimes dynastic (with the players relying on the dice to get them attached to the dynastically "right" families), and sometimes topographical (in which the stages are the stages of a journey with all the hazards of precipices, whirlpools, and the like).

In the Far East, the One and Four (or sometimes the Three and Four) on the dice are spotted in red. This practice is explained in a legendary story of a Ming emperor, who was playing sugoroku and needed One and Four (or Three and Four, depending on the version you hear) to win. He called to the dice to fall as he wanted them (thereby, perhaps, originating the superstitious practice of whispering to the dice before throwing them). They came up, and he commanded that from then on Ones and Fours on all dice used in his empire should be painted red.

In many Eastern games, dice are used on their own account rather than as motivators; and the dice are conventionally of different sizes for different games. They can range from one fifth of an inch to a full inch in cubic size. (Also, in accordance with the Eastern principle of introducing as much beauty as possible into mundane things, dice are thrown into decorated porcelain bowls instead of onto any surface that happens to be around.) The biggest dice are used in the popular game *sing luk* ("four, five, six") and three of them are thrown at a time by each player. The first player throws until he gets either of the following: three dice showing alike; a Four, Five, and Six; two alike with the third die ignored unless it's a One; or One, Two, and Three.

The smaller dice are used in *chak t'in kan* ("throwing heaven and nine"), a game in which 21 different combinations of throws are divided into "civil" and "military" ranks. Pairs of Sixes, Ones, Fours, and Fives, and a combination of One and Three are called (respectively) Heaven, Earth, Man, Plum Blossom, and Harmony.

The somewhat harsher name of *pat cha* ("grasping eight") is given to a dice game in which individual players bet against a banker. Eight of the smallest dice are used, and the banker has a facsimile plan of the six faces of a die on which the players put their stakes, as on a roulette table. The player has only two chances of winning: If among his eight thrown dice three, four, or five fall showing the number he has bet on, the banker pays him eight times his stake; if six or more duplicate his number, he gets paid 16 times his stake. With any other throw he loses. Games resembling pat cha are played in India, Manila, and Portugal (in the last, the game is called *pirinola*) with a teetotum (or spinning top) instead of a die. But the six sides of the top are marked exactly as if it were a die, with the One and Four in red.

Versions of pat cha (all these Chinese games have countless variations and offshoots) seem to be the most popular kind of dice game in settlements of emigré Chinese in other countries. In modern China, the Communist regime has denounced gambling as a subversive activity. Yet travelers in China have told me that groups of dice players can often be seen gambling in bars with apparently no attempt to hide their activity.

Dice were not always (and, indeed, still are not) exclusively cubical in form. Several European museums show Egyptian polyhedral dice of golf-ball size with so many faces that there must have been some difficulty in deciding which had fallen uppermost. Tne four-sided die—or astragal—was commonly used in the East well into the 10th century and games with natural and manufactured astragals are still almost as numerous as the games with cubes. Korea, India, and Indonesia have dice in the form of rectangular prisms (some with conical or polyhedral ends and some oblongated).

The sequence of spots on the four sides of long rectangular dice is never consecutive. Sometimes One, Three, Four, and Six are used, sometimes One, Two, Five, and Six, sometimes One, Two, Four, and Six; and rectangular dice sold in pairs will often have different sequences of numbers on each one of the pair. (This custom may be intended to imitate the slight difference in pairs of natural astragals, which are usually the right and left ankle bones of the same animal.) Even on Asian cubical dice the numbering scheme is not as rigidly adhered to as in Europe, where the Six and One, Five and Two, and Four and Three are always on opposite sides. Eastern dice occasionally have the Two and Three, the Four and Six, and the One and Five on opposite sides.

Both European and Asian countries have in the past named the different sides of the dice to suit their numerical status. In Europe the names have usually corresponded with social conditions (Slave, Peasant, Consul, Emperor, Viceroy, King); in Asia they have been linked with aesthetic or contemplative pleasures (Harmony, Nature, Beauty, Heaven, Earth, Landscape). Even today one sometimes hears the echo of such nomenclature. In London recently a policewoman discovered some young girls entertaining (if that's the right word) their boy friends in a women's public lavatory. The boys were throwing dice to decide which of them should pair off with which girl. The policewoman heard one of the boys using the phrase "eye of God," and the magistrate who tried the case was told that it was another name for the One on a dice. Similarly, modern craps players use a fairly exotic slang for various combinations of two dice: "snake eyes" for Two, "boxcars" for Twelve, "little Joe" for Four, "ninety days" for Nine, and so on.

One of the physical transformations dice have gone through is into the form of dominoes. There are Chinese legends to account for the invention of dominoes as far back as the 12th century B.C., but if they existed at that time they would probably have been used for divination rather than for gaming. In both Korea and India dominoes are still used for fortune telling, and there is a possibility that dominoes developed as a form of dice suitable for use without danger in occult matters. It was presumably thought that to use the same implements for both gambling and probing the mysteries of the unknown might have brought disaster.

There are extant rules for 47 different Eastern games using dominoes. And they show a lot more variation than the few basic games played in Western countries (mentioned in Chapter 3), because there is far more variation in the number of pieces in different sets and because color combinations of spots are introduced. As with dice games, the names are often beautiful: "Within the

Pagoda," "Leaping Gazelle," "The Little Snakes," "The Game of the Seller of Bean-curd," "The Peach Orchard," and "Carnations in the Haze."

Nowadays Indian and Chinese games with dominoes very often combine the elements of gambling and fortune telling; certain juxtapositions of pieces are of good augury even if they lose the player his bet. This mystic element has been dropped in the translation of dice and dominoes games to the Western world. We have retained only the arithmetical element, which (along with the restriction in the number and variety of the pieces themselves) naturally limits the diversity of games.

According to some American ethnological observations made in the late 19th century, the Innuit Eskimos (who came originally from the Hudson Strait) played a kind of dominoes called *a ma zu a lat*, which seems to mean "standing upright side by side." It is played with pieces of ivory (varying in number from 60 to 148) cut into irregular shapes and marked with spots arranged in different patterns. The pieces are designated by pairs, with names like *ka niu tik* ("sled"), *kaiak* ("canoe"), *kale sak* ("navel"), and *a ma zut* ("many"). The report adds that the Eskimos would stake the last article they possessed—including wives—on the issue of the game. But sometimes the wives joined the game and won themselves back to their former owners.

It is possible (though not proved) that dice games were played in Europe and Africa before they were played in Asia. But, questions of precedence aside, the Egyptians were playing dice early in civilization's history. They evidently played mostly board games, using limestone gaming boards and terra-cotta pieces in the form of disks, animals' heads, and other symbols. The names of two of the games played with them (*senet* and *tjau*) are on record, though little seems to be known of the rules of play. Without doubt, however, dice were thrown as motivators, for in the boxes made for the storage of the pieces there were compartments to hold dice made of sandstone, rock crystal, wood, or ivory.

Probably the most popular dice game in the Roman Empire was called, simply, *ten* (which may have been the game the soldiers played for Christ's crucifixion garments). After Roman troops had taken the game into Gaul and the French language had developed, it became *passe-dix*, which it still is. The rules for passe-dix are simple, and remain much the same as for ten: It is played with three dice and any number of players, each of whom becomes the banker in turn. Each time a player throws a total below 10, he and all the other players lose their stakes to the banker; but each time 10 or more is thrown the banker must double all the stakes in a payoff to the players.

Passe-dix is played almost universally with very little variation of the rules, though it has many different names: in Britain and America it is called *ten-spot, dicey, roll-ten,* or *birdie*; in Italy, *talus*; and in Turkey, *zarf* (which is also the name of a metal frame that holds a glass of hot coffee). It is usually played by groups of friends for small stakes. For instance, in Germany after the

Above, the cruciform board used for the Indian game *pacisi*. Boards for the game are today usually made of cloth; the squares are embroidered. The game is played by four players, each with four pieces; players sitting opposite each other are partners. Each player tries to complete a circuit of the board first (starting from the center); moves are controlled by three dice. Left, four sets of conical pacisi pieces, and the long dice used. At the end of the 19th-century, pacisi (in a modified form) was introduced into Europe as the parlor game ludo.

war the armed forces played it for chocolate, cigarettes, and other black-market goods; in 1946 I saw a game of passe-dix being played in a Hamburg underground train, in which about 500 cigarettes changed hands between two stations. In many European bars (commonly in Holland and Belgium) a dice box and dice are kept on the counter, the proprietor no doubt hoping that the excitement of a game of passe-dix would prolong his customers' stay and keep them drinking. (The fine he would have to pay if a policeman were to drop in would be a justifiable expense.) The simplicity of passe-dix, plus its speed and the fact that the stakes can be small, make it appeal widely—probably even more widely than *craps*, which is largely concentrated in America.

But in the years before craps was developed by Mississippi Negroes in the 19th century, even passe-dix had to take second place in popularity to the great European dice game (and ancestor of craps) called *hazard*. There is etymological evidence that hazard was originally an Arab game, for the word derives from the French *hasard*, which in turn derives from the Arabic for dice—*az-zahr*. The game's first European appearance was in Corsica, which suffered a Saracen invasion in the eighth century A.D., and from which the game's popularity may well have seeped through Italy, Spain, and France—where for three centuries it was a mania rather than a game.

In its heyday hazard was by no means a game of small stakes. A book called *Memoirs of the Lives, Intrigues, and Comical Adventures of the most Famous Gamesters and Celebrated Sharpers in the Reigns of Charles II, James II, William III, and Queen Anne* tells the story of a Colonel Panton, who in a single night won enough to bring him an annual income of the equivalent of $7500 from its investment, and who built Panton Street, near Pall Mall in London. A similar success story involved one Richard Bourchier, who, during a Grand Tour of Europe, diced his way into the high company of the king of France, the king of Holland, and the Duke of Bavaria. From all of them he won a fortune big enough to buy a huge estate at Pershore, in Worcestershire, and keep himself in luxury for the rest of his days.

Today a gambler might be able to find a game of hazard in some older casinos (usually in a variation that uses three dice), or a corrupted form of it at traveling fairs or carnivals (where the game is sometimes rigged by the use of either weighted or magnetized dice). But since the appearance of craps it has virtually been abandoned by most gamblers. Two-dice hazard is a simple game. A player bets the other players—of whom there may be any number—that he will throw any one of several specified numbers that can be thrown with two dice (the numbers are Five, Six, Seven, Eight, and Nine) and backs his choice with his stake. The remaining players must together match the amount of the thrower's stake with their own stakes.

The thrower's choice is called a "main." If he throws his main, he wins and takes all the stake money. (Such a piece of good fortune is sometimes called a "nick.") But if he throws another number he neither wins nor loses but must

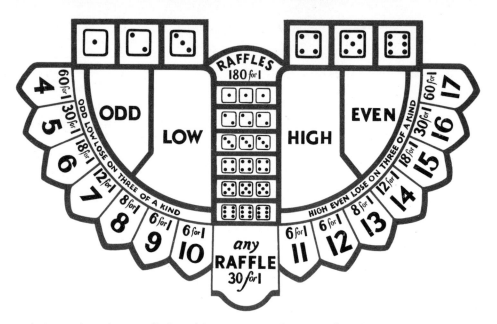

continue throwing until he either repeats that number (which is called his "chance") in which case he wins, or repeats his main, in which case he loses.

As you see, the game is basically very similar to craps (the rules for which I outlined in Chapter 5). But the hazard players of the Middle Ages had no notion of the theory of probability, nor had they tumbled to the fact that all the combinations possible with two dice (except Two and Twelve) can be thrown in more than one way. Later hazard players grasped only part of this fact; for a long time they failed to realize that, for example, there were only three ways (instead of six) to throw a Seven, and only two ways (instead of three) to throw a Four. For this reason they complicated the game by making rules that seemed to them to even out chances, but that were in fact doing nothing of the sort. During the Renaissance and later, there was a comprehension of the truth about chances and odds in relation to dice; but players tended to correct the early complications by making new ones, and hazard became a game of such complexity that its place was taken by passe-dix.

Nowadays, passe-dix (or one of its innumerable local variations) and craps are the dice games most likely to be encountered—craps in the splendor of casinos as well as in private games whose setting may be far from splendid, passe-dix typically among informal groups of gamblers. But there are many other kinds of dice games, some of which I ought to mention.

Poker dice, a variation using five dice in which the faces of the dice display card symbols instead of spots, and in which the thrower tries to make winning combinations as in card poker, is popular in Britain and America, especially in the armed forces. For the British armed forces, another favorite is *crown-and-anchor* (or *chuck-a-luck*). In this game three dice are used; each bears four card symbols plus a crown and an anchor on its six faces, and these symbols are repeated on a cloth that is spread on the table, floor, or deck and on which the players place their bets. (Incidentally, crown-and-anchor and *housey-housey*

138

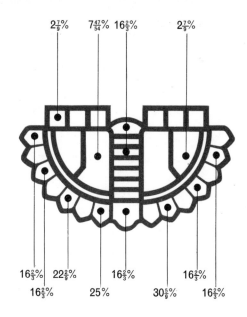

$2\frac{7}{9}\%$ $7\frac{41}{54}\%$ $16\frac{2}{3}\%$ $2\frac{7}{9}\%$

$16\frac{2}{3}\%$ $22\frac{2}{9}\%$ $16\frac{2}{3}\%$ $16\frac{2}{3}\%$

$16\frac{2}{3}\%$ 25% $30\frac{5}{8}\%$ $16\frac{2}{3}\%$

Left, a modern hazard table as used at Las Vegas. By placing chips on any of the six numbers in the area marked "raffles," a player is betting that he will throw three of that number (with three dice). Winners of this bet are paid at 180 to 1. But the correct odds are 215 to 1, so the house percentage (shown in a diagram, right) is $16\frac{2}{3}$. On an "any raffle" bet, the player tries to throw any three of a kind. If he wins he is paid at 30 to 1, true odds being 35 to 1 (and the house percentage is again $16\frac{2}{3}$). To win a bet on "low," the total count on the three dice must be 10 or under ; to win a "high" bet, the total must be 11 or more ; to win an "odd" or "even" bet, the dice must total any number (odd or even) selected by the player. (But the player loses if he makes the number with a "three-of-a-kind" ; thus the bank's edge is $2\frac{7}{9}$ per cent.) Other main bets are a "numbers bet," where a player tries to forecast the total count, and "chuck number," where the player bets on the numbers one to six.

—the original form of bingo—are the only gambling games that may be played openly on British naval or troop ships.) *Under-and-over-seven* is a variation of passe-dix that is often played as a carnival game with oversize dice : Players (obviously) bet on their throw's being less or more than Seven.

Where the early hazard players concocted complex rules to try to even out chances, modern craps players (who must accept the existing rules) have developed quite a number of ways to improve their chances. There are, for instance, a few widely held superstitions. Blowing on dice, as I mentioned earlier, is based on the notion that anything moribund (including, presumably, failing luck) can be restored by an application of healthy breath. Talking to the dice is a habit probably begun by someone like that Ming emperor who was playing sugoroku and got his One and Four up by commanding them to appear. The command is rarely used today, but whispered pleas are common in many languages and usually concern material benefits needed for poor families—for instance, "Baby needs a new pair of shoes." Stroking and kissing the dice is an obvious manifestation of the wooing spirit—with, possibly, some psychologically erotic significance, for women dice players wooing for luck often hold the dice between their breasts or touch them to their thighs.

Gamblers who find that blowing on, talking to, or wooing their dice doesn't always work may resort to more practical methods of lessening the odds against winning. The more unscrupulous will simply cheat. Some of the oldest cheating methods are still the most effective—methods like loaded dice, drilled and filled with mercury, so that the weighted side falls to the bottom when the dice are thrown. Of course, loaded dice are too easily detectable (you merely need to hold the dice by diagonally opposite corners to see if it rotates as on an axis) to be used against any but the greenest players—though there are plenty of these. But there are other ingenious methods. Sticking a short pig's bristle into one corner of a dice, or beveling the corners and sides, or making the dice slightly off their proper cubic form, will all have the effect of making the dice fall more often on one side than another.

Duplicating the Sixes on opposite sides of the dice is a method used more often than you might think, since any attempt at inspection by a suspicious player is anticipated by switching to true dice. Palming true dice and switching them for false ones at the most advantageous moment needs a lot of skill; but this rarely bothers cheats, who are always adept at palming routines. (Sometimes, of course, the other players are equally adept at spotting the palming routine. In one tough gambling circle in America, the punishment for a sleight-of-hand artist is quick, brutal, and very effective: He loses the middle finger of his working hand.)

"Topping" and "slurring" are often used in games like backgammon, where the dice are shaken in a cup or box. Topping means putting the dice in their box in such a way that the required numbers will come out on top when the dice are thrown. (The rattle is counterfeited by another set of dice in a different box concealed in the player's other hand.) Slurring requires a box with a false interior that holds the dice in one position, so they come out as they went in.

A more honest way in which gamblers try to improve their chances of making a profit at dice is by using a system. Most crapshooters use (or at any rate know of) several systems of varying degrees of reliability. But I should first reiterate and extend my outline of the terminology that crapshooters use in play before going on to the systems. A Seven or an Eleven is called a "natural" or "pass"; a Two, Three, or Twelve is a "crap" or "miss-out"; a Four, Five, Six, Eight, Nine, or Ten is a "point"; when the shooter rolls one of these numbers, he tries to repeat it before throwing a Seven. If he does so, this too is called a "pass." But if he throws a Seven before his point, this is called a "crap." The shooter's first throw is his "come-out."

Left, the board used for the game called under-and-over-seven, using two dice. Players bet that the dice's total will be under or over seven (even money is paid on each) or seven, when the payoff is at 5 to 1). True odds for either under or over seven are 7 to 5; true odds for seven are 6 to 1. Thus the bank maintains profitable advantage.

Right, one of the three dice used in crown-and-anchor ("exploded" to show all six sides) and the betting layout. The dice are marked with a crown, an anchor, a heart, a spade, a diamond, and a club. Players place their bets on the symbols of their choice. The bank pays even money on singles (i.e., if the chosen symbol appears on one die); 2 to 1 on pairs, 3 to 1 on three of a kind. True odds against the combinations are respectively 35 to 19, 25 to 2, and 215 to 1.

To "fade" is to accept a bet. In casinos, craps tables are laid out with a design of lines and boxes that allow you to bet on or against any of the shooter's possible throws; but there are considerable variations from casino to casino in the amount of the bets that may be laid, and also in rulings as to the payoffs. A "come-out bet" is a bet prophesying that a specified number will turn up on the thrower's come-out. A "come bet" is a bet that the dice will pass (i.e., win) on the next come-out throw. A "place bet" is a bet that the thrower will or will not throw a specific point. On a casino craps table the "don't pass line" is the space reserved for bets that the dice will lose; the "pass line" is the space for bets that the crapshooter will throw a pass.

(Incidentally, though there are many conflicting theories about the origin of the name of the game itself, here is the most plausible one: Both French and English hazard players used the word "crabs" to denote a throw of Two or Three. The word was probably being corrupted into "craps" at the same time that hazard was being simplified into the game of craps.)

No system yet invented can give perpetual success to the habitual casino gamblers because, as I've already said, the odds in any long run are always in favor of the casino or bank. But all of the systems described below offer varyingly limited chances of success to the casual player. And many of them have proved useful to the gambler who prefers to avoid casinos and to join his friends in a private (perhaps even "floating") crap game.

In the "six-bet" system you need a fair amount of capital, since on a casino table there is invariably a minimum as well as a maximum limit to the size of a bet. Put an acceptable bet on each of the six point numbers (place bets), thus giving yourself six chances against the shooter's single chance of throwing a natural. If he throws a natural, you lose; but if he makes a point, collect your winnings on that number and cancel the other five place bets.

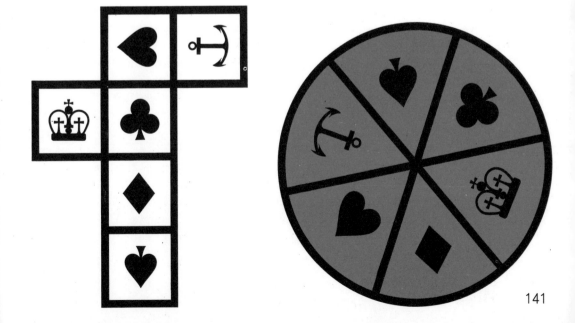

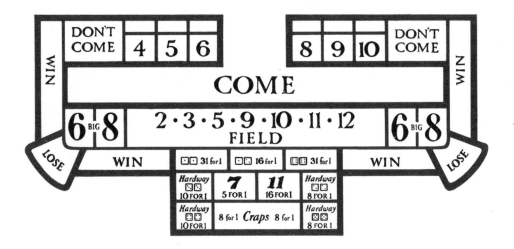

A point of Four or Ten will give you odds of 9 to 5; Six or Eight will give 7 to 6, and Five or Nine will give 7 to 5. Your advantage, of course, is that there are 24 ways of throwing Four, Five, Six, Eight, Nine, and Ten, but only six ways of throwing Seven—so the odds are apparently 4 to 1 in your favor. But the shooter has only to throw two successive naturals for you to be irreparably out of pocket, since the minimum place bet is always carefully calculated to neutralize the advantage you gain by the 4 to 1 odds.

The "win-and-lose" system can be used only in a casino, since it requires a table with a "don't pass" line. This simple process is frequently advertised as a "never-fail" system. You back the dice to win *and* lose. Put your first bet on the don't pass line, and when the shooter throws his point, make a place bet on the number he throws. You are likely to win on one of these bets unless the shooter throws a natural or crap on his come-out; and, according to the odds on the particular point you back, you will either break even or make a profit. Since you have bet that the shooter will *lose* on his come-out, the system falls down immediately if he throws a natural or crap, for the payoff odds will be considerably smaller in your winning place bet.

In the "series system" you watch for the shooter's come-out. If he throws a pass, you begin betting on him to win. If he throws a crap you begin betting on him to lose. The assumption is that each pass or crap is the first of a series of passes or craps. It is, of course, quite possible that it will be. And if you switch your bet after the first throw of the dice that begins a new series you will naturally win. Unless, of course, the thrower throws alternate passes and craps.

One craps system is an adaptation of a roulette system—called the "Martingale"—which is based on a progressive doubling of the bet each time the bettor loses (he needs a lot of capital). But it can often fail because of the limitation of maximum stakes imposed by the casino or the other players. The Martingale system adapted to dice is called the "patience" system. You must be patient

Left, the usual layout for bank craps as played in many casinos. Right, a diagram of the layout showing the bank's favorable percentages on the even-money bets. A "win" bet is that the shooter will pass (win) on his come-out (first roll) by throwing either a "natural" (Seven or Eleven) or by throwing a "point" (Four, Five, Six, Eight, Nine, or Ten) and repeating it before throwing a Seven. (The bank's edge is $1\frac{41}{99}$ per cent.) A "lose" bet is that the shooter will throw a crap (Two, Three, or Twelve) on the come-out. A "Big 6" (or "Big 8") bet is that Six (or Eight) will be thrown before a Seven. A "come" bet is that the dice will win on the next roll (which then becomes a come-out). A "don't come" bet is that the dice will lose on the next roll. A "field bet" covers seven specified numbers.

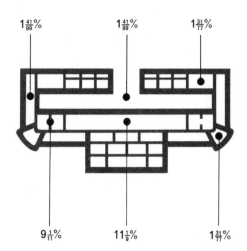

$1\frac{41}{99}\%$ $1\frac{41}{99}\%$ $1\frac{31}{77}\%$

$9\frac{1}{11}\%$ $11\frac{1}{9}\%$ $1\frac{31}{77}\%$

enough to watch the game without betting until the shooter has thrown four passes in succession. If and when that happens—and *only* if it happens—you bet that the shooter will lose next time. The odds against his throwing five Sevens or Elevens in a row are 31 to 1, which seem like very favorable odds. And indeed they are—so long as you remember that *you are not actually betting on this proposition at all*.

Because it is impossible for you to determine the point at which you are joining the periphery of that infinitely expanding circle, the true long run, you must treat every throw of the dice as a *separate entity*, unrelated to any previous throw. If, before the shooter began throwing, you bet him that he couldn't make five Sevens in a row, then the odds would be 31 to 1 in your favor—because you would be betting on the five throws *as a unit*. But in the patience system you are betting that the shooter will not throw a pass in his next throw—one more throw in the endless succession of all the throws ever thrown, which began at some indefinable point in the past. All other considerations are irrelevant. And your chances of winning or losing on a single throw are very nearly equal.

Your chances are nearly equal because on a single throw it isn't just Seven or Eleven (a natural) that will win, or Two, Three, or Twelve (a crap) that will lose. The shooter can also win (i.e., pass) by making his point—Four, Five, Six, Eight, Nine, or Ten—and, if shooting for a point, can lose with a Seven. Thus the odds on a single throw are computed by taking into consideration all the odds against making each individual point before a Seven, as well as the chances of shooting a natural before a crap. To spare you all the mathematical details, the odds against the shooter's making a pass on one throw are 1.0286 to 1—which, in practice, is the same thing as 50-50.

However, in the patience system, if your bet proves fruitful and the shooter loses on his fifth throw, pick up your winnings and don't bet again until another four successive passes have been made. If you have a successful spell at all with

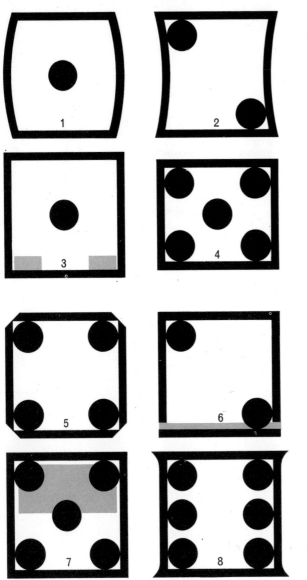

Dice cheats can be spotted if the player knows what to look for. Above, a crooked die with only three numbers on it. With two such dice the numbers Three, Five, Seven, Nine, Eleven, or Twelve could not be thrown. Above left, dice 1 and 2 have two slightly rounded sides; such dice will tend to come to rest on the flat sides. Die 3 has weights inside the corners of one side that will force the die on to that side. Die 4 is not truly square and will land most often on its long sides. Die 5 has round edges on certain sides and is less likely to land on these. Die 6 has a metal strip within one side that brings it down on that side. Die 7 is hollow at one side, so will tend to drop on the solid side. Die 8 has edges jutting out on one side that tend to stop the die rolling off that side. Below left, how to test a die for weights. Loaded dice turn over when dropped in water, landing on the weighted side.

Right-hand page: some of the dice cheat's sleight-of-hand exposed. Crooked dice are concealed in the palm of the hand (top left) when the cheat picks up the honest dice. He closes his hand, and the crooked dice drop to his fingers (top right). After palming the honest dice he throws the crooked pair (center left). Center right, the "Greek shot": The dice are thrown against a wall (not shown) so that one lands on top of the other —preventing the bottom one from rolling. Thus the bottom die can always be made to score, say six, and the cheat would always score at least seven. Bottom left and right, a "slide throw": One die is held by the little finger so that it slides rather than rolls, again ensuring that one number will appear. If the number is a Six, no lower number can be thrown—and so the shooter cannot "crap out" on a Two or Three and is more likely to make his point.

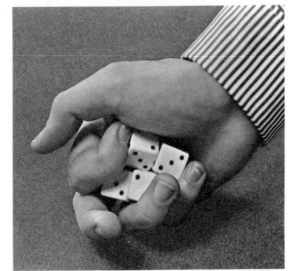

this system, your winnings will be small and widely spaced (it may be weeks between throws of successive passes) but at least they will be winnings. Of course, sooner or later you will come up against a situation where the shooter throws five, six, seven, eight, or more successive passes. The system's answer to this is to double your bet each time the shooter throws a successive pass after the fourth, so that you can recoup your losses when you win. But you may find that if the shooter has a row of eight passes you may not be able to bet any more—because to double your bet again will be either to exceed the limit the bank will fade, or to exceed your capital.

Most of these systems find their greatest use in casino play (or what some gamblers call "bank craps"). In informal games (or "private craps") the players are less likely to turn to complicated methods of improving their luck. Craps is a simple game, and most crapshooters prefer to keep it that way. In fact, its simplicity is one of its main attractions. All the players need is some money, a pair of dice, and a floor to roll them on. (To prevent some of the cheating throws already mentioned, a wall or other upright surface is necessary too. The dice must be rolled so as to rebound from the wall before coming to rest. A blanket is laid down to prevent dice from chipping.)

Crap games can be found on almost every social stratum: in the living rooms of mansions, in the smoky back rooms of pool halls, even on street corners. Of course, no matter what kind of premises it is played in, craps is illegal in most states of the U.S.A. and in most European countries. This is why Damon Runyon's famous "floating crap game" floated; it was never held in the same place twice, in order to keep one jump ahead of the police. Crapshooters have developed many ways to circumvent the law: Some years ago, for instance, the authorities in Alabama were trying in vain to put a stop to the Negroes' street-corner crap games. The police would swoop down on a group of Negroes crouched in a circle, money in their hands and on the pavement—but no dice would be visible anywhere. So no arrests could be made. The Negroes' method was simple: They used very small dice, and swallowed the evidence.

But craps is one gamble that doesn't need to rely on the danger of police raids for added excitement. It has been called "the fastest gambling game in the world"; the dice are rolled, picked up, shaken, and rolled again almost as fast as the shooter's hand can move, yet the other players always manage to cover the bets (and make "side bets" among themselves) between each throw. The pace gets even faster when a shooter begins a winning streak (i.e., when the dice get "hot"). Runs of up to 10 consecutive passes are not as uncommon as the odds might indicate (1023 to 1 against a run of 10).

The excitement engendered by a crap game was allegedly the direct cause of a tragedy that looms large in American history—the great Chicago fire of 1871, which destroyed most of the city. I say "allegedly" because the following story has never been verified; but, true or not, it has taken its place in the colorful history of craps:

146

In 1871 a man named Louis M. Cohn was shooting craps with some friends in a barn (Chicago was then presumably less urban than it is today) owned by a family called O'Leary. They were playing by the light of a lantern, and in a particularly exciting moment of the game Cohn knocked over the lantern and set the barn on fire. The fire spread across Chicago with uncontrollable rapidity. Presumably to escape the consequences, Cohn spread a story that the lantern was kicked over by Mrs. O'Leary's cow, and for many years that was the accepted story of the cause of the fire. But in 1944, two years after Cohn died at the age of 89, the dean of Northwestern University, Illinois, received from Cohn's vast estate (he had become a very successful business man) a gift of $35,000, together with the full story of the "truth" about the Chicago fire.

In his will Cohn added a postscript to his story, in the form of a deadpan comment that could have been made only by a man with the unswerving single-mindedness of the dedicated gambler: "When I knocked over the lantern," he wrote, "I was winning."

Four British youths enjoy an improvised craps game. Games of dice need no elaborate equipment—which is mainly why they are such a popular form of private gambling.

7 Take a card

One of the possibilities concerning the origins of cards—and all theories of origin are only possibilities—is that Chinese paper money was used by the Chinese as the basis for a game of chance. (The money was invented during the eighth-century rule of the T'ang dynasty, and bore pictures of emperors, empresses, and provincial governors of different degrees of importance to indicate different values.) But there is no real evidence to support either this theory or the theory that the first-century Chinese colored bricks in the Boston Museum's collection are an early form of playing cards. It is equally possible that playing cards originally evolved out of arrows, stones, bones, scraps of bark, wooden blocks, and animal teeth used by primitive men in their divinatory practices. In time some of these implements may have become pieces used in games—pieces like dice, dominoes, or chessmen—while other divinatory implements might have become printed representations on disks, squares, or circles of paper. And these last may have been the first cards. (Korean and American Indian gaming disks and similar equipment can be seen in many museums.)

Some historians believe that cards were introduced into Europe by the Saracens (or Arabs) who, it is thought, used cards mostly for divination and brought them along during the 10th-century Saracen invasion of Italy. The first extant mention of European card playing is in the manuscripts of two monks (one Belgian, the other Swiss) who were writing ecclesiastical history in 1369. The

British workmen enjoy a quick hand of cards between shifts. Countless varieties of card games are played all over the world—both as an entertaining pastime and as a major form of private gambling.

Spanish

Ancient symbol	Modern symbol
Caliz (cups)	Copas (cups)
Espadas (swords)	Espadas (swords)
Oros (gold pieces)	Oros (diamonds)
Bastos (clubs)	Bastos (clubs)

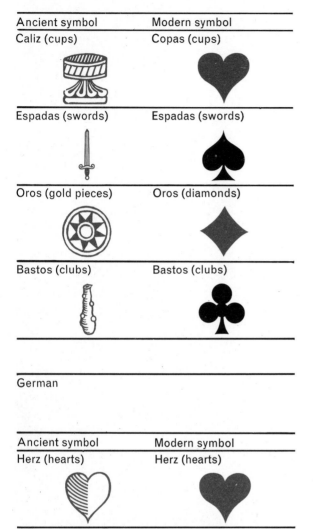

French

Ancient symbol	Modern symbol
Coeur (hearts)	Coeur (hearts)
Pique (pike)	Pique (pike)
Carreau (tile)	Carreau (tile)
Trèfle (trefoil)	Trèfle (trefoil)

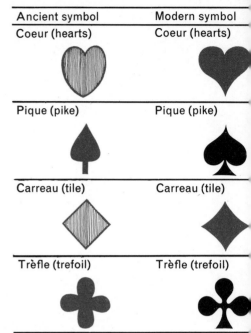

German

Ancient symbol	Modern symbol
Herz (hearts)	Herz (hearts)
Ecker (acorns)	Piks (spades)
Schellen (bells)	Karos (diamonds)
Blätter (leaves)	Treff (clubs)

Five charts showing ancient and modern card symbols, and names given to the four suits, in five European countries. Some early cards (such as the old Italian and Spanish cards represented here) derived their names and symbols for the suits from the Tarot pack, which was used for fortune telling. Elsewhere, the suits acquired other names and symbols (though all early packs in France, England, and Germany included a "Hearts" suit). Eventually, the different designs came to conform with France's representations, which today appear in most packs throughout the world—though each country still calls the suits by different names.

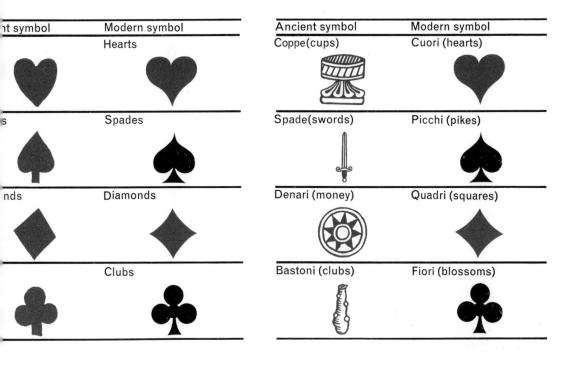

nt symbol	Modern symbol	Ancient symbol	Modern symbol
	Hearts	Coppe(cups)	Cuori (hearts)
s	Spades	Spade(swords)	Picchi (pikes)
nds	Diamonds	Denari (money)	Quadri (squares)
	Clubs	Bastoni (clubs)	Fiori (blossoms)

Belgian monk says he was horrified to find two lay brothers playing at cards "in the very shadow of St. Sauveur"; the other merely notes without comment that cards came to Switzerland that year.

The 15th-century Italian historian Angelo Covelluzzo writes: "In the year 1379 the game of cards was brought into Viterbo, which game came from Serasinia and is called by the Saracens *naib*." The Arabic word *nabaa* means "prophecy," which seems to underline the theory that the Saracens told fortunes with cards rather than playing games with them. (Incidentally, though the Spanish for "cards"—*naipes*—is a word with a lost etymology, it might be derived from Arabic, or might be a corruption of Naples, the town that is thought to have first exported cards to Spain.)

The earliest European cards were the Tarot pack, used for a now obsolete game called *tarocco* (*tarot* is the French adaptation of tarocco). So far as Europe was concerned, the Tarot pack was used almost solely in Hungary, Italy, Spain, and France. Britain (to which cards migrated about 1425) always used the 52-card pack, which had become popular by then. Only fortune tellers and philosophers clung to the Tarots for their mystic purposes.

The earliest known Tarot pack was made in Lombardy in the 14th century and had four suits: Cups (or Chalices), Swords, Money, and Batons (or Clubs). In each suit there were 10 numbered cards and four pictures: king, queen, knight, and varlet. And in addition to these 56 there were 22 trump (or triumph) cards, numbered from 0 to 21, and called: The Fool; The Juggler (or Mountebank); The Popess; The Empress; The Emperor; The Pope; The Lover; The Chariot; Justice; The Hermit (or Old Man); Fortune (or The Wheel); Force; The Hanging Man; Death (this card, for superstitious reasons, is invariably left unnamed, but there is no doubt about what the design of the card is supposed to represent); Temperance; The Devil; The Hostel (or Hospital); The Star; The Moon; The Sun; The Judgment; The World.

Later, in Florence, a pack was developed with another 20 trumps. Twelve of the additions were called by the names of the signs of the zodiac, four were virtues (faith, hope, charity, and prudence), and four were elements (earth, air, fire, and water). The fool was discarded from this pack, and the entire 97 cards were used in a game called *le minchiate,* now obsolete.

As the playing of card games increased in popularity in Europe during the 14th century (except, for the time being, in Britain, European Russia, and Scandinavia), all the trump cards of the Tarot pack were dropped—though this time the fool was retained, and still exists in modern packs as the joker. The four knights were dropped from the court cards, and the pack as used for play became the new standard one of 52 cards plus the joker. Both the 97-card and the 78-card Tarot packs continued to be used for fortune telling throughout Europe, and are still used today to some extent. (Some American magazines have carried advertisements for Tarot packs, offering them as "a fortune-telling novelty.")

The 52-card pack may have come into being for much the same reason that, in the East, dominoes were developed from dice: to separate gambling from occult explorations of the unknown. Or, more simply, a pack of 78 or 97 cards may perhaps have seemed too unwieldy and the rules too complex, so the trumps were dropped and left for the fortune tellers. Also, the change might have happened partly for practical reasons: Before printing (and indeed for some time after, until suitable techniques had been evolved), cards had to be drawn and painted by hand. Stencils were used, but the cards were so elaborately designed and gorgeously colored that they must have been very expensive —too expensive to keep pace with their growing popularity. So for economy the fewer the better.

Production problems may also have had an effect on the symbols chosen to represent the different suits and the names given to them. Both symbols and names have undergone considerable change in most countries. In the past each country had its own set (or sets) of symbols, and therefore its own names. But in 14th-century France a pack was introduced bearing the stylized symbols of hearts, spades, diamonds, and clubs. These symbols were eventually adopted by most western countries; but the names attached to the symbols have mostly remained widely different from country to country.

The French names are (and have been for centuries) *Coeur* (hearts), *Pique* (pike), *Carreau* (tile), and *Trèfle* (trefoil). The French probably took the names from appearances: A pike's head resembles the "spade" symbol; a paving tile

LE TOILLE

LE SOLE

CEVAL DE BASTON

Ten cards from a 19th-century French Tarot pack. After the 14th century, the Tarot pack was no longer used for playing but entirely for telling fortunes. All Tarot cards have traditional symbolic meanings, which can be altered by the positions in which they are dealt. Tarot packs usually consist of 78 cards : four suits of 14 (called "the Lesser Arcana"), and 22 numbered "triumph" cards (known as "the Greater Arcana"). The cards depicted here are : above, from left to right, the Star, Death (nameless for superstitious reasons), the Sun, and the Knight of Wands ; right, the Hanging Man and the Magician ; below, the Moon, the Devil, the Wheel of Fortune, and the Knight of Pentacles.

LE PENDV

LE BATELEVR

LA LVNA

LE DIABLE

ROVE DE FORT

CEVAL DE DINER

FASCINE

Fascine, est une espece de gros Fagot de branchages qu'on fait porter aux Soldats pour remplir le Fossé d'une place assiégée, afin d'en faciliter le passage. Il n'y a personne jusqu'aux officiers principaux qui ne se fasse honneur de porter la Fascine

Aside from the countless games possible with the conventionally designed pack, there are some games that are played with specially illustrated cards. These three cards are from an 18th-century French pack used for playing a now obsolete game called *jeu de guerre* (war game). They depict (left) soldiers carrying branches to fill in the ditch separating them from a besieged fort; (right) an exploding mine; and (far right) a diversionary attack. These cards correspond to the seven, eight, and nine of Clubs in today's packs.

is lozenge-shaped like the "diamond" symbol; and a trefoil is a clover leaf, shaped like the "club" symbol.

Italy's original Tarot cards, as I have said, were named according to the objects depicted on them: Chalices, Swords, Money, and Batons (in Italian, *Calici, Spadi, Denari,* and *Bastoni*). But in modern Italy, the suits (with the French symbols) are named *Cuori* (hearts), *Picchi* (pikes), *Quadri* (squares), and *Fiori* (blossoms).

Germany names the suits *Herz* (hearts), *Piks* (spades), *Karos* (diamonds), and *Treff* (clubs), using the same symbols as France. The original names and symbols for the suits were Acorns (*Eichel*) for Spades, Bells (*Schellen*) for Diamonds, Leaves (*Blätter*) for Clubs, and Herz, as today. These can crop up in packs produced today; also, the old names are sometimes applied to the new symbols.

In Spain, the suits are *Copas* (cups), *Espadas* (swords), *Oros* (gold pieces), and *Bastas* (clubs). "Copas" is applied both to the old "chalice" symbol (which was formerly called *Caliz*) and the new "heart" symbol. Until fairly recently the second suit was represented by swords, but these have mostly been replaced on modern packs by the spade symbol, though the name "swords" has remained. Similarly, the lozenge-shaped diamond symbol has replaced the representation of a coin on the third suit. But generally for the fourth suit both the old representation (that of a bludgeon) and the old name "Bastas" have remained.

English names seem to have come from several European sources. The Hearts suit corresponds to the French Coeur and the German Herz; but the name of the next suit, Spades, seems to reflect an Italian or Spanish influence (Spadi or Espadas). Or perhaps the name comes from the appearance of the symbol: It

MINE.

Mine, est une espece de Cham-
bre souterraine qu'on fait sous
le Rempart de la face d'un Bas-
tion ou de quelque autre ouvrage
à la quelle on va par detours,
et qu'on charge de la Poudre
qu'on juge estre neces faire—
selon la hauteur et la pesanteur
des corps qu'on veut renver-
ser pour aller à l'Assault.

FAUSSE ATTAQUE.

Fausse Attaque, est un travail
qu'on ne pousse point avec Vi-
gueur, mais seulement pour fa-
voriser les veritables Attaques,
en faisant diversion pour obli-
ger les Ennemys a partager
leurs forces.

looks like a spade to the English (though like a pike to the French or the Germans). The suit of Diamonds is connected with the old Italian "Money" suit, but the symbol is lozenge-shaped like the French tile. And so with the English Clubs: the name resembles the Italian (or perhaps German) but the symbol is the French trefoil.

During the last 500 years there have been many attempts by card designers to introduce new symbols. Animals, flowers, birds, fishes, cutlery, and domestic crockery have all appeared on the suits at various times. Presidents, commissars, industrialists, and workers have been used to symbolize the social distinctions in democratic and communistic regimes, as have the abstract ideas of liberty, equality, fraternity, and health. Early in the 15th century there was a German pack with the suits symbolized as offertory boxes, combs, bellows, and crowns; and Italy and Spain produced some equally original designs. A similar change recently was in South Africa where, since the break with the Commonwealth in March 1961, the suits have become Powder Horns (Hearts), Wagon Wheels (Spades), Tent Pegs (Diamonds), and Shoes (Clubs). South African court cards have also been changed—from ace to president, king to kommandant, queen to vrou, and jack to boer.

Other countries have generally retained the card monarchies without change, or at any rate without lasting change. What have often changed are the actual personalities who were the original "models" for the kings, queens, and jacks. The four kings, for instance, originally represented four great monarchs of history, the ones most likely to be remembered and admired by 14th-century Europeans: Charlemagne (Hearts), who was the king of the Franks from A.D.

Three sets of court cards are examples of the past variations in card design between different countries—variations that still existed as late as the 18th century. Left, the appearance of the four queens from a French pack (dated 1752) is already highly stylized. In contrast, the German kings (above)—also from an 18th-century pack—are of standard Tarot design, though the suit symbols are the same as those used today. The Spanish jacks (above right), dated 1800, are marked with the old Tarot symbols (as were all other Spanish cards of the time).

768 to 800 and emperor of most of western Europe until 814; David (Spades), the shepherd and singer who became the Hebrews' king; Julius Caesar (Diamonds); and Alexander the Great (Clubs).

In some packs, though, either Julius Caesar or Alexander appeared as the king of Hearts. That king has also been given a hairy skin (possibly as Esau), and has appeared as a likeness of Constantine, Charles I of Britain, Victor Hugo, and the French soldier-politician General Boulanger—though the last portrait was swiftly expunged from the series after Boulanger's suicide in 1891. All the kings of Hearts other than Charlemagne, however, have had brief tenures. The superman hero who reigned over Europe for 46 years is still identifiable in most modern packs by carry-overs from older cards: his wealth of ermine and his left-handed grip of his sword (originally a battle-ax).

The representation of David as king of Spades originally included a harp to remind everybody of the Jewish king's musical ability; but only in France has a harp remained a conspicuous feature of the drawing. During the Napoleonic wars the king of the second suit briefly became Napoleon in France and the Duke of Wellington in Prussia; but David was eventually reinstated.

Julius Caesar was never, of course, a king, though a medieval French legend named him as king of Rome (and the founder of Christianity—somewhat improbably, since he died in 44 B.C.). He is invariably drawn in profile, and in some old French and Italian cards he was given an extended hand (which might be taken as a "grasping" gesture, perhaps an attempt to relate him to the suit that was traditionally connected with money). The conspicuous hand remains in most modern cards, and the name *Cézar* is also retained in French packs.

Alexander (who was idealized in the literature of the Middle Ages and the Renaissance) is the only card king who holds an orb, the symbol of monarchy; this is a characteristic of both old and modern kings of Clubs. As the design

A German king, a French queen, and a British jack represent the more or less uniform stylized design of court cards today. Practically all cards are double-headed, reversible, and identified by an initial (like the "D" for *dame*).

has become more stylized, the hand holding the orb has dwindled to a vestigial fleshy tint. The king's appearance has also changed from that of a black man with a fierce expression and kinky hair to a somewhat effete white fellow with sensual nostrils and a curlecued beard and moustache. However, Alexander the Great he was and remains.

The queens of the card monarchies have nothing to do with the real-life consorts of Charlemagne and the others. Helen of Troy was the first queen of Hearts; St. Helena (mother of Constantine the Great), Dido, Juno, Joan of Arc, Elizabeth I of Britain, Roxane, Rachel, and Fausta have all tenanted the card from time to time. But the enduring resident of this queenship is Judith, the heroine of an Apocryphal Bible tale, who has been perpetuated on playing cards ever since the Middle Ages, when the Apocrypha was most popular.

For most of the time in the Latin countries, the queenship of Spades was held by Pallas Athena, the Greek goddess of wisdom and war (or her Roman counterpart Minerva). The Teutonic and Scandinavian countries substituted goddesses of war from their own mythologies; and France temporarily tried edging in Bathsheba and Joan of Arc, neither of whom apparently appealed to card players.

As for the queen of Diamonds, no special personality seems to have been favored in the 14th and 15th centuries, except in France, where the queen was often labeled Penthisilea (the queen of the Amazons in Greek mythology). In the 16th century, one heroine became almost universally adopted: Rachel, Jacob's love in the romantic Bible story. Since Rachel was by and large mean and grasping, her adoption as queen of the "money" suit seems reasonable enough—as does the motto that the French often printed on her card: *Vivent les bons enfants qui jouent souvent* (long live the good folk who play often).

The earliest Italian card makers called their queen of Clubs "Lucretia"—perhaps the Lucretia who was married to Tarquinius Collatinus and committed suicide after being raped by Tarquinius Superbus. No other country appears to have settled on a queen of Clubs for some time, though Hecuba (who was the queen of Troy) and Florimel (a personification of womanly charm created by the English poet Spenser) both had brief appearances in the pack. So did an allegorical being called "Disillusion," shown on old French cards exhibiting (but not wearing) a wedding ring. The French eventually stumbled on the idea of naming the queen of Clubs "Argine" (an anagram of the word Regina), and this has stuck. It became traditional to attach the name Argine to any queen or king's mistress who justified lampooning. Henry III of France, a sexual fetishist who wore women's clothes, was also picked on in this way (probably in court jokes and popular songs). When he tumbled to the *double entendre* behind the word "queen" he issued an edict forbidding any kind of written or pictured royal or political allusion—though nobody took much notice of it.

The four knights of the Tarot cards were dropped as the pack developed, so there are no reliable records of their personifications, if they ever had any. But the valets (as they were in France) or knaves (in Britain) had identities as real people just as the kings and queens did. Though "valet," "varlet," "knave," and "jack" are all words meaning men in a lowly position, the subsidiary meaning of a buccaneering adventurer, lawless but not villainous, is closely attached to the jacks of playing cards.

This meaning is certainly apt in the case of the jack of Hearts. As usual, the French choice was the personality who became most firmly established. He was Étienne de Vignoles, a soldier in the service of Charles VII of France, who called himself "La Hire" (a noun sometimes alleged to mean "wrath," sometimes "the growl of a dog"). He was an excellent soldier, generous, brutal, swashbuckling, and irreverent. (On one occasion he was being given absolution after confession and was told to pray for mercy. He knelt and said, "O God, I pray thee to do for La Hire today such things as you would wish La Hire to do for you if he were God and you were La Hire.") He became one of Joan of Arc's councilors of war, and has remained a popular hero like Till Eulenspiegel, William Tell, and Robin Hood, tacitly accepted by other nations as the personality of the jack of Hearts.

Ogier the Dane was the original jack of Spades, probably because he is known to have owned and used in battle two fine Spanish swords with Toledo steel blades. ("Swords," remember, is Espadas in Spanish.) Ogier had a legendary as well as an historical existence: In legends, he slew giants, restored kingdoms to bewitched princes, and was himself constantly being restored to youth by Morgan le Fay, King Arthur's fairy sister, who determinedly married him.

Historically, he is thought to have been the son of Geoffrey of Denmark and a cousin of Charlemagne's. (He is still the national hero of Denmark, though now called Holger Danske.)

Roland, Charlemagne's legendary nephew, became the Italians' jack of Diamonds (under the name of Orlando). But unaccountably he seems to have been quickly replaced by Hector de Maris, one of the legendary knights of the Round Table and Sir Lancelot's step-brother. At least, that is the identity now generally given this jack. But Hector de Maris seems to have been too chivalrous to have attracted the evil reputation that the jack of Diamonds has always had; it is possible that the Hector concerned was Hector de Galard, a disreputable officer of Charles VII. In fortune telling by cards, the jack of Diamonds can be considered ominous—though in fact the entire suit of Diamonds is looked upon favourably by cartomancers, possibly because of its connection with the Tarot "Money" suit.

The jack of Clubs is Sir Lancelot, top knight of King Arthur's round table and Queen Guinevere's lover. He was originally the most decorative of the jacks, but his gorgeous raiment and the elaborate arrow that symbolized his prowess in archery have been lost in successive designs through the years. It is impossible to associate the present jack of Clubs with the warrior who (as told in Malory's history) smote down 30 knights after being shot in the buttock by a huntress.

Today, so long as the suits are distinguishable and the values clear, most card players would probably be indifferent to the long-dead personalities depicted on the court cards even if they knew about them. Of course, the designs of modern court cards are hardly recognizable as having been real people. They are generally stylizations of stylizations countless times removed from the original idea (though France and Germany still link the court cards with the historical figures by often incorporating their names into the designs). Nor does there seem to be any strong resistance by card players today to new designs. For example, the modern French artist André François has designed a pack in which all the kings ride caparisoned horses and all the jacks play guitars.

In most countries the designs are not necessary to identification, since the card makers have labeled the court cards with initials. This innovation was inter-

Six cards, selected from two 19th-century packs made of hide by southwest American Indians, betray their Spanish ancestry. Left, the kings of Coins and Clubs from an Apache pack; right, the queens of Clubs and Cups and the five and seven of Swords from a pack used by Yuma Indians.

nationally adopted in the 19th century, as was the French and German invention of double-headed figure cards. Spain, also in the 19th century, was the first country to use figures as well as the number of symbols to indicate the value of a non-court card.

That, then, is a thumbnail history of the cards themselves. The fact that all modern cards have their roots in the Tarot pack, with all its occult connections, may be responsible for the permanent flavor of evil that for many people clings to these small pieces of pasteboard. John Wesley, founder of the Methodist Church, forbade the use of cards entirely among his flock. Some old shipmasters won't allow "the devil's picture-books" aboard; or, if they do, they'll have them thrown overboard at the slightest indication that anything is going wrong. (Their attitude is based on an unsubstantiated story about Columbus's sailors, who allegedly got the notion that their cards were bringing them bad luck. As soon as they flung them overboard, so the legend says, they sighted land.) Coal miners won't take cards down the shaft. Burglars won't steal them if they can help it. Of all forms of gambling, in fact, cards are the most resentfully regarded by moralizers and by those whose lives involve a special degree of risk. But, in spite of this stern disapproval on many sides, card games have remained one of the most popular of all forms of gambling.

Games played with cards have ranged through wide degrees of simplicity and complexity. Many have lost favor in some countries and kept it in others. Some have vanished altogether. New games and variations of old ones are continually being invented. In Europe, America, Africa, and Australia there are more than 50 different games currently played, excluding solitaire and other non-gambling games. In Eastern countries, where both European and many oriental varieties of cards are used, at least a hundred different games are played. Oriental cards are often elaborate and beautiful and of many shapes other than the normal European rectangles: They can be narrow strips, circular, triangular, or octagonal. The only thing they have in common is that they invariably seem to be made of pasteboard. (The word "card," as a description of a material, is derived from the Greek word for "papyrus.")

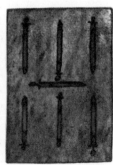

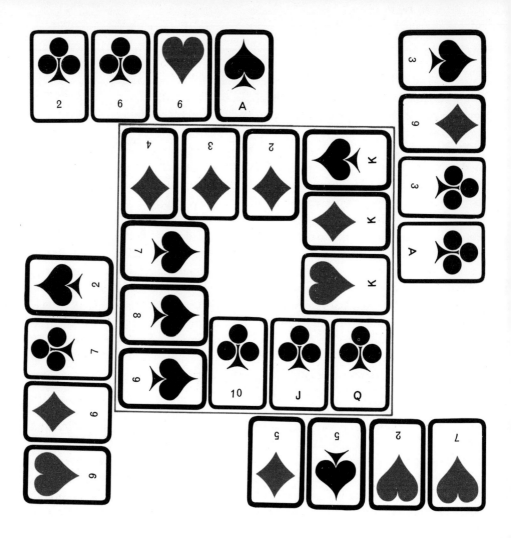

Only a very few card games exist in which chance plays no part. One of them is Russian and is called *svoyi kozin*; the other, *quintet,* is English. Both are played with 32-card packs (that is, with all the numbered cards from two to six omitted), and both require great skill. In these games, chance is eliminated because the players have identical hands.

The games involving the maximum of chance and the minimum of skill are those based on the random selection of a card from the pack. In the most elementary form of this kind of game the players simply bet and then each draws one card, and the holder of the highest (or lowest, whichever is pre-arranged) takes all the stake money. Should more than one player draw a card of the same value, the ranking of the suits decides the winner. The usual order of ranking runs Spades, Hearts, Diamonds, Clubs (though this also may be pre-arranged).

This game, probably the oldest of all card gambles, has been the occasion for some dramatic bets. Typical of these is the case of William Jones, an Englishman who emigrated to Canada in the middle of the 19th century and made a crooked fortune out of playing *three-card monte* on railway trains. He died in

In most card games, players aim either to make specific card combinations (or "melds") as in rummy, or to take tricks, as in whist. Left, a diagram sets out the basic card combinations used in games of the rummy family : the "straight" or "run," and "three (or four) of a kind." Imagine four players seated at the four sides of the red square and each holding four cards. The cards inside the red square have been arranged in three straights (10, jack, queen of Clubs ; seven, eight, nine of Spades ; and two, three, four of Diamonds) and in one three-of-a-kind (three kings). Players may add to these sets from their hands : For example, the five of Diamonds from the bottom hand may be added to the Diamond sequence. Prearranged "wild" cards can be played in place of any card in the pack. Thus, if twos were wild in this game, the two of Hearts from the bottom hand could be played as the six of Spades, and, with the five, be added to the Spade sequence.

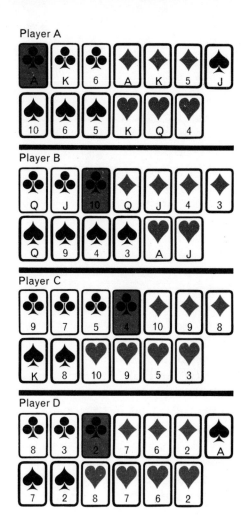

Player A

Player B

Player C

Player D

The diagram (right) illustrates the type of game in which tricks are made. A trick consists of four cards (one from each player's hand), and is won (or taken) by the player who produces the highest card. The four players—who compete in partnership, A and C against B and D—are each dealt 13 cards, which they arrange in suits. (The suit selected as "trumps" has a higher value than any of the others.) A leads with the ace of Clubs ; B "follows suit" with the 10 ; C (as A's partner) discards his lowest Club, as does D. So A wins the first trick.

poverty after staking $180,000 on the draw of one card—the only time in his life he had gambled without cheating.

A more exciting version of the same basic gamble is the game now called *chase-the-ace.* In this the players all stake an equal amount, each player's stake being divided into three equal portions (three one-dollar bills, three pound notes, three 10-franc pieces, or whatever). The dealer gives one card to each player, face down. The object of the game is to get rid of cards of low value (and in this game the ace is the lowest). The first player to the dealer's left either exchanges his card with the next player, keeps it in his hand (in which case he says "stick"), or, if it is a king, lays it face up on the table. The other players each try in the same way to get rid of low cards until it becomes the dealer's turn. He lays his card face up and may either stick or change it for the first card in the remainder of the pack. Everyone then shows the card he holds and the player with the lowest card puts one third of his stake in the middle. Similar rounds are played (the deal passing clockwise each time) until all the players except one have lost their stake money and are out of the game.

Most card games fall into two main groups. First, the games in which certain cards are "trumps" (a corruption of the word "triumph") and players can make "tricks." (A trick is a collective term for the cards—usually four—played and won in one round.) This group includes the *contract bridge* and *whist* series of games. Second, the games in which "melding" (making specific combinations of cards) is a basic principle. These are the *rummy* games, which include all forms of *poker*. There are a number of games that combine the ideas of melding and trick making. And in a few games the object is to *lose* tricks.

Games of the rummy series appear to be the oldest, but one has to remember that the Tarot pack had trump cards, so games involving the making of tricks may have preceded rummy games. There was a Persian rummy game of the 14th century called *âs-nâs*, which has been adapted by every nation without altering the structural basis of dealing a hand of five cards to each of four players. (Poker and *gin rummy* are the Western world's most popular variants of âs-nâs.) Columbus's seamen took the game from the Old World to the New (whether or not they flung their cards overboard in order to change their luck) and one of them gives an account of it in a journal he kept for his wife:

"After the Hail Mary at nightfall those not at watch played at cards, the game having been showed them by sailors from Cathay. . . . It is a game in which skill adapts to chance, each player having five cards only and these to be matched in every respect to the coat [court] cards and the as [ace]." It seems very likely that the sailors from Cathay (Cathay was the name given to the whole of the oriental empire, not just to Marco Polo's China) had taught Columbus's men âs-nâs. There are certainly several references to the popularity of this game in 14th-century Persian literature.

After the 14th and 15th centuries, references to the names of games (but not rules) crop up quite frequently. *Primero* (or *primiera*) was a 16th-century Italian game, and Charles IX of France played *gilet*, a French version of it, during the period of his remorse after the massacre of the Huguenots in 1572 ("At Gilet this day I lost my purse, but at Saint-Barthélemy I lost my soul"). Both the French *ambigu* and the English *brag* introduced the element of bluffing (i.e., betting heavily to make it seem that your hand is stronger than it is, so as to frighten your opponents and make them concede the hand before the cards are shown); but it's doubtful if either of these games was played before the 18th century. *Brelan* (or *bouillotte*) was a 15th-century French game of the rummy kind, in which hands of three, not five, cards were dealt.

Of the games combining the characteristics of melding and trick making, *piquet* is the best known. (*Kalabriasz,* a game from central Europe, is probably older; *bezique* and *pinochle* belong to the same family but are considerably later.) The suggestion (quite common in early histories of gambling) that piquet is named after its inventor is absurd. The name is derived from *pique*, meaning to prick or nettle your opponent, and is exactly the same word that gave the name to the French suit of Pikes (Spades).

The trick-losing games come in varying degrees of difficulty. *Black Maria* is perhaps the most complex: Each of the three players has 17 cards (the two of Clubs is omitted from the pack) and at the beginning of the game passes three of them to the player on his right, collecting three from the player on his left. Play then proceeds by making tricks, but the object is *not* to win those tricks that contain penalty cards. The penalty cards are all the Hearts, (each of which counts one point against the trick winner), and the ace, king, and queen of Spades, which count seven, ten, and 13 points respectively. *Greek hearts* (which is sometimes shortened to *hearts*) and *slobberhannes* are slightly simpler variations on the trick-losing theme.

The games in which trick making was of principal importance seem to have been the last to arrive. One catches glimpses of details of whist-like games in the 16th century. *Triumph, ruff, ombre,* and *honors* were all built round the idea of trumping, and are all developments of *ronfa,* an early 16th-century Italian game in which the leading player could decide to his own advantage which should be the superior or trump suit in play. (A card from the trump suit will win a trick from any card of any other suit.) Ronfa, like ombre, was usually a game for two. The Spanish adapted it for three and called it *renegado.*

Ombre was the French version and became very popular in the smart set. Descartes, who began gambling when he was 17, gave up ombre after losing for 15 nights in succession and discovering that he was more interested in the mathematical probabilities that had caused his losses than the losses themselves. And the playwright Rotrou, who wrote execrable poetry to earn money to pay gambling debts, won 400 *louis* at ombre one night and put the money in a bag and gave it to Corneille, his fellow playwright, to look after for him. Corneille immediately sallied forth with the firm intention of turning it into 1000 louis. But the inevitable happened and he returned the empty bag with a note: *"Vous n'avez pas l'ombre d'une change."*

Ruff, honors (sometimes called *slamm*), and whist were the earliest English variants of the trick-making games, and were all hugely popular by the middle of the 17th century. Ruff and honors (and later ombre) faded out, but whist—which got its name from the exclamation "Whist!" ("Hush!") demanding silence for concentration—kept its popularity until the end of the 19th century. It was partly maintained by the boosting power of *A Short Treatise on Whist* by the English lawyer Edmond Hoyle, whose name as a card expert is well known even today (though not a word of his original writings remains in rule books). More complex rules were later foisted upon it by one Henry Jones, who called himself Cavendish and wrote innumerable treatises (*Cavendish on Whist*) superseding Hoyle's and making increasing demands on the wits of those who played the game. In a more simplified form, whist today is largely played at social gatherings in England and North America (a "whist drive" is often used to raise money for churches or women's clubs); it can no longer be called an important gambling game.

Biritsch was a version of whist played in Russia, where it rivaled *faro* in popularity in the early part of the 19th century. The main difference was that in biritsch the trump suit was decided by the dealer instead of by chance as in whist, where the suit of the last card to be dealt was trumps. Also the dealer's partner became "dummy" and declared (i.e., exposed his hand) after the first trick had been made. And there was a points system of scoring that allowed doubling, tripling, and quadrupling of stakes. Biritsch appears to have come to western Europe via Turkey; General Menshikov, the Russian ambassador in Constantinople immediately prior to the Crimean war, remarks in one of his despatches that his only relaxation for 15 days had been a game of biritsch, which he lost because of "the overwhelming forces of chance."

At all events, biritsch quickly gained European ground. It reached England in 1894, and the Portland Club of London claims to have been the first to use the name "bridge" (a corruption of the original Russian name), which is today used internationally. Bridge has gone through several changes on its way to the now firmly established "contract" form. The "auction" form appeared in the Whist Club of New York in 1908. Instead of allowing the dealer to nominate trumps, auction made the suit the subject of competitive bidding. But a variation called *plafond*, popularized by the French expert Pierre Bellanger, was quickly taken up in Europe and America and became contract bridge. Contract has superseded auction in most clubs, but auction is still played privately, especially by players who prefer not to endure the marathon of skill that is a good game of contract. (As if contract weren't difficult enough with the standard pack of cards, a fifth suit called "Royals," symbolized by a crown, was added in 1938. By 1939 it had vanished.)

Bitter conflict between the British, American, and French bridge authorities waged over the rules from 1925 to 1948; and at least two socialites came to public blows (*Westminster Gazette* headline: "Fisticuffs Confound Culbertson") over the Culbertson "conventions." (Culbertson was one of the world's acknowledged bridge experts, and the one to whom modern players owe most for the development of the rules that are now internationally accepted.) Today contract bridge holds its top popularity among the games in which great skill is combined with a relatively small element of chance—which by no means implies that gambling on bridge is equally small. An Australian club owner I know estimated that Melbourne and Sydney turn over the equivalent of $300,000 nightly at the bridge tables. And an American authority has estimated that about $1,000,000,000 are bet annually on bridge in the U.S.A.

Piquet, pinochle, kalabriasz, bezique, and *cribbage* are also tests of skill in which players make tricks, meld, and claim points for their successes. The skill in all these games lies in memorizing the cards played, sensing the speed of the game, making the right decisions on the declaring of winning hands, and reckoning the scores and sacrifices it is best to make at the appropriate times. Piquet has kept its aristocratic and French terminology. In the version for two players, the complete game of six deals is a "partie," the players are "younger hand" (who deals) and "elder hand" (who discards), and the scoring sequences of cards are Tierce, Quart, Quint, Sixième, Septième, and Huitième.

Pinochle (the word is a corruption of the French *binocle* : binocular) is especially popular nowadays in Switzerland (where it originated) and in America (where it was taken by 19th-century emigrants). But it has a very small following elsewhere under that name. It is played (usually by two, three, or four players) with a 48-card pack and the scoring and betting is by points; the combination of the queen of Spades and the jack of Diamonds is called "pinochle" and is worth 40 points.

Bezique is the more widely played version of pinochle, with a big following in Britain, parts of the Commonwealth, and France. It requires 64 cards and is usually played by two players. Like pinochle, it is a game of considerable skill, and, though played for money, makes its principal appeal to those wishing to exercise their brains with figures. Again, tricks and melds score varying numbers of points and the first player to score a predetermined number wins.

Cribbage, though sometimes played by three or four, is also customarily a game for two. It has several forms, but the five-, six-, and seven-card versions are the most popular. The object in all versions is to achieve a certain number of points (the score is kept by advancing counters on a board) by collecting different combinations of cards and discarding those that will be less advantageous when the hand is played and there is a show of cards.

As in bridge, the stakes in any of these games are rarely very high; but in a long game a considerable amount of money may change hands. A bezique enthusiast of my acquaintance challenged his wife to a game of a million up with stakes of one shilling a hundred points. The game lasted three and a half years and during that time one or the other was often many thousands of points down. But the final settlement was for four shillings and sixpence only—which at least demonstrates that in *a* long run (though it is but a relatively short part of *the* long run) the chances tend to even themselves out.

A 19th-century Eskimo cribbage board from Alaska. The score in cribbage (usually a game for only two players) is recorded by pegs' being moved along the two rows of holes on either side of the board—60 holes for each player.

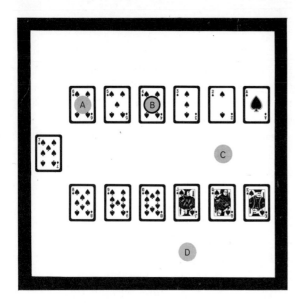 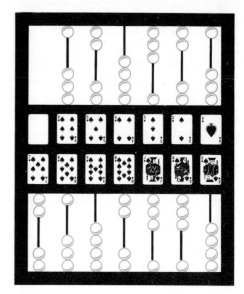

The 17th century was undoubtedly the hothouse in which all the great card gambling games were nurtured—faro, *trente et quarante, baccarat, chemin de fer, vingt-et-un,* and poker—as well as a number of other games that have long since vanished or been given different forms, like *wit-and-reason, bankafalet, bassette, gleek, bone-ace,* and *five-cards.* But their heyday lasted a century or more and colored vividly the gambling scene.

Bassette, the great banking game that gave way to faro, was invented by Pietro Cellini, a Venetian, about 1593. It took Italy, Spain, and France by storm and caused such havoc among the fortunes of the rich that complaints were laid against Cellini and he was banished to Corsica. The king of France (Henry of Navarre) and the pope (Paul V) both issued edicts forbidding the game unless the banker was of noble birth (which seems a strange solution, since it was the nobles who were doing all the complaining). As played in France the game flourished well into the 17th century, edict or no. In England small and large stakes were permitted and there were no edicts. In fact, after his restoration Charles II put it around that bassette losses were fashionably laudable, perhaps because his own had made some steep inroads into the treasury.

Then came faro. The exact time when it took over from bassette in the European gaming rooms is uncertain, but it and the older game were certainly running side by side during the middle years of the 17th century. In bassette, basically, each player bets that his chosen card will turn up in a deal before the cards that are the dealer's choice. Faro is broadly the same. Thirteen cards from ace to deuce are painted on the layout (suits are irrelevant) and players bet on cards of their choice. The banker draws one card at a time from a dealing box: The first card is not bet on; the next is a *losing* card; and the next is a *winning* card. The deal continues thus, alternate losing and winning. Players bet on each card—i.e., whether it will win or lose. If the banker draws successively two cards of the same value, he takes half the bet on that card. A gadget like an

Faro—perhaps the oldest "banking" game in the world—has only recently been replaced (by baccarat and craps) as the most popular casino gamble in Europe and America. Right, a faro game in Reno, Nevada, during the 1920s. Players place their bets on the faro layout (far left), painted with a suit of cards, usually Spades. The banker deals two cards: Players with money staked on the first card win; any bets on the second card go to the bank. (Players may bet with the bank, in which case they win on the second card and lose on the first.) Bets can also be laid on a card's being odd or even; and, in the last round, on the sequence of the three cards that remain. Cards that have been dealt are recorded on the dealer's counting rack (left) by moving the four wooden markers beside each card. The positions of the various bets are shown by the blue counters (far left); A is staked on the six—"winner"; B on the four—"loser"; C is a "split" between the two and the Queen; D is staked on the odd.

abacus keeps track of dealt cards, so players can know what cards remain. When three are left (the "last turn"), players bet on the order of their appearance.

Faro requires almost as little skill as chase-the-ace, but as it became more and more popular the players needed a good deal of skill to stop the cheating tactics of bankers. Marked cards, sleight-of-hand dealing, etc., became highly important in faro, because the banker could then deal cards that were to his advantage.

Although cheating has a history as old as gambling, it might be said that it became really worth while in the big banking card games. Conjurers who had amused audiences at fairs and entertainments found a new outlet for their prestidigitations. Chemists and opticians came to the aid of sharpers with bleaching and other marking processes, including cards with luminous spots on their backs that revealed their face value but that were visible only when viewed through specially tinted spectacles. And codes of signals between bankers and collaborators among the onlookers became schoolboyish in their complexity. All these methods, and numerous elaborations of them, are still used today. You need only riffle through the catalogues of carnival outfitters to find endless varieties of cheating packs, gadgets, and signal codes "for entertainment only." (One recent optical development is a contact lens form of the tinted spectacles for reading the luminous betraying cards, at $300 a pair.)

The faro days were a gambler's paradise. The whole world seemed faro-mad. Pawnshops glittered with jewels whisked into custody by wealthy women—and their husbands—to raise money. Robbery with violence was rife in the dark alleys of every town that had a gaming house. Fortune tellers specialized in a new branch of their art that conveniently foretold the cards the banker would turn up for the players. Syndicates found surprising amounts of money from surprising sources to furnish and equip gaming houses. (One of them, in Hamburg, was floated on the profits from the huge sales of a periscopic device enabling *vôyeurs* to peer into upstairs windows from downstairs apartments.)

Though the game eventually became a standby of gamblers on every social level, it was at first the favorite of the glamorous and fashionable society gamblers. One leader of 18th-century British society, Mrs. Fanny Westmacott, remarked in a letter: "The game of pharoh has stolen from society much of the fashion of assemblies and balls, but it is an advancement that society is hereby grouped into houses every bit as genteel and with better opportunity for the close proximity of suitable ladies and gentlemen."

In Paris, the First Secretary at the British Embassy thought it worthwhile to inform his government in diplomatic correspondence that "agents would be well placed at the faro tables here, for nowhere else is there quite such a splendour of foreign ladies and gentlemen revealing quite so much of the fortunes of their countries." And in Lyons an enterprising coachbuilder named Chabrier put on the market a highly successful carriage that he called a *dormeuse*. It was fitted with a bed and was specially designed for faro players exhausted from gambling, who could thus snatch a few hours' sleep without bothering to go home.

America became faro-wise somewhat later than Europe, though cards were widely played—particularly during the Revolution. (The first president himself is said to have played the game at one time, but presumably disapproved, for he later wrote out an emphatic edict to his army that stated: "All officers, non-commissioned officers, and soldiers, are positively forbid playing at cards, or other games of chance. At this time of public distress, men may find enough to do, in the service of their God and their country, without abandoning themselves to vice and immorality.") The card games most played were *loo* (a trick-making game of the whist family), and *post-and-pair* (a bluffing game with similarities to poker), which had been imported from France and Britain by the first colonists. (Jefferson apparently filled in the intervals in his composition of the Declaration of Independence with games of post-and-pair.)

Faro didn't come into its American own until the beginning of the 19th century, when the Louisiana Purchase brought thousands of exploiters into the valleys of the Mississippi and Ohio rivers and ramshackle towns harbored them in unaccustomed proximity—a state of affairs that encouraged many activities, including gambling. After that, faro remained the big gamble until well past the middle of the century, with poker running alongside it and only gradually ousting it from the carpet joints and sawdust joints of American towns.

Just as the terms "carpet joint" and "sawdust joint" meant broadly the degree of luxury or squalor to be expected in American gambling saloons, so the names "poker" and "gin" once signaled the degree of skill needed by the players of two distinct branches of the same card game family. Poker was (and is) the connoisseur's game, demanding several skills beside that of keeping a straight face; gin poker, whisky poker, and rum poker were variations that used fewer skills but offered almost the same high degree of excitement. (The bibulous names were probably applied to the variations on poker because of the saloon

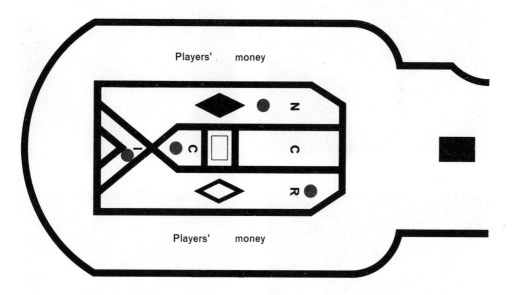

Above, a diagram of the layout for trente-et-quarante. The dealer lays out two rows of cards (*le noir* and *le rouge*) until each totals 31 or more (right). Players bet that one or the other row will be nearer to 31 by placing chips on *rouge* (R) or on *noir* (N). They also bet on *couleur* (that the first card in each row will be the color of the row) or *inverse* (that the first card will be the opposite color).

atmosphere in which they were played.) Gin, whisky, and rum poker became gin rummy, and "rummy" subsequently became a family name to be applied to any of the numerous games involving the principles of melding and sequence collecting.

But first things first. Poker, as I say, had appeared under that name in America by the middle of the 19th century. It is, like all rummy games, a version of the 14th-century Persian game âs-nâs. The origin of the name "poker" is far more obscure than the game itself. The popular explanation is that it derives from *poque*, a French card game of the 18th century; but such information as there is about poque suggests that it was a game of the whist family. A German adaptation of the English bluffing game *brag* is a more likely origin, for its name was *pochspiel* and involved a call by non-bidding players: *"Ich poche."* And even more likely is the theory that the name owes something to "poke," a 19th-century American, Australian, and South African slang term for pocket or wallet. And the cheats and cardsharps that infested the poker tables of those days were great emptiers of pockets and wallets.

There are two main strains of poker—"draw" poker and "stud" poker. The principal difference is that in stud poker some of each player's cards are revealed

 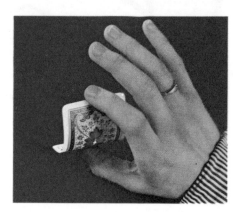

while in draw poker all remain secret. Within these two strains there are innumerable and quite different parochial, regional, and national variations. Draw poker is usually considered the most basic form. Each player is dealt five cards and, if he decides to join the betting, he may discard up to three of them (four or five in some variations) and draw other cards from the remainder of the pack. (In stud poker, however, the player must play the cards he is first dealt.) Here are the nine poker hands (in descending order of value):

Royal flush: ace, king, queen, jack, and ten of one suit.

Straight flush: five numerically consecutive cards of one suit. A straight flush led by a king defeats one led by a queen, and so on down the scale.

Four of a kind: any four cards of the same value. The fifth card in the hand counts for nothing.

Full house: three cards of any one value plus two of another. It is the ranking of the trio that determines which of a number of full houses wins.

Flush: any five cards of the same suit, the competitive value of the flush being decided by the value of the highest card.

Straight: five numerically consecutive cards of any mixture of suits, with the highest card of more than one straight determining the competitive value.

Three of a kind: any three cards of the same value. The remaining two cards count for nothing.

172

On the opposite page are depicted some of the card cheat's crooked practices. Far left, glancing at the second card from the top when dealing the top card to himself. (In blackjack, for example, the dealer would now know the value of the first card dealt in the next round.) Left, inserting a card that has been trimmed at an angle, so that its corners will protrude slightly from the rest of the pack. The pack can now be cut at a particular point to that player's advantage. Bottom far left, a dealer, under cover of looking at the two cards in his hand, bends the next card to see whether it is worth drawing. Bottom left, bending a card to see the corner. Top right (this page), dealing off the bottom of the pack.

One precaution against suspected cheating is to give the pack a thorough shuffle. The laborious "overhand" shuffle (as in the three pictures right and below) often fails to redistribute all the cards. Here the cards patterned in blue and yellow have, despite shuffling, remained undispersed among the other cards with blue backs. On the other hand, the "waterfall" shuffle (bottom pictures) successfully mixes the cards.

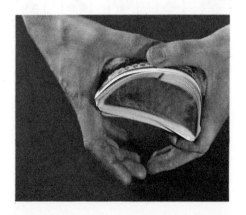

Royal flush

♣A	♣K	♣Q	♣J	♣10

Straight flush

♥6	♥5	♥4	♥3	♥2

Four of a kind

♠J	♥J	♦J	♣J	♠8

Full house

♥9	♦9	♣9	♠3	♥3

Flush

♦Q	♦10	♦7	♦5	♦3

Straight

♣J	♦10	♥9	♦8	♠7

Three of a kind

♠Q	♣Q	♦Q	♦7	♠6

Two pairs

♣K	♦K	♣5	♠5	♦7

One pair

♥J	♦J	♥9	♣8	♠3

High card

♦K	♠J	♥8	♠6	♣2

Royal flush	4	1 in 649,740
Straight flush	36	1 in 72,193
Four of a kind	624	1 in 4,165
Full house	3,744	1 in 694
Flush	5,108	1 in 509
Straight	10,200	1 in 255
Three of a kind	54,912	1 in 47
Two pairs	123,552	1 in 21
One pair	1,098,240	1 in 2

In the basic form of draw poker, players are first dealt five cards; they can discard up to three (sometimes four) and can take others in their place. The chart (left) sets out the various poker hands in order of value from the highest (royal flush) to one of the lowest (king high). Above, the left-hand column of figures lists the number of possible ways in which the different hands can be made up. For example, there are 3744 potential full houses in every pack. The right-hand column sets out the odds against a player's receiving each of the hands at the first deal.

Two pairs: two cards of one value (any suits) and two of another. In this case the fifth card is not worthless, for it can be the deciding factor in two competing pairs of equal value.

One pair: two cards of one value and any suit, the highest ranking pair being the winner in any competition. The remaining three cards count for nothing.

Betting begins before the cards are dealt. A widely-used betting procedure (especially in America) begins with the first player betting one chip or a pre-arranged sum of money (called the "ante") and the second two chips or twice the sum (the "straddle"). Then the cards are dealt and the third player decides whether his hand is worth betting on. If it is, he doubles the straddle; if not, he throws his hand in. Successive players now decide whether they want to bet and, if they do, may bet four or eight chips. Increasing the stakes even more (called "raising") is allowable for those players who remain in the game, but a limit is often imposed—by the house in a casino game, or by the players' mutual consent in a private session.

A simpler betting method is often used in private poker games where the accent is on the fun of the game as much as on the chance for profit. Before the deal each player bets an *equal* amount (which is still called the ante) in chips or money. After the deal the players bet again (in draw poker the first bettor is often the player on the dealer's left, but in stud poker and its variants the player with the highest cards showing must bet first). After the draw betting continues in earnest, with added tension provided by raising, the possibility of bluffing, and so on. The betting is halted either when the limit is reached or when the players end the raising by "calling" (i.e., simply covering the last bet without increasing it), or, sometimes, when all the players except one throw in their hands when the betting gets too high.

Poker players should know that there are 2,598,960 different five-card poker hands; that the chances of being dealt a royal flush are approximately one in 649,740, of a straight flush one in 72,193, of four of a kind one in 4165, of a full house one in 694, of a flush one in 509, of a straight one in 255, of three of a kind one in 47, of two pairs one in 21, and of one pair one in two. And players should also be able to calculate their chances of improving their hands in any way by discarding and drawing from the stock. What, for instance, are your chances of making a full house when you already have three of a kind? About 15 to 1 against. At the other extreme, the odds against making four of a kind when drawing three cards to a pair are 359 to 1. Or against making four of a kind when drawing two cards to a pair, 1080 to 1. Or against making a straight open in the middle when drawing one card to a four-card straight, 11 to 1. But it should be added that the usefulness of these or any other calculations will be limited if your opponents' play is unpredictable, if your understanding of the game (or of your opponents' play) is faulty, or if there are "wild" cards (i.e., cards that can be substituted for any other cards).

Gin rummy is less involved than poker, but is a game of great excitement and nice proportions of skill and chance. It is played with a full pack of cards and the ace ranks low. The dealer is decided by the lowest cut and deals 10 cards to each player and one face up on the table. The remainder of the pack forms the stock and lies face down. Each player now tries, by discarding and replacing, to assemble collections of one value (such as fours, sixes, kings, etc.) in different suits or sequences in the same suit. (Incidentally, there are 15,820,024,220 possible gin rummy hands.) Court cards count 10 and every other card its face value, ace counting one.

A player may declare his hand ("go down") when the unmatched cards in his hand count 10 or less, and the strategy of the game lies in watching his opponents' discards and deducing from them the weakness or strength of the hands against him. Twenty points are awarded to the player who wins each deal, and a 20-point bonus goes to the player who scores "gin"—i.e., who does not go down until he can meld all 10 cards. The first player to score 100 points wins, with stakes predetermined at so much a point.

As I pointed out earlier, the attractions of the great banking games (faro in particular) gave way, around the middle of the 19th century, to the attractions of the great rummy games (poker in particular). The signs are that now the banking games are coming into their own again. One rummy game recently

reached an international height of popularity—*canasta*, a Spanish game that had only a mild initial success in Spain when it was introduced in 1946 but that, translated to Uruguay a year or so later, left everyone dizzy with enthusiasm. "Canasta" is the Spanish word for "basket"; it has been suggested that the game is so called because the players must "weave" their cards into complex and high-scoring combinations.

The game is most usually played by four players in partnership. Two complete packs of cards, plus four jokers, are needed. Deuces are "wild," red threes may not be melded, and black threes may be melded only by a player declaring at the end of a game. Various melds gain bonuses in points: A "canasta" (a meld of seven of a kind) is top flight and scores a bonus of 500 if it is a "natural" meld or 300 if it includes wild cards.

Canasta whisked through America and back to Europe in no time and has spread now virtually all over the world—though I don't mean by this that the other universally popular rummy games, poker and gin rummy, have lost ground. But at the same time banking games have found a lot of new followers in most of the world's gambling centers.

The three modern banking games—baccarat (or chemin-de-fer), *blackjack*, (or vingt-et-un or *pontoon*), and *seven-and-a-half*—are all complicated versions of European games of the 15th and 16th centuries. The principle underlying all of them is the same: to assemble cards whose value does not exceed a specific

Left, gamblers in Las Vegas face the house dealer (who is also the banker) in a game of blackjack (or twenty-one), which today is America's top banking card game.

The major banking game chemin-de-fer is based on the same principle as blackjack, except players aim for a total of nine and take the bank in turn. Right, the *sabot* from which the "chemmy" cards are dealt; below, the palette used to collect cards and chips; below right, the cylindrical container that takes the cards after each deal.

HAVING		Draws if dealing	Does not draw if dealing		OPTIONAL
	3	1 2 3 4 5 6 7 10	8	9	
	4	2 3 4 5 6 7	1 8 9 10		
	5	5 6 7	1 2 3 8 9 10	4	
	6	6 7	1 2 3 4 5 8 9 10		

In chemin-de-fer, the banker and the "active" player may draw cards after the deal if neither has a count of 8 or 9. The player draws first; his card (dealt face up) determines the banker's play. Left, a chart (attached to *sabots* in most casinos) sets out the procedure that the banker must follow. For example: If the banker holds a count of 3 (in the "having" column), and if the player draws 1, 2, 3, 4, 5, 6, 7, or 10, the banker *must* draw. If the player draws an 8, the banker *cannot* draw. If the player draws a 9, the banker *may* draw.

Right, a diagram of the chemin-de-fer layout (the numbered sections are for players). After every deal, the croupier pushes tips into the slits on the left, used cards into the center cylinder, and the bank's winnings into the *cognotte* on the right.

number—nine in baccarat, 21 in blackjack—and, of course, to bet on the probability of player or banker being successful. (The older French, Spanish, and Italian games were called variously *baccaro*, trente-et-quarante, *trente-et-un*, and *quinze*, and had target numbers to fit.) Only blackjack has any potential for skills on the player's part, but these skills (i.e., the mathematical system that was outlined in Chapter 5) may be too esoteric for ordinary players.

Blackjack and seven-and-a-half are found more rarely in the casinos of Europe than those of America; but as private games played by friendly gamblers in their homes and in the armed forces they are extremely popular. Both continents have baccarat, America having given it a big welcome in the early 1920s. Its European popularity has been of longer duration, since it was recorded as being played in Italy in 1500.

The chief difference between the two baccarat games—chemin-de-fer and baccarat *banque*—is that in banque the players play against an appointed banker and in chemin-de-fer among themselves. Otherwise the method of play is much the same in each, and can be outlined as follows:

Any number of people between three and 11 may play. The cards bear their face value (10 for each court card). Six complete shuffled packs are used and are dealt from an open-topped, open-ended box called a *sabot* (or shoe). (This is the item of equipment that gives the game its name in the chemin-de-fer version, for it is passed round the table from banker to banker and looks somewhat like a toy train.) One player is banker and dealer and puts his stake before him at the head of the table. The other players set themselves on the two sides of the table in equal numbers. Any player may bet against the whole of the banker's stake·by calling "banco"; but if no player does so the players may combine their bets to match the amount of the banker's stake. The player staking the highest sum takes upon himself the responsibility of representing the others against the bank, and is called the "active" player.

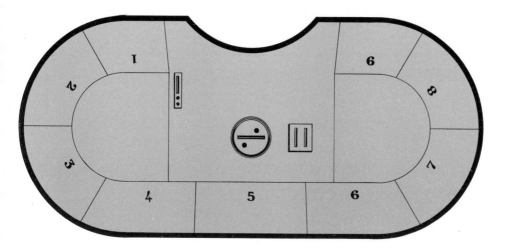

The banker deals one card each to the players on his right and left and one to himself, then repeats this operation while the suspense mounts up. The cards are then examined by the players and if any pair totals eight or nine the holder of that pair says so and wins, and bets are settled at once. If not, the banker offers a third card to the player on his right, who may refuse it, as may the player on his left—in which case the banker himself must take it. All cards are exposed again and the banker pays the player who is nearer nine than himself, or vice versa.

A player who has declared himself against the bank by saying "banco" and who loses his stake has the right to lead against the bank on the next deal, and he announces that he will do so by saying "banco suivi."

This is just a sketchy outline of the rules of baccarat—which are in fact extremely intricate and demand a high degree of concentration, particularly if a system is being followed. Baccarat, like roulette, is a game of pure chance, and many of the same systems are used in both games (some of which are outlined in Chapter 9). But since the house takes a percentage (sometimes five per cent, but it varies considerably from casino to casino) of every winning bank after the first one, it is difficult to end up in pocket after any extended period of play, system or no system.

To wind up this survey of cards and card games, let me again stress that the rules of all the games I have written about here are as variable as the English weather. You are unlikely to find play exactly the same in Wisconsin as in Beirut. But card players generally prefer variety; and this preference has been in large measure the reason for the development of so many different card games over the centuries. For in cards rules must be malleable enough to suit tradition, regional or national character, and the convenience of the millions for whom the card table is the central focus of relaxation or hard and fast gambling.

8 Win, place, or show

For most gamblers, racing means horse racing. What they put their money on is *Equus caballus,* of the perissodactyl family *Equidae,* an ungulate (or hoofed) mammal having a variation in the number of toes on its back and front feet. The first horses probably appeared in the Lower Eocene period, about 70,000,000 years ago, and were no bigger than small dogs. Even when the world had moved on enough for man to appear, catch his horse, and domesticate it, the animal was still only 13 hands (52 inches) high. But after that there was rapid development until today the animal can range in size from the Shetland pony (about 36 inches high) to the massive Clydesdale (about 72 inches high).

Everything is older than you think, including horse racing. The Metropolitan Museum in New York has a statuette of an Egyptian race horse and jockey from 2000 B.C.; the Hittites of Asia Minor recorded on their cuneiform tablets instructions for training race horses; and even earlier (about 3200 B.C.) there was some racing going on between Arab steeds that the Arabs had trained by tethering them, making them thirsty, and then freeing them to run to distant water.

One of these Arab races had far-reaching consequences for two tribes whose sheiks were steady rivals but who managed to keep the peace for a long time. Both sheiks (like most rulers in the Middle East at the time) owned studs of horses tens of thousands strong and both liked the spectacle of the thirsty animals speeding across the plain to the waterhole. But lesser nobles on each side upset

Horses and riders flash by the camera at the climax of a race at Britain's Ascot summer meeting. Horse racing combines both speed and excitement, which perhaps explains its unchallenged position as the world's greatest gambling sport.

the status quo by matching selected horses from their masters' studs against one another in a 12-mile race for a stake of 100 camels. When the two best horses began drawing ahead of the rest, the onlookers surged onto the course and began hurling missiles at the other horses to speed them up. This led to a free-for-all in which horses, tribesmen, and camels were all involved. No winner was announced because the judges also joined the battle. The fight led to a war that lasted for a century, and the two tribes virtually destroyed each other.

The Greeks (who had no horses until invading Arab and Persian cavalry brought them) turned the animals to sporting use almost immediately—first (about 2500 B.C.) in chariot races around a circular course a mile long; later, in the first horse races with riders, which were often combined with javelin throwing, torch bearing, or the pursuit of a ball in a development of the old Persian riding game, *savlajan* (polo). The Romans held spectacular horse races in their circuses; in the Circus Maximus, 380,000 people would sit daily and watch 50 horse races (with riders or chariots) between sunrise and sunset, betting money, slaves, women, and reputations on favorite horses and riders.

For the early Teutons and Scandinavians, horses were bred for work and war. Although there exists (in the Morgan Library in New York) a printed poster advertising a horse race sponsored by the Duke of Würtemburg on December 21, 1511, Northern Europe showed little widespread interest in horse racing until the early 19th century, when some rich noble families built a course at Mecklenburg and imported stock from England.

In one form or another horse racing had been popular in Britain since the Roman invasion, when Arab horses (imported by the invaders) were matched in chariot races against Celtic ponies belonging to the Iceni and other tribes. There are historical references to racing at Smithfield (now part of the City of London) in the 12th century, where the crusading Richard I offered "forty pounds of redy gold" to the winner of a three-mile race.

Later monarchs (such as Henry VII, Henry VIII, and Elizabeth I) were keenly interested in horse breeding and in hunting but did little to encourage racing. But, in the early 17th century, James I made up for the relative indifference to the sport shown by his predecessors. He built stables at Newmarket, instituted the idea of a racecourse with a place for spectators, had a great deal to do with the founding of prizes for winning owners and jockeys, and even attempted to organize a horse race on ice when the River Ouse froze over in 1605. Also, he began a royal interest in the sport that has continued in Britain to the present day. Charles II rode his own horses in race meetings, and Queen Anne inaugurated the first Royal Ascot meeting in 1711.

The Mediterranean countries have produced great horses and horsemen from the earliest days. Spain's particular breed—the Andalusian—rivaled the Arab for endurance and grace. In Italy a somewhat sturdier stock was raised, though there was a great deal of crossing with Arab and Spanish breeds. In France, lines of splendid horses were bred from the days of the early Saracen invasions;

182

A first-century A.D. horse and chariot in bronze. The Romans were renowned for their sensational chariot races, which attracted enthusiastic crowds. These circus races of classical times were the forerunners of the harness or trotting races that are popular today in Europe and North America.

but racing didn't gain a popular following until 1681, when Louis XIV inaugurated a meeting at St. Germain and offered to buy the winning horse for its weight in gold. (The offer was apparently turned down by the owner, an English aristocrat named Chevesey.) After the publicity attending this offer, the French nobility began establishing racing studs of their own, with great success. A close liaison between the racing fraternities of Britain and France was also established, and the French never relaxed their interest in the sport until the Revolution. Then it struck them that racing had been the sport of kings as well as of commoners, and they fanatically ordered the slaughter of every race horse in the country. Napoleon re-established breeding to some extent (though naturally for his cavalry) but the Revolutionary destruction took many years to repair. Today, however, France has again achieved greatness on the turf. Several fine French horses have won world-famous events—including the English Derbies of 1947, 1950, 1955, and 1963.

There were no horses at all on the American continent until the Spanish expeditions at the end of the 15th century left some there—specifically, five stallions and seven mares of the Andalusian breed. By 1700 these had become several thousands and had been crossed with imported Arabs to produce mustangs. These were the horses with which racing was inaugurated on the American mainland at the end of the 17th century on the quarter-mile tracks in Virginia, though a race track on Long Island had been laid out in 1665 and English horses had run there. Canada, Africa, Australia, New Zealand, and India were (like America) innocent of horses until colonizers or invaders took them there. But once horses were imported, interest in racing them for money was eventually bound to arise. India recorded her first race in 1791, South Africa in 1795, Australia in 1810, Canada in 1830, and New Zealand in 1837.

Horse racing throughout the world can be divided into three major forms: The first and probably the most familiar to everyone is generally called *thoroughbred racing*, in which horses ridden by jockeys race on a flat track. The second, in which horses ridden by jockeys jump obstacles (natural or contrived) in the course of the race, is commonly called *steeplechasing*. And in the third, known

France's Longchamps racecourse in the Bois de Boulogne is one of the most attractive in the world ; it is also the scene of Europe's most valuable and sought-after racing prize, the Grand Prix de Paris. Above left, a board detailing the runners and riders in the next race ; above, bettors confer between races before placing their bets with the tote (in the background). Below left, the climax of a race as the horses speed across the finishing line. Right, the winning horse and jockey parade in the winners' enclosure.

as *harness racing,* horses pull a light vehicle and a driver and run at a fast trotting pace, not a gallop.

Britain can claim not only the oldest extant thoroughbred race in the world (the Chester Cup, first run in 1512) but the most famous as well—the Derby. This race was instituted by the 12th Earl of Derby in 1780 ; since 1784 it has been run annually—usually on the first Wednesday in June—at Epsom Downs racecourse, about 14 miles from London (except during each of the world wars, when the race was run at Newmarket).

The Derby's popularity ensures that it is a big-money race in gambling terms. In 1962 the combined intake of only three London bookmaking firms during the last few days before the race totaled the equivalent of over $2,000,000. Derby fever isn't only urban : In eight small towns in the north of England, bookmakers recorded an average of 3600 Derby bets placed in each town on the two days before the 1961 race. Derby betting totals are usually the sums of a great many small bets made by occasional gamblers who have been tempted to "have a flutter" by the prestige of the Derby and the ballyhoo that precedes its running. Individual bets are seldom as lavish as they were 100 years ago, when noblemen like Lord George Bentinck would often bet hundreds of thousands on Derby horses. Bets of over $5000 would create something of a

stir in today's gambling circles—understandably, for with around 27 horses running, only a tycoon would risk thousands on one of them. (Of course, occasional
tycoons have been known to do so: In the 1946 Derby an American millionaire
used $6000 that he had made on a stock-exchange deal to back a horse called
Airborne. The horse won at "long shot" odds of 50 to 1, and the millionaire
went home $300,000 richer.)

After the Derby, many other British races rank high among the world's great
thoroughbred events—races like the St. Leger (which was first run in 1776), the
Oaks (first run in 1779), or the Ascot spring and summer meetings. (The last
are famous as social events as well as races: They are usually attended by the
monarch and the cream of British high society.) But perhaps the closest runner-
up to the Derby in fame is America's greatest race, whose name indicates England's influence on the world's horse racing but whose traditions are entirely
American. This is the Kentucky Derby (first run in 1875), a race for three-year-
olds held annually at Churchill Downs near Louisville, Kentucky.

Surrounded by all the pomp and elegance of the Old South (including the
traditional sipping of mint juleps), the Kentucky Derby is one of the American
gamblers' major annual events. An economic survey published by the *New York
Times* showed that in 1958 bettors placed $1,635,500 on this race alone. The

writers went as far as to suggest that the country's whole economic trend was manifest in the amount of money bet on this race: In 1932, for example, at the depth of the depression, only $277,000 were bet.

In 1866 the first Irish Derby was run at Curragh, the headquarters of Irish racing. Nearly a century later, in 1962, the first Irish Sweeps Derby was run on this same course, in connection with the Irish Sweepstakes (see p. 244), which established a new tradition; the Sweepstakes had always previously been held in connection with the English Derby. Many other countries have, like Ireland and America, their own Derby races—such countries as Germany, South Africa, India, and Japan.

France's major race, the Grand Prix de Paris (held at the great Longchamps course in the Bois de Boulogne), was first run in 1834 at Champ-de-Mars at the instigation of a group of sports enthusiasts. Following an agreement with the Town of Paris the inferior course of Champ-de-Mars was abandoned and on May 31, 1863, the race (for three-year-olds) was run for the first time at the Longchamps racecourse. It has been run there annually on the last Sunday of June ever since. Betting for this race is heavy: The equivalent of about $4,000,000 was staked in 1962; the equivalent of over $7,000,000 in 1963.

No international survey of horse racing should ignore the big events that take place in the two oldest British dominions, Australia and Canada. In Australia, the Melbourne Cup (held at the Flemington course) is the biggest annual event. In Canada, the Queen's Plate (run at Toronto's Woodbine Park) takes precedence. This race (first run in 1860) proudly claims the title of "the oldest consecutively run race in North America"; it is accompanied (like Britain's Ascot) by pageantry that includes a parade of the Governor General's Horse Guards.

All the races so far mentioned take place on flat tracks. But the definition of "flat" in relation to race tracks varies considerably. American tracks conform to a standardized pattern: They are nearly all ovals of smooth dirt enclosed by white rail fences. British courses (which are rarely called tracks) are much more individualized; they are turf rather than dirt, not always entirely level, and usually irregular in shape.

Continental courses vary greatly. Examples of the stylized American track can be found in Scandinavia, Germany, Italy, and France. But there are also many irregularly shaped and variably sized turf courses (similar to Britain's) all over Europe. One of the finest racecourses in Europe is the Hippodrome Côte d'Azur at Cagnes, between Nice and Cannes. Evening harness races, with the failing light supplemented by floodlights, are held there from December to March and during the whole of August. The grandstand has a view over the track to the sea, and the social ambiance resembles that of Ascot. The betting, much of it by millionaires, is understandably enormous; a typical day can bring in the equivalent of over $1,000,000.

The flat track is also used for harness racing (or trotting), which is especially popular on the continent of Europe, in North America, and in Russia. (It has never gained much following in Britain, though an English horse named Messenger, imported into Pennsylvania in 1788, was the progenitor of one of the greatest lines of trotting horses. Many trotting horses were bred in the North of England, but the idea of racing them without ever allowing them to break into a gallop is American.) In harness racing each horse pulls a lightweight, two-wheeled buggy (called a "sulky"); the driver sits up close behind the horse with his feet in "stirrups" attached to the shafts.

America's biggest trotting track is the Roosevelt Raceway on Long Island, which in the 1961 season accommodated over 2,500,000 spectators who spent about $196,000,000. (In New York state, harness races are more popular than thoroughbred races: In 1960, trotting races at various tracks drew over 7,000,000 spectators, while only about 5,000,000 went to see the thoroughbreds.) Canada, too, delights in trotting races, and spent nearly $40,000,000 on them in 1962. The Hippodrome in Moscow has a 60-day season of floodlit harness events complete with totalizator betting. In 1961 an English journalist, in Moscow on an assignment for his paper, visited the Hippodrome and won the biggest prize of the year—the equivalent of nearly $4800—on a bet of about $5.

Steeplechasing (the form of racing in which horses jump obstacles on the course) is generally thought to have evolved from the sport of hunting—i.e., the pursuit of a fox, stag, or hare by hounds and mounted hunters in traditional garb, who jump intervening hedges, fences, brooks, and so on during the chase. But hunting's most direct descendant is a form of horse racing called "point-to-point," which originated in the 18th century when hunters who had run down their quarry early in the day would continue their sport by challenging one another to races over all obstacles to some distant landmark—often the church steeple in a neighboring village. (Point-to-point meetings are still held in many countries, but attract horse enthusiasts rather than gamblers.) Modern steeplechasing probably owes more to European military trials in which the skill and endurance of horse and rider were tested by facing them with artificial hurdles. Britain, again, can lay claim to the best-known steeplechase in the world—the Grand National, which was first run in 1836 at Aintree, near Liverpool.

The Grand National is one of the most exciting races in the world, and from the bookmakers' point of view one of the most remunerative. There are usually well over 40 runners (the record for horse races everywhere is 66 runners in the 1929 Grand National) but the number of falls can put half the horses out of the race. A Liverpool bookmaker told me that, if he could attend only one more race before he died, he would choose the National "because at least I'd be sure of making my funeral expenses."

The same bookie also mentioned that, in his experience, "more people stick a pin into the list of runners for the National than any other race I know. They bet blind." But, with this race, such a method of choosing a horse to bet on seems to be as useful as any: The 1963 winner was a "long shot," with odds of 66 to 1 against its winning; and the 1962 winner carried odds of 44 to 1.

There is an American Grand National (held at Belmont Park, N.Y.) that tempts over 1,000,000 people into making bets totaling over $113,000,000. France's steeplechasing counterpart to the National is the Grand Steeple de Paris, which is run at Auteuil and can draw about 30,000 spectators and the equivalent of over $12,000,000 in betting money annually. (Incidentally, that bookmaker whom I quoted before told me that in his experience the French bet on the Grand Steeple in a much less haphazard fashion than the British do on the National: "The Steeple de Paris public knows its horses like nobody else. You wouldn't find many of them pricking race cards with a pin.")

As all the figures that I have been quoting indicate, there is nothing like the sight of some horses thundering along an enclosed track for emptying people's pockets. In fact, in many countries more money goes on horse racing than on any other form of gambling. Britain, for instance, spends over $900,000,000 annually on the horses; the next most popular form of gambling, greyhound racing, draws only $450,000,000. Australia is proportionately even keener than Britain; it spends about $850,000,000 on horse racing and about $400,000,000 on *all* other forms of gambling combined.

In 1960, 46,000,000 Americans placed over $3,000,000,000 on the horses in legal bets (i.e., through the facilities provided on the tracks). The amount bet illegally (through off-track betting with bookmakers) cannot be determined

Originally, steeplechases were improvised cross-country runs over hedges and ditches to some convenient landmark (often a church steeple). These three illustrations (from an 1839 edition of the British magazine *Sporting Life*) record an early steeplechase that was run from an army barracks (left) over fields and fences (below left) to the village church (below).

Right, the start of a Finnish harness race. In the background is a tote board. All racing bets in Finland must go through the tote, since bookmakers are illegal (as they are in many European countries).

exactly. Estimates range from $7,000,000,000 to $50,000,000,000; the true figure is probably somewhere in between. Canada, a small country in terms of population, spends about $200,000,000 legally each year on pari-mutuel horse-racing bets.

The highest gambling expenditure in many European countries goes on various forms of lotteries and pools (see Chapter 10). West Germany, for instance, is extremely lottery conscious: Gamblers there spend the equivalent of over $50,000,000 annually on lotteries and pools, and only about $10,000,000 on horse racing. Italy spends the equivalent of over $75,000,000 on various lotteries in a year, more than 13 times the amount bet on the horses. In France, however, the equivalent of over $400,000,000 is staked yearly on the horses, while the national lottery draws only the equivalent of about $150,000,000.

In countries like Britain, France, and America, where horse racing has been a top betting draw for a great many years, traditions have grown up that have made the race track into a world of its own—a world as unique and self-sustaining as a high-class casino, but by no means as exclusive. A would-be race-track bettor needs to know how to use the highly streamlined betting facilities; and he must become familiar with some of the jargon and with the roles of some of this world's permanent denizens.

First, the bettor must learn where to find the information he needs in order to place his bet. He can turn to the sports pages of the newspapers of the day,

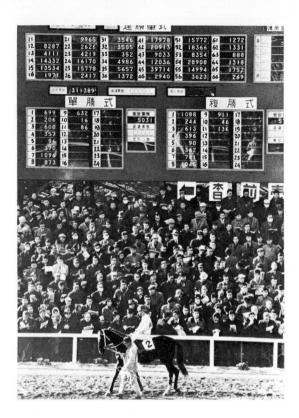

Left, eager racegoers crowd below a huge tote board in the parade ring at Japan's *Fuchu* track—scene of the annual Japanese Derby. Above, two standard American tote tickets include a heart and other symbols to deter forgers. Right, a grandstand view of a typical American tote board. The board has been labeled to show the information displayed on each section: For example, the money that has been placed by bettors on various horses "to show"—i.e., to finish either first, second, or third.

which in most racing centers provide complete lists of the day's horses, jockeys, their past form, and tips (i.e., "selections") on likely winners. Or he can look at one of the more specialist publications—like the *Daily Racing Form,* an American newspaper dedicated entirely to the nation's horse racing. Britain's enthusiasts turn to the daily *Sporting Chronicle* or *The Racing Calendar.*

Also, spectators at most race tracks can buy programs that list the horses for each race by numbers, the jockeys (giving their weights and colors), the owners and trainers, a selection of horses likely to finish first, second, and third in each race—and even such specialized pieces of information as equipment changes: for example, if a horse is running in blinkers for the first time or has had blinkers removed for the first time.

One of the most colorful (if not the most reliable) kinds of assistance that a gambler can get in choosing his horse comes from the tipsters, or touts, who make a living by selling tips on likely winners and other information that, they assure their customers, comes "straight from the stables." (It seldom does; racing authorities generally ensure that the people directly concerned with the horses keep any information they have to themselves.) Tipsters are not of course dishonest: Their knowledge of the racing world can make some of their advice more valuable to a bettor than sticking a pin into the program. And, even if they're wrong every time, no race track would be the same without them. Every tipster looks for a gimmick to distinguish him from his rivals, and some have thus become world famous—like Prince Monolulu, an impressive Maori whose

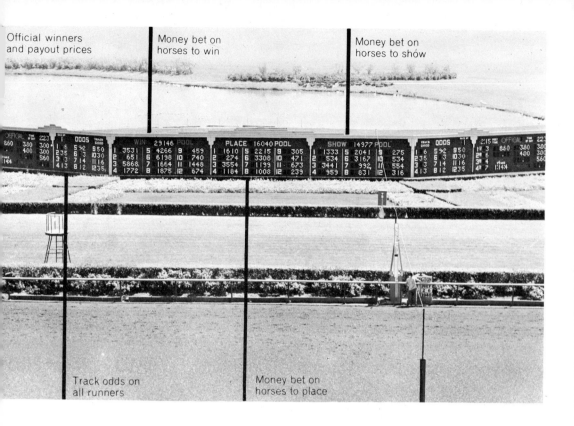

Official winners and payout prices

Money bet on horses to win

Money bet on horses to show

Track odds on all runners

Money bet on horses to place

exotic robes and business call of "I gotta horse, I gotta horse" are known on every racecourse in England and are the joy of thousands of visitors.

Aside from the newspapers and tipsters, the racegoer gets the basic information he needs in order to bet (i.e., the odds given on the horses) from the same apparatus with which he makes his bet—the *totalizator* (or "tote" machine). The original tote—a hand-operated calculating machine—was first used to operate a pari-mutuel betting system in New Zealand in 1880. In 1913 (also in New Zealand) an electrical calculator was put into use for the same purpose; and in this form the totalizator came to Europe in 1928, when it was tried out at France's Longchamps track. England adopted it two years later, and used it first at Newmarket and the Northolt greyhound track. A similar machine was produced independently in America in 1932, and this machine in turn was developed into the complex electronic computer that it is today.

The totalizator is a nearly fraud-proof method of distributing the wealth acquired from the bettors according to the pari-mutuel system (which was devised in 1872 by a French chemist named Pierre Oller). As the name indicates (*pari*, wager, *mutuel*, among us all) the system is based on a pooling of the total amount staked by the players, and an equitable distribution of the pool among the winners (less a proportion deducted to pay the government's tax). The intricate mathematics that are required to make the distribution equitable are less important to the average gambler than is the fact that they work. The computer that is the tote rarely errs and never cheats.

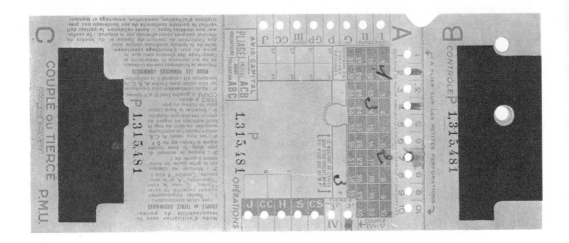

Above, a Tiercé ticket—issued by France's Pari-Mutuel Urbain organization—on which a bettor has marked three horses for first, second, and third places. Tiercé tickets are sold at any P.M.U. office (left) for certain races run on Sundays and holidays; the P.M.U. also accepts bets for weekday racing and is the only form of off-track betting permitted in France.

In America and many countries other than Britain, the only way a bettor can back a horse legally is through the totalizator. When he has chosen his horse he turns to the tote to learn the odds. The focal point of his study is the "tote board," which in America is a long, low board set in the middle of the infield (the area encircled by the track) clearly visible to everyone. The day starts with the numbers of the runners in the first race posted in order, with the "morning line" odds in lights opposite them. The morning line is the odds established by the racing officials for each horse (on the basis of its past performance) on the morning of a particular racing day.

When betting opens on the first race, the odds begin to change as the money comes in. A ticket is issued to the bettor for each bet, and the amount is immediately recorded and computed, in terms of the odds. In the 30 minutes between each race, the odds will usually change about six or eight times, depending on the volume of betting.

All odds except those below 10 are figured to one (11 to 1, 20 to 1, etc.) but only the first figure is actually shown in lights on the board. For instance, if horse number five is running at 14 to 1, the board will show the figure "5" and in the column next to it the figure "14." Odds below 10 are figured to two (like 5 to 2) or four (7 to 4) or five (6 to 5), and are shown thus: 5/2, 7/4, and so on. These are "approximate odds" (as a sign on the board admits)—approximate because the electronic system would be even more complicated if it was necessary to show three or more figures. But payouts to winners are at exact odds.

Bets on American tracks are as standardized as the tracks themselves. You place your bet at a row of windows, and you can choose a $2, $5, $10, $20, or $50 window. You must bet these sums, or combinations of them: If you want to bet $500, you must place ten $50 bets (10 separate tickets). If you want to bet $17, you must get tickets from the $10, $5, and $2 windows. Obviously you can't bet such amounts as one or three dollars.

Still with regard to American racing: The bettor can back a horse to win, or to "place" (i.e., to come in first or second), or to "show" (i.e., to come in first, second, or third). The windows are thus further subdivided into $2 win, $2 place, and $2 show: and so on for the other amounts. There are a few other kinds of bet: You can put your money on a "daily double," which is usually run on the first two races of the day; to win you must pick the winners of both races. Or there is the "quiniela," in which the bettor tries to pick the first and second horse of a race. In Canada, the two horses must be picked in their order of finish; but in the U.S.A., if there are more than eight horses running, the chosen two can finish either way. (With fewer than eight horses, the bettor must predict their order; in New York state, this bet is called an "exacta.")

Of all the systems devised to "beat" the daily double, one of the most popular is called "wheeling" or "locking" the double. The bettor takes a likely winner (i.e., a favorite) in one race and places double bets on it with *every* horse in the other race. Thus if the chosen horse wins its race, the bettor automatically wins the double. (But he may make little profit if each race is won by a horse with short odds.) "Wheeling" can be applied to the quiniela as well: The bettor chooses an obvious winner and links it with every other horse in the race, one of which is bound to come in second.

Bettors can also gamble on the "six-dollar combine," which is also known as betting on a horse "across the board." You stake six dollars that your horse will come in somewhere in the first three. But this is just a convenience, not a special bet; the payment is no more than if you bought separate win, place, and show tickets. The daily double and quiniela are special features of a day's racing, and there are separate betting windows to deal with them. Also, the money bet through them goes into separate pools, not connected with the ordinary betting on the same races.

At the end of a race, the tote board shows the prices that will be paid for the first three horses, and winners take their tickets to another set of windows to

2/6 Win "Yankee" = 27/6 Invested			
Fitzroy	Abermaid	Hill Royal	Anzio
Epsom	Chepstow	Ripon	Ayr

6 x 2/6 Win Doubles			
Fitzroy	Abermaid		
	Abermaid	Hill Royal	
		Hill Royal	Anzio
Fitzroy		Hill Royal	
Fitzroy			Anzio
	Abermaid		Anzio

4 x 2/6 Win Trebles			
Fitzroy	Abermaid	Hill Royal	
	Abermaid	Hill Royal	Anzio
Fitzroy		Hill Royal	Anzio
Fitzroy	Abermaid		Anzio

2/6 Win Accumulator			
Fitzroy	Abermaid	Hill Royal	Anzio

Above on a British racecourse a bookmaker (extreme left of photo) takes money from bettors while his clerk (extreme right) records the bets. The current odds are shown on the board at the back. Left, a diagram showing the "Yankee bet" (a permutation bet covering four horses) that can be made with off-course bookmakers in Britain. The bettor has staked a total of 27s. 6d. on his four chosen horses with 11 separate bets of 2s. 6d.—the bets consisting of six "doubles," four "trebles," and an "accumulator" bet.

Right, the hand-signaling code used by British tic-tac men to relay changes in odds to bookmakers across the course. For example: By placing his right hand on his right shoulder the tic-tac man signals odds of 5 to 1. (This signal can also mean "horse number five.")

receive their winnings. Three payout prices are shown on the board for the horse that came in first, because anyone who bet that horse to place or to show still collects. Two prices are shown for the second-place horse (if you bet it to show you still win some money), and one price for the third horse.

That, in a simplified form, is the basic procedure that is familiar to every gambler who plays the horses legally in North America. Much the same procedure is followed in totalizator betting elsewhere, with certain local variations. In France, for instance, bettors can also get their money down in small establishments off the course that are collectively called Pari-mutuel Urbain (P.M.U.) offices. But these offices are in fact merely extensions of the on-course totalizators. All bets placed through the P.M.U. are recorded, transmitted to the racecourse, and included in the pari-mutuel pool as if they had been placed on the course. P.M.U. betting must end before the day's races begin. (It should be remembered that, in France, bookmaking is illegal; and the law against off-course, non-totalizator gambling is strictly enforced.)

The French have developed a special way of betting that has much in common with the American "across the board." It is called "Tiercé" and involves the selection of three horses to finish first, second, and third in specified races held on Sundays and holidays. For three francs (about 60 cents) the bettor buys a ticket at a P.M.U. office that contains (among other things) squares numbered from one to 39. The bettor makes his selection by writing the figures 1, 2, and 3 in the squares that correspond to the numbers of his chosen horses. The money thus staked is pooled and divided among the winners. The big wins, of course, go to those who predicted the right horses in the right order; but a bettor still receives some payment by choosing the three winning horses in any order.

No. 1	No. 2 or 2:1	No. 3 or 3:1	No. 4 or 4:1	No. 5 or 5:1	No. 10 or 10:1	Odds on	11:8

Evens	11:10	6:4	7:4	9:4	5:2	7:2	9:2

In Germany, bookmakers are allowed to operate, but money staked with them annually (in 1961, the equivalent of under $4,000,000) amounts to only about half the total amount staked with the totalizators. Britain is practically the only country where bookmakers are both legal and dominant in the racing world. Totalizator betting exists, of course, but takes a back seat to the bookies. (Its relative unimportance is indicated by the fact that the tote board itself is rarely in as prominent a place as in America. On some courses it cannot even be seen from the grandstand.)

A British bookmaker at the racecourse usually operates a stand or "pitch," dominated by a large blackboard on which he writes his odds (which change as frequently as the tote's). His clerks handle the money, record the bets, and issue the tickets to the bettors. The bookmaker also has in his employ several "runners," who are in effect private information bureaus. Runners know everything worth knowing in the racing game, are experienced in recognizing "blind" bets that are put on by big bettors to mislead bookmakers about betting on other horses, have sources of information about bets being laid by stables, and similar kinds of expertise. One bookmaker told me: "A runner with all the snippets you can use is worth fifty [£50] a meeting. He keeps you from doing a lot of silly things like shortening the odds too soon."

On the course the runner often passes his information to the "tic-tac" man, who communicates it by hand signals to the bookmaker elsewhere on the course. The code used by the tic-tac man consists of gestures with the hands to the head, throat, and nose, and is a complex form of semaphore that varies from place to place and even from bookmaker to bookmaker.

From the information passed to him the bookmaker adjusts the odds, sometimes "hedges" (i.e., lays off) his bets, and in general tries to keep just a little ahead of the bettor, who is looking for the same sort of information to aid him in his object of winning. Lay-off bets often become necessary when a bookmaker receives heavy betting on a horse with sizeable odds: If the horse were to win, the payout would ruin the bookmaker. So he places several bets of his own on the same horse—enough to help him out if the horse wins, but not enough to prevent him from making a profit if the horse loses.

A major percentage of British betting takes the form of legal *off*-course betting with bookmakers (or turf accountants, as many of them like to be called) at their betting shops. A great deal of this betting is done by post and telephone by customers who have credit accounts, but any special racing event like the Derby brings the crowds of occasional gamblers in to have a flutter. In general, British betting shops are like other shops in having a counter, a cash register, and a number of clerks to take the money. A bettor writes on a slip of paper the name and time of the race, the name and number of the horse he has chosen, and the size of his bet. Then he hands the paper and his money to a clerk and receives a ticket, which he will exchange for his payout if the horse wins. A blackboard shows the latest odds, and copies of racing newspapers are available for customers to look at. Attempts are seldom made to persuade customers to increase the size of their bets. Instead, the staff behind the counter is usually quite anxious to make sure the inexperienced customers know the basic facts about bets and odds.

There is no "show" betting in England. A gambler (whether betting with a bookie or through the tote) backs a horse to win, to place, or "each way." On an each-way bet he wins if his horse comes in either first or second—unless there are fewer than five horses running, in which case the payout is only on "win" bets. In races with over eight horses running an each-way bettor receives a payout if his horse comes first, second, or third; in races like the Derby or Grand National, if over 22 horses are running, payouts are made to four places. A British bettor can also put his money on a special combination bet called a "forecast" (the same thing as the Canadian quiniela).

Bookmakers everywhere set their own odds for a race, largely by the horses' past performance. Then the odds are "lengthened" or "shortened" according to the volume of betting. In America, a bookmaker will usually pay at track odds until they go too high; then he puts an upper limit on his payout, to protect himself against a big loss that might put him out of business. For example, if several hundred dollars (or, in the case of a bigtime bookie, several thousand) comes in on a particular horse (whose track odds are, say, 100 to 8) the American bookie would be very unlikely to pay out at longer odds than 10 to 1. This upper limit for odds and payouts is in effect the bookie's favorable percentage, the profit-ensuring technique that keeps him in business. The British bookie, however, is obliged by law to pay the "starting price" of the horse—the price as set out by the bookies at the track—no matter what it is.

One more thing should be noted in this quick look at racing odds. In cases where a particular horse in a race is almost certain to win, it would be foolish for bookmakers to bet against its victory. So they offer odds "on" instead of "against"—which means that your stake money will be more than your win. If the odds are 2 to 1 *on* and you bet $2, your total payout would be $3—your $2 stake money plus your $1 win. A classic example of "odds on" was the odds of 100 to 1 on offered by bookmakers on the great American horse Man O'War in three races in 1920. In other words, a bettor would have had to stake $100 to make a profit of $1. Odds on would appeal only to those bettors who could afford the large stake necessary to make such a win worth having. Nevertheless, the horse that runs with odds on is the closest to a "sure thing" in racing.

But not always—or, anyway, not according to that knowledgeable American author Damon Runyon, who used the idea of odds-on to build a dramatic climax for his short story "All Horse Players Die Broke." The story concerns a down-and-out gambler named Unser Fritz who has a fantastic streak of luck at the races and nets himself $100,000—almost enough to buy a gift of emeralds that, he hopes, will win back to him his former girl friend, "Emerald Em." But the emeralds cost $101,000. So Unser Fritz looks for and finds a safe bet—a

horse running at 100 to 1 on. He stakes his entire capital in order to win the extra thousand. Needless to say, the horse accidentally falls during the race, Fritz loses, and the girl rejects him.

On the other hand, the bet probably furthest from a sure thing is a special bet called an *accumulator* in Britain and a *parlay* in America. This bet transfers any winnings from horse to horse in different races at the same meeting. Assume that there are six races in the day: You choose a horse in each race and then bet on the first one. If it wins, your entire winnings are placed as a bet on your chosen horse in the second race. If *it* wins, your winnings are again transferred, and so on. As can be seen, your winnings can snowball immensely; but the chances of any bettor being right six consecutive times are more than slim.

Nevertheless, here too the improbable often happens: Before the war in the Normandy village of Saint-Saens there was an inveterate gambler who was in debt to the local landowner for taxes, owed for the food he and his wife had last eaten, and had lost his job as a tractor driver because he could never be relied on to be in the fields if there was any racing going on within 50 miles. He borrowed a few francs from his brother-in-law, saying that since he was determined to give up gambling anyway he might as well have one last fling, and put the money into an accumulator bet. All of his horses won and he cleared 500 francs. (He must have been less inveterate a gambler than he seemed, for he never made a bet after that day. He persuaded the owner of a cellar to let him have it at a nominal rent, started a café, and made a success of it. It was called *Café Cheval*.)

But even this bettor wasn't so vastly lucky as a man from Coventry, England, who in 1951 won the equivalent of $8500 for a 14-cent bet on an accumulator on four horses. The odds against this quadruple win were 60,640 to 1—the highest ever recorded on a horse race.

Systems are not so common in horse racing as they are in such games of pure chance as roulette or dice. I have mentioned the system associated with the American daily double; another is the popular "doubling" or "progressive" system. An Australian gambler who must remain nameless uses it (and makes a regular living with it) in the following form:

A game called "horsey-horsey" (a corruption of "housey-housey," another name for bingo) is simply public betting on old films of American horse races (far left). Mostly popular in Britain, it is usually played in disused cinemas (left). Right, players place their bets on the horses, which are represented by numbers on the betting slips to avoid possible recognition. After the film winning bets are paid off at the odds that were quoted for the original race.

He sets himself a specific goal for his day's win—usually £10. Then he bets on the favorite to win the first race (his bets are always placed at the last minute, to be sure of the starting price). The size of his first bet is calculated to ensure him a £10 profit if he wins; thus, if the favorite's starting odds are 5 to 1, he bets £2. If the horse wins, he collects his money and bets no more that day.

If the favorite loses the first race, he bets on the favorite for the second race, staking enough money both to recoup his £2 loss and to win his goal of £10; i.e., if the second race's favorite goes off at 3 to 2, he would bet £8 in order to make a £12 profit. And so on. If none of the favorites at one day's meeting won its race, he would presumably aim at a £20 gain the following day.

This system stops being workable when the capital required to recoup losses and make a profit becomes impossibly large—which happens after a lengthy losing streak. But in Western Australia such a streak is a rare occurrence. There are a limited number of race horses in that part of the world; many of the same horses run in every day's races, and some horses may run two or three times in the same day. So the choice of favorite is usually more soundly based than in most other countries where many of the horses running in a race may be unknown in terms of their past form—or may be untried, with no past form. At least *one* favorite is likely to win in a day on a Western Australian track.

Methods of cheating (i.e., of fixing races) figure much more largely than systems in the lore of the race track. Some of the well-known fixing methods of past years have today been made almost impossible by new strict rules, developed and enforced by powerful authorities (like Britain's Jockey Club or America's State Racing Commissions). For instance, substitution of a bad horse for a good one (or vice versa) has virtually been stopped on most tracks by such rules as the American one that demands the tattooing of a registration number on the inside lip of every horse.

Doping or drugging a horse to make it into a winner is another method of fixing that has been inhibited in recent years. The track officials today invariably make saliva and urine tests on every winner. Of course, doping a good horse to make it lose is less easy to detect, since tests can't be run on every horse in every race. But an experienced veterinarian will usually be suspicious when a normally fast horse comes in last—and he can order a test if he wishes. Punishment for convicted dopers is stiff; jail or fines, plus being ruled off the tracks for life.

Probably the closest thing to a sure method of fixing a race is by bribing the jockey to "pull" his horse or otherwise discreetly to lose the race. A skilled professional jockey would know a million subtle ways to discourage his horse (whether he ever uses them or not)—ways that go unnoticed by his fellow riders, by the crowd, and even by the "film patrol" (movie cameras placed at intervals around American tracks that keep a film record of the entire race).

So far, I have merely tried to sketch the broad outline of the racing world's important features—but an outline that should be enough to make even a novice bettor feel at home on most race tracks anywhere. For the rest of this chapter, I will turn away from horses and take brief looks at some of the other most popular forms of racing. Foremost among these is greyhound racing.

Greyhounds have a wide and numerous following in America, Britain, and many European nations. There are eight states of the U.S.A. (Arizona, Arkansas, Colorado, Florida, Massachusetts, Montana, Oregon, and South Dakota) that allow greyhound racing, and in 1962 about 10,000,000 gamblers spent nearly $500,000,000 on legal pari-mutuel betting. American greyhound racing was first begun in the 1920s in Florida, which is still the greyhound mecca of North America; that state alone accounts for about one third of the betting total of greyhound racing in all eight states.

Britain was once the home of the world's most avid greyhound backers: In 1946 the British spent the equivalent of $1,200,000,000 on the dogs. But the rising popularity of the football pools and bingo attracted a lot of gambling money away from the dogs, and today the greyhound tracks draw only about $375,000,000 annually in bets.

Several European countries list greyhound racing among their gambling interests (for instance, Belgium, France, and Holland); but in these places it is of minor importance compared to such gambles as numbers games, football pools, and horse racing. In Spain, however, greyhound racing has an enthusiastic

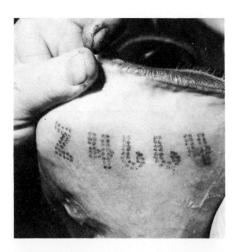

Left, the lip tattoo that is compulsory identification for all horses racing in North America. Tattooing is a foolproof method of foiling the "ringer" racket, in which a good horse is substituted for a poor one resembling it, allowing gamblers to collect at long odds. Right, a camera patrol at work at Canada's Woodbine Park. It is one of several cameras distributed along the track to detect any unfair tactics among the jockeys. Far right, a jockey takes a numbered ball from a "keno goose" (see p. 249) to find his position in the line-up at the start of the race.

following; it has been estimated that the equivalent of almost $1,700,000 is spent annually at the greyhound tracks.

Greyhound racing is an adaptation of the ancient sport of *coursing,* which was flourishing as far back as the fifth century B.C. (when Xenophon, the Greek soldier and protégé of Socrates, wrote of it in a manual of hunting). Coursing is the pursuit of live quarry—usually a hare—by greyhounds; originally the chase was across open country, with judges and spectators following on horses. For centuries in Europe it was the exclusive pastime of the aristocracy, for only they could afford to keep horses and greyhounds. But in the 19th century Britain initiated the idea of enclosing the course so that spectators could watch the chase from a covered stand. The idea met with immediate success not only in Britain but also in Australia and America. Coursing is still a popular minority sport in all three continents, but its following is regional rather than national, and there is little or no gambling.

But greyhound racing with a mechanical hare, when it was first thought of, received acclaim from people who knew nothing whatever about the finer points of greyhounds—people who simply liked to watch (and bet on) races. The electrical hare now in common use was perfected in America in 1919 by a man named O. P. Smith, and was first tried out on a track at Emeryville, California. (Actually, a mechanical—clockwork—hare had been used in coursing much earlier in England in 1876, but the idea didn't catch on; it lay dormant until Mr. Smith brought out his version, which first arrived in Britain in 1927.)

At first, greyhound racing was almost completely uncontrolled, and therefore offered plenty of opportunities for crookedness. Many phony promoters cheated gamblers out of millions by organizing the doping and substitution of dogs. But today the various national greyhound associations and the individual state governments are in full control. In America, to prevent substitutions, every racing greyhound is registered at birth; its paw prints are recorded and it must wear an identity disk. Also, greyhounds are taken from their owners several hours before a race, and are inspected on the track by a state veterinary officer. A similar precautionary procedure is enforced in Britain by the National Greyhound Racing Association.

The typical British track has an iron-roofed stand, floodlights illuminating the turf track, and six traps at one end in which the dogs are imprisoned: When the hare is about 10 yards ahead of the traps, the dogs are released simultaneously. Betting on greyhounds in Britain follow very much the same procedure as on horses—tote, bookies, and betting shops. In America and much of Europe, of course, only totalizator betting is legally permitted. The standard bet on most American tracks is $2.

Automobile racing attracts very little gambling money in most countries, mainly because it has largely become the realm of manufacturers who pay highly skilled professional drivers to exploit the possibilities of their machines. Thus gamblers, reasonably enough, are probably hesitant at the thought that their chances may be affected by mechanical alterations that apply to some machines but not others. Few bookmakers bother to acquire the knowledge necessary to quote odds on drivers like Graham Hill or Farina; if you want to stake some money on a driver in a car race, you can most easily do it in a private bet with a friend. The nine biggest races that you can have your personal bets on are the Grands Prix of Monaco, Holland, Belgium, Great Britain, France, Germany, Italy, South Africa, and the United States.

Organized betting is minimal on motorcycle races as well (though these are highly popular as spectator sports). And as with car and motorcycle racing, so

with bicycle racing—at least in the Western world. There is no organized gambling on Europe's many bicycle races: The races are sponsored by manufacturers and other advertisers, who pay the prizes. (The prize money for the most famous European race, the 2750-mile Tour de France, rarely amounts to more than the equivalent of $4000.) The French are the most ardent bicycle-race fans in Europe; the Germans, Belgians, Dutch, and Italians are close behind them. All four nations have developed the sport with enthusiasm, both on specially built circular tracks with heavy banking on the corners and on ordinary roads.

But in the East—specifically, in Japan—bicycle racing is one of the most important sports for gamblers. Japanese bicycle racing was instituted in 1948 to aid the recovery of the bicycle industry from a post-war depression. By 1955 sixty tracks had been built; today more than 1,000,000 racing cyclists compete each year, with sometimes a dozen races taking place daily on every track. The local governments sponsor the races and sell, in one year, over 60,000,000,000 betting tickets. (A small proportion of these, about 1,500,000,000 are for motorcycle races.) Twenty-five per cent is deducted from the sale of the tickets by the government; after deducting the costs of building and running the tracks, the sponsors are left with a net profit of nine per cent—the equivalent of about $15,000,000. The remainder is pooled and divided among winning bettors; in 1954 the winnings totaled the equivalent of about $163,000,000.

Left, racing greyhounds round a corner at one of America's many greyhound tracks. Above, the dogs are released from numbered "traps" in pursuit of electrical hares (right). Sometimes the greyhounds are allowed to sniff at a dead hare after the race, as compensation for the deception.

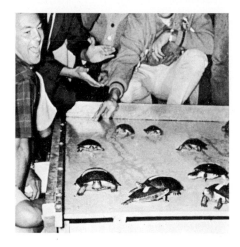

Some bizarre examples of animal races: Top left, uncovering hermit crabs (distinguished by painted shells) at the start of a race across the floor of a smart Puerto Rican hotel. Top right, a tortoise race at San Francisco. Left, a race between goats paced by runners—a local sport of the West Indies that draws heavy tote betting.

Right, the French bicycle marathon the Tour de France. As on all European bicycle races, there is no organized betting on the Tour, though private betting is widespread among the race's many enthusiastic followers.

Yacht racing, like horse breeding, is mainly a pursuit for the rich (since racing yachts can be extremely expensive); and in their time the rich have staked their friends and themselves with big wagers. Charles II of England started the sport after being presented with a yacht by the Dutch East India Company, and he and his brother, the Duke of York, raced on the Thames for 100 guineas. The 18th-century diarist Samuel Pepys speaks of his colleagues at the Admiralty wagering on the results "as merrily as they do on any dice." In 1866 three American schooners raced across the Atlantic in very heavy weather for a stake of $90,000 contributed by all three owners, and it was reported in the New York papers at the time that interest was so keen that it was "impossible to enter any gambling saloon without finding a person who would offer you odds on whether the *Fleetwing, Henrietta,* or *Vesta* would first arrive at her destination." (*Henrietta* won with a crossing time of 13 days, 21 hours, 5 minutes.)

Today there is still considerable private betting between members of the various yacht clubs; and recently a remarkable achievement involved such a wager. In 1960, two yachtsmen, Francis Chichester and H. G. Hasler, had a five-shilling bet on which of them would be first to make a solo crossing of the

Atlantic. Chichester won the race in his yacht *Gipsy Moth III*, completing the trip in 40 days.

Motor-boat racing is another sport that is pursued for glory and trophies rather than gambling victories—except in Japan, where, like bicycling, it has a national betting following. National and local governments sponsor the sale of over 13,000,000 betting tickets a year (not only to the spectators but to anyone who cares to buy them) in tobacconists, pin-table saloons, and cafés.

The amounts lost and won over the centuries by betting on which of a number of moving bodies would reach a determined point first have certainly been astronomical. For example, in the 13th century, the affluent Persian Sultan El Naseri paid out the equivalent of $250,000 a day for bets on horses. And in more recent times (specifically, 1961) racing fans in the state of New York bet a total of over $1,000,000,000—the second consecutive year in which the state betting total topped the billion mark. Between these gamblers of the Old and New Worlds one might imagine a valley about as deep as the Grand Canyon, filled with the money bet on racing. To the people who bet it, however, it was in no sense metaphorical money. It was very real.

9 Faites vos jeux

The word *roulette* derives from the French *roue,* a wheel, and literally can mean any kind of caster, roller, or small wheel. The idea of a wheel (or balanced pointer) spinning and stopping in an unpredictable position is as basic to games of chance as the drawing of lots. The ancient Greeks gambled on the spin of a battle shield balanced on the point of a sawn-off sword; the Roman emperor Augustus used a chariot wheel that spun on a vertical axle in the floor of the gaming room of his palace; the American Indians and Greenland Eskimos played a gambling game (which I mentioned in Chapter 2) with a revolving pointer.

The Indian *teetotum* (a spinning top) is a variation on the same theme, as was the once-popular Western game of *put-and-take,* which also used a top. Today the carnival game known as "the wheel of fortune" (in America sometimes called "crown-and-anchor," but not to be confused with the dice game of that name) employs the same basic principles of these ancient gambles. A numbered and usually upright wheel is spun and players bet on which number will come to rest against a pointer (see p. 66).

Roulette obviously belongs to the same family of games, though the line of descent is less direct. In roulette the winner is not chosen by the wheel's final position in relation to a pointer. Instead, the choice is made when a small ivory ball falls into a numbered slot *on* the wheel. The wheel is divided into 37 of these equal radial slots (38 in America), which are colored alternately red and

Roulette players in action at an American casino. Bets may be placed after the wheel has started to spin—but not after the croupier has called "rien ne va plus" (no more bets).

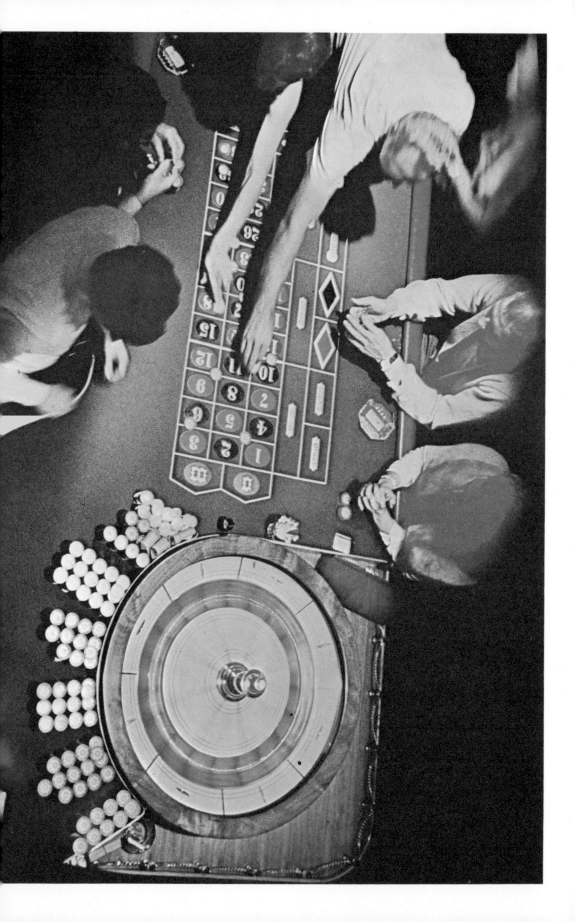

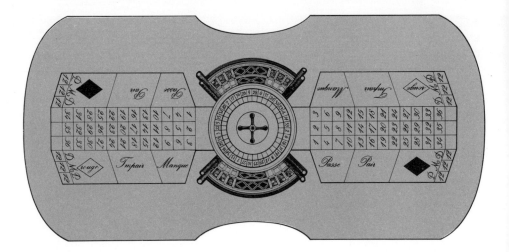

black and numbered irregularly. The wheel revolves clockwise inside a fixed circumambient ledge around which the ball is thrown in a counterclockwise direction. As the wheel slows, the ball falls into one of the slots.

History is vague concerning the origins of this variation on the spinning game. There is the usual abundance of theories, including the erroneous idea that the 17th-century French philosopher-mathematician Pascal invented roulette during a monastic retreat. In fact, Pascal was experimenting with a device concerned with perpetual motion and saw no connection at the time between a possible game and his ball-and-wheel experiment But his experiments did employ a wheel, to which (it is thought) he gave the name "roulette." Presumably others saw its commercial possibilities.

The first wheels specifically designed to throw a ball into a numbered slot for gambling purposes were used for an early version of roulette called *hoca*. These wheels were used in the early 18th century at casinos in France (Saint-Cyr), Germany (Baden-Baden), Austria (Baden bei Wien), and Hungary (Pest). These early wheels, of course, were much cruder than the delicately balanced mechanisms used today. They consisted of a circular flat bed with numbered pockets around the periphery and a spindle projecting upward through the center, with a six-spoked rimless wheel pivoted on the spindle. In the game of hoca that was played with this wheel, the ball was placed between the spokes (which were about half the radius of the bed); when the wheel was spun, the ball was thrown by centrifugal force toward the 40 numbered pockets on the edge, at the same time being forced clockwise around the bed. A rim around the edge of the bed prevented the ball from flying off.

Hoca was sponsored on a grand scale by the French statesman Cardinal Mazarin, who saw in it an easy way to increase the fortunes of the youthful Louis XIV. He authorized the opening of innumerable casinos in France and then collected the profits for the royal treasury (and no doubt the Mazarin treasury too, for he was immensely rich when he died in 1661). Since there were three zeros among the 40 pockets, and all the money on the table went to the bank every time the ball fell into a zero, the profits were ludicrously large. After

Left, an etching of a late 19th-century European roulette wheel (with one zero) and its layout. Right, an American wheel of the same period. Below, two wheels and layouts of the kind used in American casinos of the 1890s. Early wheels varied considerably in size, style, and accuracy—and the players' chances varied accordingly.

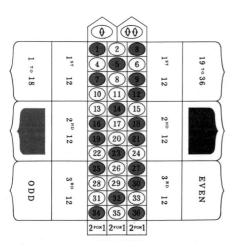

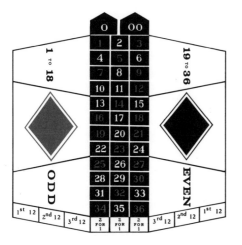

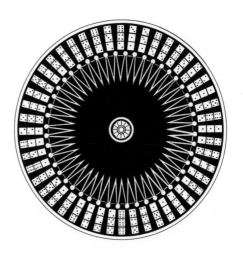

Left, the wheel used for the 18th-century society game E.O. (Even-Odd)—a forerunner of roulette. The wheel was divided into 40 compartments; 20 of these were marked E, the other 20 were marked O. The banker spun a ball around the wheel, and players bet on whether it would drop into an E or an O compartment. Above, a cartoon by the 18th-century British artist Thomas Rowlandson shows an E.O. game in full swing.

Mazarin's death the government decreed that anyone running a hoca casino should be executed.

Other variations of roulette had phases of popularity in the 18th century, and some have lasted until today. *Petits chevaux*—which still flourishes in Northern France and Ireland—indulged the fancy of horse-racing enthusiasts in an effort to tempt them from the courses into the casinos. The number of spokes in a hoca wheel was increased to 19 (and later reduced to nine), and small ivory or china horses were fixed to the other ends of the spokes. The wheel was placed on an elaborately painted cloth depicting a country scene (rather after the manner of old maps) with a "winning post" marked at one end. The horses were numbered for betting purposes, and the player whose horse stopped nearest the winning post took the money.

Another variation was *E.O. (Even-Odd)*, in which a wheel (again with 40 compartments) was set in the middle of a round table marked for the placing of bets. Twenty of the compartments were marked E, the other twenty O. If the ball came to rest on an O compartment the bank took all the bets staked on E, and vice versa. Like petits chevaux, this game might have been as monotonous as a coin-tossing session, though it did offer the spell of a spinning wheel and ball without the complication of roulette odds. Possibly for this reason it was immediately popular with women. At the English resort of Tunbridge Wells, for example, where the most fashionable ladies went to take the waters, an E.O. casino was set up in 1739 and was considered part of the cure. One of the many shrewd doctors who took up residence at the spa prescribed this remedy for an ailing patient: "Of a morning and post-noon, the waters; and in the evening the excitement of the Roly-Poly [E.O.] tables: watching which, brings out the vapors."

Incidentally, aside from the question of society ladies' vapors, there are circumstances in which gambling *does* have a definite therapeutic value: in cases

A modern "track" and the four betting layouts (which are identical) for the racing game *petits chevaux*. Nine numbered horses (attached by rods to cogs beneath the table) are set in motion by the croupier (the starting handle is bottom right of the track) and "race" around a central figure. Each horse revolves independently. Players may back one horse to win (i.e., to stop nearest the winning post, shown bottom left of the track) or can back four horses at once—by staking money on either of two bands on the layout numbered 1, 3, 6, 8 and 2, 4, 7, 9 respectively. They can also back the odd numbers (1, 3, 7, 9) or the even numbers (2, 4, 6, 8). When 5 wins, all money staked on any of the groups of numbers goes to the bank. Odds of 7 to 1 are paid for a win on a particular horse, and even money for a win on any of the groups of numbers.

of enforced boredom, for instance, or at times of extreme tension or danger. And ingeniously contrived roulette games seem a favorite at such times. During the 1939-45 war, prisoners of both sides proved themselves to be very skillful in making mechanisms that supplied all the excitements of roulette. The British artist John Worsley, a wartime naval officer who was captured by the Germans, has described and depicted the gambling activities that went on in the Milag Nord prison camp, a merchant-navy camp near Bremen to which Worsley was transferred from a naval prison camp at Westetinke. Discarded bicycle wheels salvaged from dumps were ingeniously divided into segments with the aid of wood, canvas, cardboard, and anything else at hand. The segments were then numbered and the wheel spun on a fixed pivot, like the Emperor Augustus's chariot wheel; a more or less perfect roulette resulted. The prisoners gambled for the currency called "Lagermarks" that was issued in the camp, or for a vicious form of alcohol secretly distilled from fruit and vegetable parings. But though the effect of alcohol can hardly be called therapeutic, there is no doubt that the action of gambling itself, like escape attempts, gave some point to an otherwise pointless existence.

Returning to the 18th century: A variation of roulette called *boule* became popular in many European casinos at this time. Like roulette, boule is played with a numbered wheel set into a bowl, and a ball that is spun around the rim of the bowl—only in this case the wheel is stationary and the ball does all the moving. On the boule wheel there are no zeros and only 18 compartments, numbered 1 to 9 twice (i.e., each number between 1 and 9 occurs twice). The number 5 is reserved for the house, which can thus expect to win one ninth of all the money bet against it; this is the casino's "edge" or favorable percentage. Players may bet on any number (including 5), and the payoff on each is 7 to 1. Or they may bet on odd or even numbers, or on either of two "bands" (numbered 1, 3, 6, 8 and 2, 4, 7, 9); the payoff on any of these is even money.

Left, the typical boule wheel used in many European casinos today. Right, a boule layout comparing the odds paid on the various bets with the correct odds. Players may bet on any one of the nine numbers, on all the even numbers 2, 4, 6, 8 (pair), on all the odd numbers 1, 3, 7, 9 (impair), on all the numbers 1, 2, 3, 4 (manque), and on all the numbers 6, 7, 8, 9 (passe). Because the odds are simple and the minimum stake low, boule has become extremely popular as a small-scale gambling game in Europe.

Boule is still extremely popular—particularly among women—partly because of its comparative simplicity and partly because the minimum stake is always low. It is one of the few forms of gambling that are allowed in Switzerland (where casinos, most privately-run lotteries, numbers games, and betting on horse races are all forbidden). But Swiss boule would not attract many dedicated gamblers, since the *maximum* stake allowed in the resort hotels and similar places where games of boule occur is only two Swiss francs (about 50 cents).

The fascination of roulette made itself felt almost everywhere during the 18th and 19th centuries. In the court of Catherine II of Russia roulette tables were set up not only in the sumptuous reception rooms of the palace but also in the kitchens, where the chefs played for Ukrainian serfs as well as for money. Selim III of Turkey heard about roulette from French prisoners of war captured at the battle of the Pyramids in 1798, and instructed his artificers to construct a wheel for him. The British diplomat Edward Clive introduced the game to India during his governorship of Madras in 1799. And in Switzerland the game began to make an important contribution to the country's economy since the Swiss aptitude for manufacturing delicate machinery brought in many orders for properly balanced wheels. None of these, however, was put into action in Switzerland itself.

In 1854, the Duc de Vallombrosa took some English friends in his yacht to visit the principality of Monaco where, under the direction of a young Parisian named François Blanc, a new gaming house had been opened. After some searching, the Duc and his party eventually found the gaming tables—two roulette and one trente-et-quarante—installed in a barn. Yet within just a few years, Blanc (who was described by the Lord Chancellor of England as the most brilliant financier of his time) had transformed this barn into a glittering casino, and people from all over the world were clamoring to try their luck at its tables. Even today, when casinos can be found in many cities and fashionable holiday

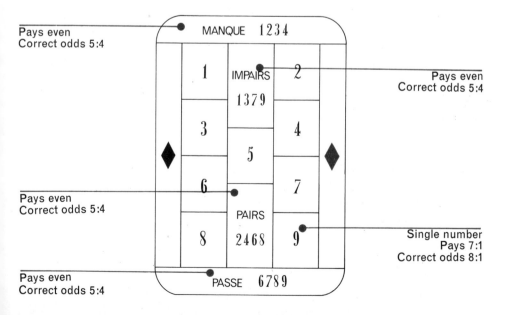

Pays even
Correct odds 5:4

MANQUE 1 2 3 4

IMPAIRS 1 3 7 9

Pays even
Correct odds 5:4

Pays even
Correct odds 5:4

PAIRS 2 4 6 8

Single number
Pays 7:1
Correct odds 8:1

Pays even
Correct odds 5:4

PASSE 6 7 8 9

centers, Monte Carlo retains its position of supremacy (though its annual betting turnover—the equivalent of about $20,000,000—is small compared to that of a top Nevada casino—usually about $300,000,000). Throughout the world its name is considered synonymous with gambling at its most expensive and most glamorous.

If this widespread view of Monte Carlo has any basis in reality, much of the casino's magic probably emanates from the roulette tables. For roulette is as much a spectacle as a game, a challenge that most sportsmen can't resist—even though the chances of winning at roulette in the long run are less than even, as a detailed look at the game itself will show.

Practically all casinos except those in the U.S.A. use a wheel with 37 spaces—one zero and the numbers 1 to 36. The American wheel has two zeros (38 spaces). Odd and even numbers are alternated around both wheels, and (except for the zero or zeros) the slots are colored alternately red and black. Apart from this, the arrangement of numbers on the European wheel seems entirely haphazard. The American double-zero wheel, however, *does* have a definite pattern. Consecutive numbers appear opposite one another; also, successive pairs of numbers of the same color total 37—pairs like 14 and 23 (red) or 4 and 33 (black). (The presence of the zeros causes exceptions to this rule : The numbers 9 and 28, both red, are side by side by the single zero instead of being separated by a black number; and the black 10 forms a pair with the adjacent red 27, beside the double zero.)

A roulette game is operated by two or three *croupiers*—according to whether it is played on a single or double-ended table. (The only advantage of the double-ended table is that it can accommodate more players and take more bets. The layout is the same at each end.) The word "croupier" originally meant a person who rode tandem on the back end of a horse, either to instruct the rider in the

Left, the wheel and layout for *roulca* (or card roulette). The wheel (modeled on the roulette wheel) has 25 compartments, each marked with a card symbol. Players may bet on individual cards, on suits, and on high, low, even, and odd numbers. Roulca was invented and first played at Germany's Baden-Baden casino.

Right, the roulette wheel that is used in American casinos today. Unlike its European counterparts, the American wheel has two zeros working for the bank.

saddle or for a free ride. The word was adopted for gaming use in France in the early 18th century, when novice card players could hire the services of an expert to stand behind them and advise them on play. Today, croupiers are, in the gaming sense, representatives of the casino, and the conduct of the game is their responsibility entirely.

In roulette, one of them spins the wheel, rakes in chips from the losers, and hands out chips to the winners. His colleagues help by sorting out the chips into their different values (usually ranging from 25c to $25 in America, and from five to 500 new francs in Monte Carlo), and keep an eye on the betting. Croupiers will also place bets for novice players who have not yet learned the betting procedure and terminology.

The European betting table is divided into six areas labeled *pair, impair, passe, manque, rouge,* and *noir* (even, odd, high, low, red, black). At the bottom of the table there are nine smaller spaces; the middle three are blank and each of the others is labeled 12. By placing chips in various prescribed positions on this table a player can bet on one or more numbers or combinations of numbers. If he wins, he will be paid off at prescribed odds. (Casinos, of course, give themselves a slight advantage—or favorable percentage—on all bets by making the actual payoff odds slightly less than the mathematically true odds, as explained in Chapter 5.)

If you put chips on *pair,* you're betting that the winning number will be an even number; on *impair,* that the winning number will be odd. Chips on *passe* are a bet that the winning number will be between 19 and 36; on *manque,* that the winner will be between one and 18. Chips on *rouge* are a bet that a red number will win; on *noir,* that a black one will. All these are "even money" bets—i.e., the player is paid the same amount as his bet if he wins. In even money bets the true odds are $1\frac{1}{18}$ to 1 ($1\frac{1}{9}$ to 1 on an American wheel); the zero provides the bank with its slight edge.

The croupier in action : Above left, the roulette wheel has been spun in a counter-clockwise direction (with the left hand) and the ball thrown clockwise around the wheel (with the right). Above, after spinning the wheel the croupier shows the players that his hands are empty. Left, the croupier removes the ball from the winning compartment (keeping his hand turned so that players can see the ball at all times). Below left, the croupier pays out to winners ; below, he sorts out the money collected from losers and drops "tips" from winners into a special slot. (It is customary for big winners to give the personnel a chip from their winnings.)

Other bets are as follows:

En plein (in America, *straight*): A player can stake any single number or zero by putting his chips on a chosen number. If that number comes up, he will be paid 35 times the amount he staked. The correct odds are 36 to 1 (on an American double-zero wheel, 37 to 1); reducing the pay-out gives the bank its favorable percentage. If zero comes up the bank takes all the money on the table except the bets placed on the "even money" spaces. These bets neither win nor lose; they are left to "ride" for another spin. If either of the zeros on an American wheel comes up, the bank will pay 35 to 1 odds to players who have bet on either zero and will take in every other stake on the table.

A cheval (*split*): Any two adjacent numbers can be staked by placing chips on the line seperating them. In this case, if either of the two numbers comes up, the player will be paid 17 times the amount of his stake. Correct odds are $17\frac{1}{2}$ to 1 (on an American wheel, 18 to 1).

Transversale pleine (*street*): In this bet any horizontal row of three numbers is staked by placing chips on the outer line of the chosen row. If any of the three numbers comes up the bettor will be paid 11 times his stake, correct odds being $11\frac{1}{3}$ to 1 (on an American wheel, $11\frac{2}{3}$ to 1).

Carré (*square*): Any square of four numbers can be staked by placing chips on the + formed by the intersecting lines of the chosen squares. Any one of the four numbers coming up will bring the bettor eight times his stake. Correct odds are $8\frac{1}{4}$ to 1 (on an American wheel, $8\frac{1}{2}$ to 1).

Sixaine (*line*): By placing chips on the intersection of the outer vertical line and the line horizontally dividing any two columns of three numbers, a player will be dividing his stake among the six numbers of those two columns. If any one of the six comes up he will be paid five times his stake instead of the correct odds of $5\frac{1}{6}$ to 1 (on an American wheel, $5\frac{1}{3}$ to 1).

Colonne (*column*): The stake can be divided among the 12 numbers in any single vertical row by putting chips in the small space at the bottom of the chosen row. If any one of the 12 come up, the payoff odds are 2 to 1 instead of the correct $2\frac{1}{12}$ to 1 (on an American wheel, $2\frac{1}{6}$ to 1).

Douzaine (*dozen*): The stake is placed on one of the six small outer spaces at the bottom of the table; according to which space is chosen, the bet will be in the numbers 1–12, 13–24, or 25–36. The payoff odds are the same as for colonne. The stake may be divided between two adjacent columns, or two series of 12 numbers; in this case the bettor will be paid half the amount of his stake if he wins, instead of the true odds of $\frac{11}{13}$ to 1.

At the beginning of each round the croupier invites players to place their bets with the phrase *faites vos jeux*. Then he spins the wheel and flips the ball around the bowl. Players continue to place their bets while the ball is in motion until the croupier calls *rien ne va plus* (no more bets). This is the moment of drama. The spinning wheel slows, the ball hovers over two or three numbers: All eyes are riveted to it. Eventually it settles in a compartment. The spell is broken.

The croupier brusquely announces the result—say, *"dix-sept, rouge, impair, et manque"* (i.e. 17, red, odd, and low)—pays out to the winners, and rakes in the money staked by the losers. Players with their chips on 17 will win at 35 to 1; players with their chips on the rouge, impair, or manque will win at even money.

The exotic nature of roulette, with its French terminology, mechanical apparatus, complicated betting patterns, and (often) luxurious casino surroundings is sufficient cause for its vast popularity. But there are other causes. For one thing, absolutely no skill is needed; for another, cheating is apparently impossible, for there is no human intervention from the moment that the wheel and the ball are set in motion until the ball falls into a compartment. Or, at any rate, there is no *visible* intervention. In the 19th century crooked operators invented several hidden devices to control the wheel, and these became widely used in most of the more shady gambling houses—especially in those of Middle West America.

One of the earliest and most ingenious types of crooked roulette wheels was the "needle wheel." By means of pressure on a secret button, tiny needle points came up in front of the red or black compartments, a different button controlling each group. If the needle blocked the "reds" the ball was deflected into one of the "blacks," and vice versa. Since the needles were out of sight before the wheel stopped, they were almost impossible to spot.

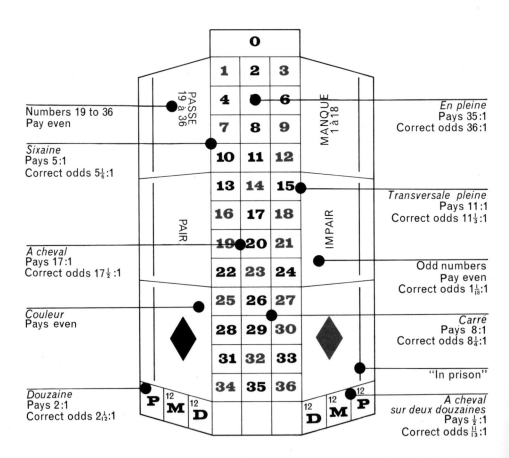

The needle device went out of fashion with the introduction of the more efficient electromagnetic wheel. This had small electromagnets installed under certain numbers, and the ball used had a steel core. When the croupier wished to insure against a heavily backed number, he touched a concealed switch controlling one of the magnets and drew the ball into a number not covered by heavy betting.

Even some extremely crude and obvious devices have proved successful in milking unwary roulette players of large sums of money. These include simple friction brakes that slow the wheel as the croupier presses a hidden pedal in the floor, or adjustable table legs that tilt the wheel to favor the house. Though some of these devices still survive today, they would never be found in any reputable casino or club—only in the most dubious of gambling dens, if there.

It has been said that the player can never cheat at roulette, since he is unable to control the wheel. But in the history of roulette, incidents are recorded in which players did come out on top through some ingenious and crooked approaches. Alexander Woollcott's short story "Rien ne va Plus" is a fictional account of a supposedly factual case of such ingenuity. In the story the author and some friends are sitting one night on a terrace at Monte Carlo "eating a soufflé and talking about suicide." Earlier they had watched a young man in a dinner jacket in the *Salles Privées* lose all his money. Now they hear that he has been found on the shore with blood staining his shirt front and a smoking

Left, a diagram of a European roulette layout showing the bets that may be made, the odds at which winners are paid on each bet, and the correct odds. (The true odds shown for impair—$1\frac{1}{18}$ to 1—are the same for all other "even-money" bets like pair, passe, manque, rouge, and noir.) Below, a representation of the European (one zero) roulette wheel. Right, a chart for the system player, showing each number from 0 to 36 (center column) in relation to its left and right-hand neighbors on the wheel.

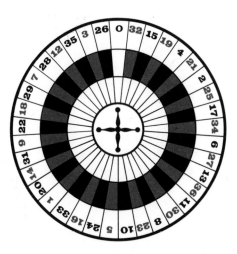

12	35	3	26	0	32	15	19	4
5	24	16	33	1	20	14	31	9
15	19	4	21	2	25	17	34	6
7	28	12	35	3	26	0	32	15
0	32	15	19	4	21	2	25	17
30	8	23	10	5	24	16	33	1
2	25	17	34	6	27	13	36	11
9	22	18	29	7	28	12	35	3
13	36	11	30	8	23	10	5	24
1	20	14	31	9	22	18	29	7
11	30	8	23	10	5	24	16	33
6	27	13	36	11	30	8	23	10
18	29	7	28	12	35	3	26	0
17	34	6	27	13	36	11	30	8
16	33	1	20	14	31	9	22	18
3	26	0	32	15	19	4	21	2
23	10	5	24	16	33	1	20	14
4	21	2	25	17	34	6	27	13
14	31	9	22	18	29	7	28	12
26	0	32	15	19	4	21	2	25
24	16	33	1	20	14	31	9	22
32	15	19	4	21	2	25	17	34
20	14	31	9	22	18	29	7	28
36	11	30	8	23	10	5	24	16
8	23	10	5	24	16	33	1	20
19	4	21	2	25	17	34	6	27
28	12	35	3	26	0	32	15	19
25	17	34	6	27	13	36	11	30
22	18	29	7	28	12	35	3	26
31	9	22	18	29	7	28	12	35
27	13	36	11	30	8	23	10	5
33	1	20	14	31	9	22	18	29
35	3	26	0	32	15	19	4	21
10	5	24	16	33	1	20	14	31
21	2	25	17	34	6	27	13	36
29	7	28	12	35	3	26	0	32
34	6	27	13	36	11	30	8	23

revolver still in his hand. The watchman who discovered him has reported post-haste to the casino (he is probably paid a commission for such information). Quickly and discreetly an official goes down to the beach and tucks ten 1000-franc notes into the corpse's dinner-jacket pocket "so that the victim would seem to have ended it all from *Weltschmerz*." But the casino has been tricked. The young man has merely fired the gun in the air and smeared his shirt front with tomato sauce. Before long he returns to the table and uses the 10,000 francs with which the casino bought off his "suicide" to win 100,000 more.

Woollcott's story is by no means farfetched. Casino entrepreneurs everywhere naturally live in dread of scandal of the wrong kind. They all keep extensive black lists of unwelcome visitors, and—as Woollcott's story shows—will always attempt to dissociate the casino from any suicide that might appear to be the result of gambling losses. In actual fact, however, the number of suicides attributed in gossip to losses at roulette is out of all proportion to the facts known. Monte Carlo has suffered more than any other gambling center through this kind of innuendo; but, though people die as often in Monaco as elsewhere, very few do so mysteriously—and fewer still by their own hand as a result of gambling. (Certainly none of these incidents involve native Monagasques, for they are forbidden to gamble in the casino.) Over a period of 50 years the number of suicides due to gambling losses—plus, sometimes, the guilt preceding the discovery of embezzlement—has been 285. There were 200 additional suicides, but these were not attributable to gambling. The total number of visitors and foreign residents during the same 50 years was around 50,000,000.

Incidentally, suicide, faked or threatened, isn't the only form of blackmail that has been used against the casinos. One blackmail story in particular (though unsubstantiated) has long held a prominent place in roulette lore. It concerns a gambler who, in 1884, is supposed to have threatened to contaminate the water supply of New York City with bubonic plague if he wasn't repaid $20,000 he'd lost at roulette. Of course, no one believed him; the croupier sent for the police and he was arrested. But it was found that the threat could easily have been implemented: The man was a laboratory assistant who had been experimenting on ship's rats and was, in fact, carrying the bacteria of plague in a phial in his pocket. (The phial was later restored to the laboratory without having at any time been opened.)

There is one kind of roulette player whose name is very unlikely to appear on a casino's "blacklist" of unwelcome visitors. This is the system player, the man who devises methods ranging from the mathematical to the mystical that, he is convinced, will succeed in breaking the bank of the casino. This man is welcomed with open arms at the roulette tables, since the tables' owner realizes what the system's owner apparently never does: that the bank must always win in the long run, because it pays slightly less than the true odds on any win, has the advantage of a zero (or two), and always limits the amount of the stake.

These are the advantages the bank must give itself if it is to remain in business against the unlimited time and unlimited capital it faces. So any kind of doubling-up system (one of the most common) is in the long run doomed to failure as far as breaking the bank is concerned. A system may work wonderfully for one game, or even for a series of several games—as one did for Charles Deville Wells (the original subject of the song "The Man who Broke the Bank at Monte Carlo") who in 1891 turned £400 into £40,000 in three days' play as a result of his adoption of the Martingale system. But if your "system" is to bet haphazardly you may find that the results are equally marvelous. Dependence on systems is always psychological: System bettors prefer to dazzle themselves with the blinding light of mathematical "probabilities" rather than face up to the fact that they are the slaves of chance. The most any system can do is *minimize losses* over a long run of play—i.e., a gambling career of many years.

The Martingale relies on the false reasoning that, when a series of even chances have resulted in similar outcomes, the odds are in favor of a different outcome next time. If, for example, a red number has come up five successive times, then money is placed on black for the sixth spin. If red comes up again— thus making six successive reds—the bet is doubled and put on black. But if the first bet on black wins, the player waits for a further series of five manque numbers, five passe, five pair, five impair, five rouge, or five noir numbers before betting again. A succession of five similar outcomes may not be enough for him; on the other hand he may think two or three enough. It's just a question of personal psychology.

The Reverse Martingale is played in a similar way—i.e., bets are always doubled up after a loss—but after each successive win stakes and winnings are left in place—the hope being for a run of eight successive wins, which would bring a profit of 127 times the original stake. Since all Martingale bets are on even chances the bettor's profits, if any, will be small. But losses may well be big—for no matter how long a preceding "run" may be, the probability of his winning any one bet remains $\frac{1}{2}$. Also, gamblers intent on doubling up bets after each successive loss will find that sooner or later they are checked by the bank's maximum limit.

Although this system was first used in the 17th century, it became popularized and more widely known as "the Martingale" in 1850 when the British novelist William Thackeray published *Pendennis*. In this novel one of the characters, Sir Francis Clavering, suffers enormous financial loss through his blind faith in the Martingale. (Actually, the system's name is thought to derive from the name of a particular kind of "checking" rein intended to prevent a horse from rearing its head when excited. Similarly, the system is supposed to "check" disaster by recouping losses.)

The Martingale and the innumerable other variations of the doubling-up systems are called collectively the *d'Alembert systems*—rather unfairly, since this 18th-century French mathematician was the first person to point out the fallacy

Six system bets for European roulette that appear to cancel out or reduce the house advantage. (The red spots represent the placing of a system player's chips.) Top left, the player has placed one chip on *impair* and one on *noir*, thinking to gain an advantage by covering 28 numbers in this way and leaving nine to work for the bank. He would thus make a profit only when a number that was both black *and* odd came up: I.e., he would win on eight numbers, break even on 20 numbers, and lose on nine. Left, the player has placed chips on 35 of the 37 numbers, reasoning that with only two numbers against him (i.e., the zero and the uncovered 9) he has a $17\frac{1}{2}$ to 1 advantage, and will win one unit per coup. This system would not work in the theoretical long run, since zero and 9 would be expected to come up once in every 37 spins—so in 37 rounds the player would win 35 (and 35 chips) and lose two (and 70 chips). Below left, the player has backed 22 *en pleine* and also (with its eight neighbors on the layout) *à cheval, en carré, sixaine*, and *transversale pleine*. Though the player would win at odds of 123 to 1 if 22 came up (and would also win or cut his losses if one of the other eight numbers came up) he still has 28 numbers against him. Above, zero has been backed *en pleine,* and *à cheval* with 1, 2, and 3. This is no more than a "hunch" bet that zero or a low number will come up. Above right, the system player has backed zero, 26, and 32 *en pleine*—a bet that might be made if the player believed that the croupier was throwing for zero. Above far right, another way of covering zero and its neighbors: The player has backed 15 and 26 *en pleine*, zero *à cheval* with 3, and 32 *à cheval* with 35.

222

in what was then known as the "Law of Equilibrium." "This law," d'Alembert wrote in his *Traité de dynamique,* "supposes a balancing of events in an interminable series, not in a brief array of events limited by the mind and time of man"—a brief array like five or six spins of a wheel. Yet somehow he has been saddled with the responsibility of applying the Law of Equilibrium to doubling-up systems in gambling.

The *Biarritz* system is more for players who find the even-chance systems too slow and too tame—players who would rather try for the 35 to 1 rake-off on an *en plein* win. The Biarritz system is based on the assumption that any given number of spins of the wheel over 111 (that is, three times 37) should give each *en plein* number a chance of appearing at least once. To follow it, the gambler must watch at least 111 consecutive spins of the wheel without betting. He must note every number that comes up and count how many times each occurs. He then chooses a number that has occurred fewer than 10 times and backs it *en plein,* on the assumption that if it has come up only nine (or fewer) times in 111 spins of the wheel, it's likely to appear again during the next 34 spins.

He now permits himself up to 34 successive bets and if the number doesn't come up in that series he loses. (If zero comes up he also loses, for then all except the even-chance bets are seized by the bank.) Should the number come up on the 34th spin, 35 units of money are won—one more than originally staked. But if the number came up on the first spin the profit would be 35 units of money.

Some of the followers of the Biarritz would have the bettor go on for 111, not 34, spins in an effort to back the lucky number; and not only go on, but actually increase the stake every 10 losing bets after the 30th. So if another 111 spins went by before the number came up, he would have staked 530 units of money for a return of 195 units of money. All this assuming—most rashly—that the bank would accept a stake of 500 times the minimum and—just as rashly—that zero wouldn't show up once in 111 spins!

Stake	Win/Lose	Capital
1	Lose	− 1
2	Lose	− 3
4	Lose	− 7
8	Lose	− 15
16	Lose	− 31
32	Lose	− 63
64	Lose	− 127
128	Lose	− 255
256	Lose	− 511
512	Win	+ 1

Charts showing four popular roulette systems for even money bets. Left, the bettor doubles his stake after each loss until he finally wins one unit—which is his goal. (In practice the house limit would probably stop him after a few rounds.) Center left, the bettor adds one unit to his stake after a loss, and subtracts one unit from his stake after a win. Below left, the bettor adds one unit to his stake whether he wins or loses, with the object of winning only one unit—which is why he bets seven units instead of nine after the eighth coup. (Again he would be stopped by the house limit.) Below, after every winning coup the bettor reduces his stake to one unit ; after every losing coup he doubles his stake and adds one.

Stake	Win/Lose	Capital
1	Lose	− 1
2	Lose	− 3
3	Win	0
2	Lose	− 2
3	Lose	− 5
4	Win	− 1
3	Win	+ 2
2	Lose	0
3	Win	+ 3
2	Win	+ 5

Stake	Win/Lose	Capital
1	Lose	− 1
2	Lose	− 3
3	Lose	− 6
4	Lose	− 10
5	Lose	− 15
6	Lose	− 21
7	Win	− 14
8	Win	− 6
7	Win	+ 1

Stake	Win/Lose	Capital
1	Win	+ 1
1	Win	+ 2
1	Lose	+ 1
3	Lose	− 2
7	Win	+ 5
1	Lose	+ 4
3	Win	+ 7
1	Lose	+ 6
3	Lose	+ 3
7	Win	+ 10

Wealthy roulette players often prefer to back a single number until it wins—and when it does, they leave the 35 to 1 payoff to run on the same number for another spin in the hope that it will win twice running, and give them a 1225 to 1 (35 x 35 to 1) payoff. Other more cautious players are convinced that they can get an edge by using a system called the *Cuban*. It is based on the assumption that because there are only three black numbers (as against eight red ones) in the third column of the table layout, a steady profit can be made by placing two bets on each spin of the wheel: one on *noir*, and a *colonne* bet on the entire third column. (The *noir* is an even-money bet, the *colonne* bet pays at 2 to 1.) The mathematical theory behind this system seems to indicate that a simultaneous coverage of *noir* and the numbers 3, 6, 9, 12, 15, 18, 21, 24, 27, 30, 33, and 36 will result in an excess of profits over losses after every 37 spins. But the system seems to ignore the fact that for every win there could be an equal or greater loss on the alternative bets: And then, of course, there is the ever-present threat of the zero.

A more down-to-earth system is called variously the *cross-out, top-and-bottom,* and *cancellation*. This involves writing down the figures 1–10 in a vertical column. The player then stakes the total of the top and bottom figures 10 + 1 = 11 units of money) on any even chance. If he wins, he crosses out the top and bottom figures and stakes another 11 units (9 + 2). If he wins again he crosses out the 9 and 2 and stakes another 11 units (8 + 3). Should he lose at any time in this process, he adds 11 units to the figure that is at the bottom of the column at that time, and stakes this new total. He continues in this fashion until all the figures in the column are crossed out. If he doesn't reach either the limit of his pocket or the limit of the bank by the time all the numbers are crossed out, he will have won 55 units of money.

But, as in every roulette system, both the zero and the bank's percentage are major stumbling blocks.

Right, a variation of the "cross-out" system. The bettor takes a group of consecutive numbers (here 1, 2, 3, 4) and bets the total of the two end numbers (1+4). If he loses the first coup he places the total (5) at the end of his group (which then becomes 1, 2, 3, 4, 5) and again stakes the total of the end numbers (1 + 5). If he then wins, he crosses off the "used" numbers and bets the next two end numbers (2 + 4). He goes on betting in this way until he reaches the center two figures of his group, or is checked by the house limit.

Stake	Win/Lose	Capital
1 2 3 4 .	Lose	− 5
1 2 3 4 5	Win	+ 1
1 2 3 4 5	Lose	− 5
1 2 3 4 5 6	Win	+ 3
1 2 3 4 5 6	Win	+ 10

Other systems are constantly being invented and re-invented under different names—often names that imply some kind of mystique, like *black magic, the gambler's heaven, the planets,* and so on. These are sometimes suggestions that by adding seven or nine or some other symbolic number to the number that last came up, the player will benefit from some mysterious occult influence. Some of these are described in a book called *The Sealed Collection of Systems* written by a man who signs himself "Croupier X." "I am a person," he writes, "who believes in the inevitability of patterns, cycles, sequences: I am of the firm opinion that there is a sort of recurring order in life that, taken at the right turn, must lead on to enduring and overwhelming fortune."

Most gamblers have their own pet systems, often extremely ingenious and occasionally very profitable—as was the system devised by an English engineer named William Jaggers and used by him to win 1,500,000 francs (about $180,000) from the Monte Carlo casino. Aware of the difficulty of maintaining a perfectly balanced roulette wheel, and knowing that the slightest inaccuracy would cause some numbers to appear more frequently than others, Jaggers employed six assistants to stand at different tables and note the numbers that came up at roulette all day long. Meanwhile he made an elaborate analysis of the results. After a month's play it became obvious that certain numbers were predominating out of all proportion to the laws of probability. So Jaggers proceeded to play on these numbers, and won his thousands in four days' play. The casino soon realized what was happening and adjusted the wheels—which

put an end to Jaggers' scheme. (This happened at the end of the 19th century. To prevent any similar occurrences, roulette wheels in most casinos are now carefully tested and examined every day.)

The 19th-century French textile magnate Stefan Heller—obviously sharing Croupier X's belief in the inevitability of patterns, cycles, and sequences—used an eccentric system of his own invention that was based on daily reports from his factories concerning the number of bobbins in use on certain looms. He played roulette only on alternate evenings, spending the intervening time working out which numbers the bobbins told him to back. (He had to take his mathematical secretary with him to the casino to help him with the intricate calculations that had to be made.) Heller died a multi-millionaire; but, considering the system he put his faith in, it is more likely that he made his millions by the loom rather than by the wheel.

And in January 1963, the British actor Sean Connery—who in his film roles portrays James Bond, the secret agent and top-flight gambler created by the British author Ian Fleming—was reported to have made a roulette coup quite worthy of James Bond himself. In the casino at St. Vincent, Italy, Connery won the equivalent of about $30,000 in three consecutive spins of the wheel. He was betting on number 17.

The odds against any number coming up three times running are 46,656 to 1 —which only goes to show that when it comes to winning (or losing) large sums of money at roulette, chance can be as reliable as any system.

Left, the actor Sean Connery (the screen's James Bond) at Italy's St. Vincent casino, where he won $30,000 at roulette. Connery backed number 17 three times running. Right, the "equipment" needed for the more eccentric system that a player once used at Monte Carlo's casino. He imprisoned a spider in a match box (painted half red and half black on the inside) removed the lid after a few minutes, and bet on rouge or noir according to the spider's position.

10 Lucky numbers

A lottery in the sense of a gamble for pleasure is basically a distribution of prizes to winning bettors who are decided by the drawing of numbered slips from a container; the prizes, of course, go to the people holding duplicates of the slips drawn. A ticket-holder's bet is the money he pays for his ticket. All the tickets not actually drawn from the container are worthless (i.e., "blanks") and a ticket-holder's chances are decided by (a) the total number of tickets in the container; (b) the number of prizes; and (c) the number of tickets he has bought. In a true lottery (as opposed to a "pool" or a "sweepstake"), there are specified prizes that remain the same irrespective of the number of people who buy tickets. In pools or sweepstakes, however, winners share all the money in the pool (i.e., the stakes), which varies according to the number of tickets sold. (Of course, running expenses are deducted first, and a certain prearranged percentage may go to a cause for which the lottery was held.)

All lotteries are basically simple, though the means of administering them may be enormously complex, as in the case of the Irish Sweepstakes (of which more later). The simple principle of the lottery has a great variety of manifestations, including sports pools, *bingo*, government bonds, raffles run by private and usually charitable organizations, *keno* (a variation of bingo), and various forms of the numbers game (based on some arbitrary figure such as a stock-exchange daily balance). But none of these requires more effort on the

A Parisienne, selling tickets for the French National Lottery, invites passers-by to try to win a fortune in the next day's draw. Such booths can be seen in any busy French street. The prospect of winning a huge sum with a small stake leads millions of people to gamble regularly on lotteries.

gambler's part than simply buying a ticket, or going through a simple routine like watching a numbered card (as in bingo) or filling in a coupon (as in the various kinds of sports pools).

A lottery can be complicated slightly by being linked with some other event— such as some kind of race. A number of tickets are drawn equal to the number of entrants in the race (all other tickets are then blanks); and the ultimate winner out of these few is decided by the entrant who wins the race. Additional prizes diminishing in value are usually awarded to those who have drawn the second, third, and fourth entrants, and consolation prizes are sometimes awarded to all who have drawn entrants. This is the basic principle by which winners of the Irish Sweepstakes are chosen.

Lotteries involving the placing of stakes (as distinct from acts of sortilege to make important decisions) are not very old. The Romans had a form of lottery that had no blanks and required no stakes, but this was virtually a distribution of free gifts given by rich emperors and aristocrats during the Saturnalian feasts. The first recorded lottery to involve the buying of tickets and the distribution of prize money was held in Bruges on February 24, 1466. It was organized by the widow of the Flemish painter Jan van Eyck in order to raise money for the poor of the town.

Europe's next lottery didn't appear until 1520, when King Francis I of France signed a bill that legalized *loteries blanques* and authorized the setting up of five wheels (that is, containers of tickets for the draw) in Paris, Lyons, Strasbourg, Bordeaux, and Lille. In Genoa and Venice, also in the 16th century, merchants began to organize public lotteries whenever they had some especially

Public lotteries have been popular in Europe from the 16th century onward—popular with the people as an enjoyable gamble, and with the organizers as a nearly foolproof way to raise money. Left, a 19th-century engraving shows a French state-run lottery being drawn. Two armed guards keep order; a blindfolded man draws the winning numbers from a barrel and the numbers are then put on a board on the wall for all to see. Right, an 18th-century German engraving depicting a public lottery in Nuremberg. Orphan children draw the winning tickets from a barrel; the names of the winners would then be called and cash prizes awarded by public officials.

valuable produce to dispose of; in this way their profit would always exceed the sum that they would normally have got from an individual.

By 1566 the lottery idea had caught the imagination of the English. The southeast coastal towns of Hastings, Romney, Hythe, Dover, and Sandwich (known as the Cinque Ports) all needed costly harbor repairs. The people of these ports, losing time and money through constant labor at makeshift repairs to combat the ravages of stormy winters, threatened an uprising; the mayor sought advice from the Warden of the Ports, who went to Queen Elizabeth I. And it was she who, as it were, set the first English lottery wheels in motion by authorizing a state lottery to pay for repairs to the harbors. It was launched in 1567. There were 400,000 tickets, with a top prize of the equivalent of about $17,500 in cash and lesser prizes in the form of goods worth the equivalent of about $7500 altogether.

All over 16th-century Europe private and public lotteries soon got a strong grip on the people. The lottery fever raged so strongly in Italy that in 1590 Pope Gregory XIV ordered the excommunication of anyone who bet on the election of a new pope or on the duration of the conclave (such bets usually taking the form of pools). At the instigation of Louis XII of France (who was also duke of Milan), tickets were sold for a lottery to be held on the date of the completion of Milan cathedral (which had been begun in 1386). Half a million tickets were sold but no one drew a prize: The cathedral wasn't completed in Louis's lifetime—or, indeed, anyone else's in that century—and the ticket-holders were given their money back. (The cathedral was completed by Napoleon in 1805, so he could be crowned king of Italy in it.)

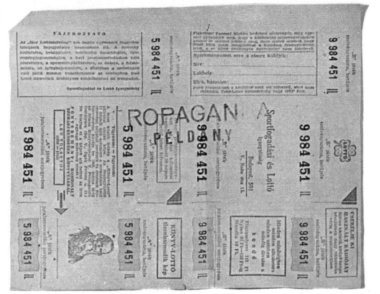

Specimen tickets from past and present lotteries : 1. and 2. The Hungarian state lottery. 3. The Czechoslovak sports pools. 4. An early 20th-century French charity lottery. 5. The Spanish national lottery. 6. The Louisiana state lottery, which ended in 1895 (the last of the big legal lotteries in the U.S.A.). 7. A Spanish national sweepstake held for the blind. 8. The Irish Sweepstakes. 9. Netherlands' state lottery. 10. A special drawing of the French national lottery. 11. A Spanish hospital sweepstake. 12. The Swiss *Romande* lottery. 13. A Dutch wartime lottery. 14. Britain's premium-bonds lottery. 15. Sweden's national lottery. All of these lottery tickets are of an elaborate design intended primarily to baffle would-be forgers.

Some of the early lotteries were run for purely philanthropic reasons, like Mme. van Eyck's. An English lottery sanctioned by James I in 1612 raised the equivalent of about $140,000 for some American colonists. Other lotteries were run for more dubious reasons, and often people hesitated before buying tickets because they feared (sometimes justifiably) that the outcome might be fixed. Louis XIV of France drew the tickets for a lottery in the 17th century, and landed a 100,000-franc prize for himself and smaller prizes for the queen and the dauphin. The people's anger was stilled only when the king graciously handed the money back and requested that it be drawn for again.

One thing was evident: Whether they were honest or crooked, philanthropic or profiteering, lotteries offered a reliable source of income. Hard-pressed governments couldn't ignore this fact for long, and so state-run lotteries gradually began to make their appearance throughout Europe. Italy organized the first one in the 19th century; then France and Germany followed suit. Today most European countries and many non-European ones have state lotteries that offer regular (often weekly) draws, large prizes, and the comforting knowledge that everything is run in an efficient and honest fashion. Stakes are invariably small, and generally a certain prearranged percentage of the income from tickets sold is handed out as prize money while the rest (after the deduction of running expenses) goes to the state.

Seeds were sown for the first state lottery as such—Italy's *Lo Giuoco del Lotto d' Italia*—by early government lotteries run in the various Italian states

before the country was united. The *Lotto de Firenze* in 1528 was one of the first; then, in Genoa in 1576, the admiral-statesman Andrea Doria persuaded the government to approve a law providing for the selection of five names from the 120 members of the Genoese nobility for election to the senate. The twice-yearly drawing of the five names aroused interest among the public, and soon betting became an important side issue of the draw. Half of all the money staked was given to the bettors who had guessed the five names correctly; the remainder was kept by the organizer of the game. Some years later the number of names was reduced to 90, and eventually numbers were substituted for names.

By the middle of the 17th century the idea had spread to many other Italian towns, but it was no longer based on the election of senators. A twice-yearly draw didn't meet the public demand. A weekly lottery was what was wanted, and the various regional governments were quick to see the revenue possibilities. On September 27, 1863, with the proclamation of the united kingdom of Italy, *Lotto* was made a legal source of national income. Today, the Italian ministry of finance (which administers the lottery) states in a bulletin on Italian affairs: ". . . The game of Lotto is firmly established among the sources of income of the state budget, which absolutely cannot do without it considering the high figure it yields every year."

The figure referred to (the state's income from Lotto) is 50 per cent of the total annual income from the sale of tickets. This total has increased rapidly in recent years. In 1954 it was the equivalent of about $45,000,000; today it is

Lotteries and pools can be held in connection with almost any event—even a papal election. Left, a Roman *totopapa* board in 1963: on June 19 betting favored Cardinal Montini. (He was elected two days later.)

Right, the day's winning number in Italy's state lottery is displayed in a Naples street. Below right, a lottery "tipster" (who makes his living in Naples by predicting winning numbers) advises a bettor. Below, a blindfolded boy picks the five winning numbers in the Italian lottery from a rotating container. Drawings take place weekly in Italy's principal cities.

Above left, a winning number in the French national lottery is drawn. The six steel cages spin the numbered balls until the winning ones fall into the wire cups. Above, one of the orphaned children who usually make the draw shows the winning number to the audience. Left, the special notice boards used to advertise the lottery. Below left, at a booth on a Paris boulevard, a man gambles on the "wheel of fortune" for the prize of a national lottery ticket. Below, in a café, a Parisian checks the list of winning lottery-tickets that always appears in the daily papers.

Tickets for the Greek state lotteries can be bought in shops, or even at pavement shoe-shine stands (above right)—as well as from licensed lottery agencies (far right).

well over $75,000,000. The introduction of mechanical ticket-issuing machines in various parts of the country has undoubtedly helped to increase expenditure. Aside from the state's profit, the prizes account for about 40 per cent of the total income from ticket sales, and the administrative expenses for 10 per cent. Among the Italian regions Campania holds the betting record—the equivalent of $13,000,000 in 1953. Lombardy, Sicily, Latium, Piedmont, and Liguria are runners up.

There is at least one lottery office in every Italian town. Each office is under the control of a manager who runs it as an individual business, and who is responsible for all running expenses. He makes a weekly return to the ministry's General Inspectorate, which controls all the legal forms of gambling in Italy, including casinos, football pools, small raffles, and games organized for charity.

In each of Italy's 2200 registered lottery offices a draw is held weekly. Tickets bearing the numbers one to 90 are put in an urn and five numbers are drawn by the manager. There are several different kinds of forecast that a ticket-holder may try to make: He may try to predict any one of the five drawn numbers (which is called "simple extraction"); the order in which any one of the five numbers is drawn ("specified extraction"); any two of the five numbers ("*ambo*"); any three ("*terno*"); any four ("*quaterna*"); or all five ("*cinquina*"). In simple extraction the chances of winning are one in 18, in specified extraction one in 90, in ambo one in 400, in terno one in 11,748, in quaterna one in 511,038, and in cinquina one in 43,949,268. The prizes for simple extraction are $10\frac{1}{2}$ times the stake, for specified extraction $52\frac{1}{2}$ times the stake, for ambo 250 times the stake, for terno 4250 times the stake, for quaterna 80,000 times the stake, and for cinquina 1,000,000 times the stake. Anyone may buy as many tickets and make as many different forecasts as desired. In most towns the price of a ticket is one lira (about one sixth of one cent)—such a tiny sum of money that even the poorest investors buy 100 tickets at a time.

France, too, has its own state-controlled lottery (the *Loterie Nationale*) with weekly draws as well as special draws at Easter *(tranche de Pâques)*, the government's summer vacation *(tranche de vacances)*, Christmas *(tranche de Noël)*, and various arbitrarily chosen occasions (known as *tranche de la double chance*) when the prizes are increased enormously. An ordinary ticket costs the equivalent of $5.60 and the prizes can range as high as the equivalent of $150,000. A bettor can buy a share in a ticket; a tenth of a ticket, for instance, costs about three francs (60 cents).

The French take their lottery very seriously. Few streets in Paris lack their little booths set up on corners, under café awnings, or other approachable places, with the ticket-sellers who manage the booths calling *"tentez votre chance!"* The equivalent of about $128,000,000 was given away in 1962 in prizes, and from this the government added about $50,000,000 to the treasury.

Bonn, Frankfurt, and Hamburg may be taken as typical of the centers in the West German Federation whose governments run and control regional lotteries. Bonn records that in 1962 the equivalent of about $6,000,000 was spent every week on lottery tickets, and that about $120,000 were paid out to each week's winners. Frankfurt, which claims a sixth of all gambling money staked in the country, gathered in the equivalent of about $58,000,000 as government revenue in 1961. Frankfurt encourages both lotteries and thrift by offering a lottery ticket worth one mark (about 25 cents) for every eight marks deposited in national-savings accounts. A draw takes place, on the average, every other weekday. These lotteries pay handsome dividends to the West German authorities—the equivalent of about $57,500,000 from all lotteries and football pools, which is about four fifths of the total state income from all forms of gambling. Hamburg's three lotteries (including a football pool) yielded nearly the equivalent of $4,000,000 profit in 1961 from the sale of 128,068,900 tickets.

An analytical article in the *Frankfurter Allgemaine Zeitung*, November 1962, stated (without giving figures) that the total expenditure on all forms of gambling in the Federal German Republic had quadrupled since 1950, and that

Far left, a girl draws one of the six winning tickets in the North West German lottery ; a public official supervises. The tickets are folded inside perspex capsules, which are whirled round in the glass drum. Left, after the drawing, all the remaining tickets in the drum are invalidated by a seal to avoid cheating or confusion.

Ten drawings of the *Loterie Romande* are made each year in five cantons of Switzerland. Right, the numbered balls are spun around in wire cages, and a lever releases the winning ones. Above, an official announces a winning number. Results are then given out on radio and television and in the press. The top prize in the Swiss state lottery is the equivalent of $23,000 ; profits are either spent on public utilities or donated to charities.

Above, in Barcelona, Spain, a woman checks
the day's winning numbers from the official
list outside a national-lottery agency.
Many disabled people make their living
selling lottery tickets (left) ; they are
licensed and paid by the government.
Below, a woman sells lottery tickets from a
stall in a Barcelona market.

Right, Britain's "Ernie" (Electronic Random
Number Indicator Equipment) picks the
month's winning premium-bond numbers.
The machine was installed in 1956 when the
government began the lottery. Prizes and
the state's profits are derived from interest
that accrues on the money invested.

the increase was due to the introduction of lotteries and pools in 1955. This enthusiasm for lotteries is explainable when it is noted that, in the first 40 draws of the Frankfurt lottery in 1962, 110 people won prizes of over $100,000 each.

The Swedish state lottery, drawn once monthly, has been enormously successful since its inception in 1897. The state employs 4544 commissioners to sell tickets, and invariably all available tickets are sold; in 1962 sales totaled 17,980,000. Profits from the lottery go to the government and are included in the national budget, and a part of them is redistributed by the government for cultural purposes. It is illegal for private persons to organize lotteries in Sweden unless the profits are to be used only for charitable or cultural purposes.

In Britain, lotteries have had a rough passage. "Lotteries exist to the utter ruin and impoverishment of many families, and to the reproach of the English laws and government," says a law prohibiting lotteries that appeared in 1700, toward the end of the reign of William III—who had himself been fighting his Augsburg battles on the income from a lottery. Throughout the succeeding centuries, different British governments had different ideas about lotteries, some allowing them, some outlawing them. The present law permits a state lottery and such allied kinds of gambling as football pools and bingo.

Britain's government-run lottery (introduced in 1956) is totally unlike the various state lotteries in Europe. It is commonly called "Premium Bonds," and is in effect a form of investing money in the state. The bonds themselves can be bought for £1 each at post offices and banks. Three months after their purchase, bonds become eligible for the monthly draw: Bond numbers are selected by an electronic machine known as "Ernie" (Electronic Random Number Indicator Equipment) and tax-free prizes from the equivalent of $75 to $15,000 are won by the holders of drawn numbers. A bond carries $4\frac{1}{2}$ per cent

interest, which (instead of accruing to the bond holder) goes into a pool that provides the prize money. Unlike lottery tickets, bonds are not excluded after a single drawing: They go back into the draw again and again unless they are prizewinners or are sold back to the state for their face value. So in fact Premium Bonds are not a full-fledged gamble. All that the holder stands to lose is the interest his money could be earning if invested elsewhere.

In 1962-63 nearly 73,000,000 bonds were sold; but since people can hold up to 800 bonds each, the actual number of purchasers was considerably less. (In that same year almost 31,000,000 bonds were sold back to the government for their face value.) The total number of bonds bought in the years 1956-63 was 514,800,000.

The communist countries of eastern Europe have by no means ignored the fund-raising potentials of the state lottery. Generally, all forms of gambling other than those based on the lottery principle are forbidden in most communist states (though the Black Sea holiday resorts have small-scale casinos for roulette and baccarat). The permitted forms of gambling include ordinary raffles, sweepstakes, number games, and football pools. Prizes of goods instead of money are popular in communist countries. In August 1960 the Russian newspaper *Izvestia* published the following list of prizes for one lottery, together with the names of the winners: a Moscowitch car; a Volga car; a two-room apartment; a smaller two-room apartment; a sewing machine; two cooking stoves; a TV set; a plot

of land; and several motorcycles, watches, cameras, bicycles, and radios. These were in addition to cash prizes totaling the equivalent of about $10,000.

With this kind of temptation, it can easily be seen why filling in football-pool coupons and working out possibly lucky lottery numbers are serious activities for workers behind the Iron Curtain. A protesting letter from the chief of an industrial plant, in the Czechoslovakian paper *Prace* in January 1958, shows how serious they are: His workers, he says, "manage to squander office time over Sportka and Sazka. Such a 'sports week' begins as early as Monday morning, when there is a great debate over the previous week's wins and losses. From Tuesday to Thursday tickets are hunted for. No one is satisfied with filling out two or three forms, but takes at least ten. It goes without saying that he does not fill them out in five minutes; moreover, he has to consult with the other bettors. Whole collectives are formed to cut down the risk and the cost. All this is at the expense of working time. On Thursday and Friday the bettors have to make an 'official' trip to the city which they extend according to the length of the line that their co-bettors have already formed at the counter. Then they spend Sunday yearning for the results, and on Monday the whole merry-go-round begins again...."

The Hungarian state lottery (which followed the successful introduction of a football pool in March 1957) provides a good example of how these enterprises work in communist countries. Lottery coupons have 90 numbers on them of which the bettor must choose five. Each coupon costs the equivalent of about

Left, a woman selling lottery tickets from a stall in downtown Tokyo. A 15-cent ticket may win a prize of over $5000. The Tokyo lottery, held every 10 days, is run by the city governments; most of the profits are spent on public utilities.

Right, in one of Hungary's "toto-lotto" shops a man buys a ticket for the weekly lottery. Below, a child draws the winning tickets from a glass drum.

25 cents; 50 per cent of the money taken is allocated for the weekly winning fund, and 10 per cent for a further monthly prize raffle. Operating expenses come off the remaining 40 per cent, and the net profit is then handed over to the state for various public enterprises. There are four classes of prizes, and the winning fund is divided equally among them. The "fiver" is the real money-winner, since there are obviously fewer people to share the pool, but prizes are also paid for "fours," "threes," and "twos." If there are no winners of the "fiver," the total amount of this pool is shared among the winners of "fours," who thus share a double pool.

The sale of tickets in Hungary has shot from the original weekly total of 1,500,000 in 1957 to a weekly figure of over 5,000,000 in 1963. As the new gamble expanded, the National Savings Bank established a special organization called the Sports Betting and Lotto Management, and a country-wide network was set up to meet the growing demand. There are 125 shops throughout the country selling lottery and football-pool coupons. In addition, coupons are sold at all post offices, National Savings Banks offices, and tobacconists; and news vendors, postmen, pensioners, and housewives sell coupons on a commission basis. The draw is held every Friday morning, following a special program of music or a fashion display. Usually the draw is held in a different town or village each week. There are also monthly prize raffles for which all the coupons from one week of the previous month (decided by lot) are eligible. The prizes vary in number and value depending on the number of coupons; but usually there are more than 800 prizes each month, and the lottery organizers issue a 16-page weekly journal that contains official bulletins of the results.

Aside from the representative state-sponsored lotteries that I have looked at, this form of national gamble flourishes in such countries as Australia, Spain, Japan, Brazil, Greece, Israel, and in many more. Apparently these governments know a good thing (in economic terms) when they see one. Add to this picture the

Left, before an assembly of government officials and journalists and under police supervision, six nurses draw winning tickets in the Irish Hospitals Sweepstakes from the millions of slips in the huge revolving drum. At the same time, from a smaller drum (right), another nurse draws a slip bearing the name of a horse that will run in the determining race. The ticket number and the horse's name are recorded, and the procedure is repeated until the small drum is empty. Each holder of a drawn ticket gets a prize, but the amount depends on the horse's final position in the race.

proliferation of private lotteries of every kind (shipboard pools on the time taken for an Atlantic crossing, "door prizes" given away on admission tickets in American dance halls, raffles in clubs with prizes ranging from cars to chickens) and it becomes very clear that all the world loves a lottery. But the one that the world seems to love most of all is that famous and highly international gamble called the Irish Hospitals Sweepstakes (more familiarly known as the "Irish Sweep").

Although the sale of Sweepstakes tickets is legal only in Ireland itself, the sales there amount to no more than about one twenty-fifth of the total. About two thirds of the tickets are sold in America (where, in most of the 50 states, all forms of lottery are illegal); and there is a big demand for tickets all over Europe, Britain, Scandinavia, Australia, and elsewhere.

The Irish Hospitals Sweepstakes is organized by a private company, Hospitals Trust Ltd., and has been held three times a year since 1930 (the year when the government of the Republic of Eire passed an act legalizing a lottery for the benefit of Irish hospitals). The Sweep is drawn three times in connection with three horse races—England's Grand National and Cambridgeshire, and since 1962 the Irish Sweeps Derby. (Before 1962 the third race was the English Derby.) The biggest Irish Sweep so far recorded was the 91st—for the Grand National in 1957—when 6455 prizewinners were paid the equivalent of nearly $7,500,000, and the first prize was $1,050,000.

On each ticket is the following declaration: "The amount of money received from sale of tickets under the Public Hospital Act of 1933 to 1940 will be distributed as follows: Twenty-five per cent will be paid to the hospitals. The balance after deduction thereout of the expenses as sanctioned by the Minister for Justice under the scheme for the Sweepstakes will be distributed in prizes. The amount provisionally certified by the auditors on the day preceding the draw to be available for prizes, if exceeding £120,000 [about $350,000], will be divided into as many prize units of £120,000 as the sum permits. The remainder . . . will be distributed into 50 cash prizes of equal amount."

The drawing of the lottery at the Hospitals Trust headquarters in Dublin is carried out under close supervision by the government and police. Several days before the relevant race is due to be run, all the ticket counterfoils (which are until this time held in sealed safe deposits under armed guard) are put in wind machines that blow them around continually for three days. Thus there can be no question of inadequate shuffling. Then, on the day of the draw (which takes place in public), all the counterfoils are put in a long drum with eight rows of six holes in its circumference and the drum is revolved slowly to mix the counterfoils thoroughly.

A team of pretty nurses is lined up beside the holes. As each nurse draws a numbered counterfoil from the drum, a second simultaneously draws a slip from a smaller glass drum. On these last slips are written the names of the horses. Both the number of the counterfoil and the name of the horse are announced, and the counterfoil and slip are then scrutinized by the director of the draw and photostated. The first, second, and third prizewinners are naturally decided by the horses; but everyone who draws a horse gets a prize whether the horse is placed (i.e., finishes among the winners) or not, and there are in addition some 200 consolation prizes.

Ticket sales, as I have said, are illegal practically everywhere. (Many countries with state lotteries—among them Brazil, Cambodia, Finland, Ghana, Hungary, Italy, Israel, and Peru—forbid all other lotteries, except small ones for good causes, to avoid competition.) But nevertheless a surprising number of tickets make their way past a great many national boundaries and are promptly sold in spite of the law. In America, for instance, occasional raids on the mails and the impounding of tickets and remittances (even, sometimes, of prize money) have been ineffective in stifling the sale of tickets. Even when, in 1935, U.S. post-office officials seized many thousands of letters addressed to the Dublin office of the Sweep's headquarters and returned them to the senders with a terse warning about using the mails for illegal purposes, there was no stopping the Sweep. Consignments of tickets were smuggled into America and counterfoils and money were smuggled out again. This often involved hiding the packages in innocent goods: The customs authorities who inspected the holds of the liner *America* in 1948 were amazed to find about 2,000,000 counterfoils concealed in bales of flax being exported for processing into Irish linen.

Until recently, no legal lottery existed in the U.S.A. except in the dependency of Puerto Rico. But since 1957 eleven states have permitted bingo and small raffles, and in April 1963 the governor of New Hampshire authorized a state lottery that he hopes will raise $4,000,000 a year for state education. But this is not to say that lotteries don't flourish illegally elsewhere in America, and not only in the form of importations like the Irish Sweepstakes. There is a native American lottery gamble that turns over about $5,000,000,000 a year—the *numbers game* (which is also known as the *numbers racket,* the *policy game, bolita, mutuel numbers,* and *negro numbers*).

Players of the numbers game gamble by attempting to predict some apparently unpredictable number. This used to be the final three digits of the daily balance figures of a city's stock exchange; but now it is nearly always one of the payoff prices at a specific race track. The numbers game had its beginnings in Harlem in the early 1900s. At the time it was a small-scale gambling game that usually involved a simple prediction of the numbers in the final totals of the Cincinnati clearing house. Tickets could be bought for as little as 10 cents and the prize for an all-correct forecast was never more than $300. But this harmless picture was soon to change. When Prohibition was repealed in 1932, the big-time racketeers who had made fortunes bootlegging liquor suddenly had their incomes cut off. So they looked around for a new field of action; and their attention turned to Harlem and the numbers game. Within a very short time the game was turned from a poor man's gamble into a nation-wide racket of immense magnitude. And the man mainly responsible for this transformation was a top New York gangster named Dutch Schultz.

At the head of a gang of toughs and killers, Schultz had become one of the richest "beer barons" of the Prohibition years. Now he sensed a new gold mine. He and his gunmen invaded Harlem, took over the numbers game, and expanded its organization throughout the city. Numbers tickets were soon on sale almost everywhere; and Schultz's men were always on hand to see that people bought. By 1933 a would-be player could find about a dozen different numbers-game depots operating on practically every street in Harlem, and the game was quickly spreading to other districts and cities.

Schultz awarded prizes for the lottery at his own discretion. Very often winners weren't paid at all, and dissatisfied customers were left to argue with his henchmen. If this approach caused business to begin to fall off in certain districts, Schultz would award some prizes. (It was at this period that the game became known as "the numbers racket.") But obviously an explosive situation of this kind couldn't last for ever, and Schultz's reign ended in typical gangster fashion when an unknown gunman shot him down in October 1935.

But the numbers game continued to flourish. Other big gang leaders took over control and there was considerable gang warfare that only settled down when each city was divided into sections, each gang controlling a particular section. Today the racketeers still have a large number of local policemen and politicians in some of the smaller cities on their payroll, which gives them a certain amount of freedom to operate.

Naturally an elaborate and well co-ordinated organization is needed to run an underground activity on the scale of the numbers game. Although "controllers" have their own favorite methods of operating, the pattern is generally this: Books of numbered tickets are distributed to agents by an intermediary known as a "runner"; a second runner collects the money from the agent; a third collects the receipts or "money slips." Each runner works for a different controller, and each controller operates from a different office or "bank." The operation is carried out in three separate stages in order to confuse the police, who cannot make a conviction unless they obtain both the money *and* the slips: Money alone is not considered proof enough. From time to time, of course, the operators slip up. In July 1960, for example, the New Jersey police raided a private home and discovered $281,283 in cash, together with number slips, tapes, and adding machines—all the evidence they needed.

In spite of the law, then, America seems just as lottery-conscious as any other country. And, in the U.S.A. as elsewhere, the lottery principle is sometimes put to some strange uses. The American author Roul Tunley, in his book *Kids, Crime, and Chaos*, writes: "In one of Philadelphia's better suburbs, a group of well-to-do youngsters developed an ingenious twist: a car-stealing lottery. The game was played as follows: Each day the kids in the group stole a certain number of automobiles, after each youngster had kicked in a certain amount of money for the 'privilege' of doing so. . . . When the police announced over the radio the license numbers of the stolen cars, the kid who had stolen the car that was mentioned first took the day's pool."

Bingo is another kind of lottery gamble that is widely popular in America. It is legal in 11 American states (New York, Nevada, New Jersey, Rhode Island, Vermont, Connecticut, New Hampshire, Minnesota, Maryland, Maine, and Alaska) but it presumably is played in all states; and it attracts nearly

Left, "Dutch" Schultz, gangster king of the illegal numbers racket in Harlem (New York) in the 1930s and one of the richest racketeers in American gambling history. Schultz only occasionally paid out prizes to "winners" of the numbers game, so for a time made immense profits. At the height of the city-wide racket he was said to be worth $7,000,000. (Eventually a Federal indictment for tax evasion was served against him, but he was murdered before he could be tried.)

Right, the front and back of a betting slip used by a "runner" (the intermediary between agent and bettor) in the New York numbers game. To evade arrest, runners usually use slips made of specially treated paper that will ignite at the touch of a cigarette, and keep the slips minutely folded in the backs of their rings, watches, etc. Numbers at the top of the columns are the betting choices; in the columns are the bettor's initials and the money staked. Bets are placed daily before noon and pay-outs to winners are made the next day.

$2,000,000,000 each year. In Britain too, bingo is big business. When the British government passed laws in 1956 and 1960 legalizing its own lottery (Premium Bonds) it had to legalize lotteries in general to some extent—i.e., those held for "charitable, sporting, and cultural purposes." This easing of restrictions opened the way to an annual British expenditure on bingo of $70,000,000. France does not permit bingo in any form; elsewhere in Europe it is of minor importance.

The Italians first played bingo in the 18th century and called it *lotto* (not to be confused with the Italian state lottery). The procedure was simple: The operator called out numbers drawn from a container and a player crossed them off when the numbers called coincided with numbers on the printed card he held. In Britain and America lotto was played as a parlor game in the 19th century and was taken up by English troops at the beginning of the 20th. It then became known as *house* (possibly because of a tenuous connection with the stock exchange, known in slang as "the house"), and the call used to assemble a group for a game of house was "housey-housey." This catch phrase soon became the British name for the game itself. The Americans adapted the French word *quine* ("set of five") and called the game keno. Today, the cry of the winner on completing a line on his card—"Bingo!"—is used in most places as the name of the game. But whether the game is called lotto, housey-housey, keno, or bingo, the play is essentially the same.

The modern bingo player buys a card bearing a selection of numbers (24 in Britain, 25 in America); the purchase price is his stake money. The focus of his attention is the bingo operator and the container in which are 90 disks or balls (75 in America) numbered consecutively. These are drawn one at a time by the operator and the numbers called out. A card-holder covers each number on his card that coincides with the called number and wins a prize when a certain pre-arranged series has been covered (a straight line or some special design). Since every card sold has a different selection of numbers printed on it, one card-holder is bound to be successful before the others. (In Britain and other countries where bingo is played, a machine called the "kenogoose" is usually used to stir up numbered celluloid balls and then to project them through a funnel. The operator does no more than call the number of the balls as they are presented to him by the machine.)

British entrepreneurs have converted most of the nation's failing cinemas into thriving bingo halls: About 13,000,000 bingo players have replaced film fans since 1956 (of these, 10,000,000 are estimated to be women). British Railways run highly successful "Bingo Special" trains during the summer months, which provide trips from London to seaside towns and back, with practically non-stop bingo sessions held on board both ways. The majority of these trains' passengers are women.

Lotteries and numbers games are one form of gambling in which no mathematical system can possibly have an effect on the outcome—simply because every ticket has the same chance as every other (unless the lottery is crooked). But, as in so many other "pure chance" gambles, this undeniable fact has never prevented gamblers from trying to find some systematic way to beat the odds—gamblers like George Massy, owner of the ship *Sofala* in Joseph Conrad's short story "The End of the Tether." Massy won a lottery prize and bought the *Sofala*

with the money; but for years afterward he ruined himself financially by buying far more lottery tickets than he could afford, convinced that sooner or later he would win again. Conrad describes Massy's obsession thus:

"... He opened the writing desk, spread out a sheet of thin greyish paper covered with a mass of printed figures and began to scan them attentively.... It was the list of the winning numbers from the last drawing of the great lottery which had been the one inspiring fact of so many years of his existence.... A great pile of flimsy sheets had been growing for years in his desk, while the *Sofala* ... wore out her boilers....

"For days together, on a trip, he would shut himself up in his berth with them ... and he would weary his brain poring over the rows of disconnected figures, bewildering by their senseless sequence, resembling the hazards of destiny itself. He nourished a conviction that there must be some logic lurking somewhere in the results of chance. He thought he had seen its very form.... Nine, nine, nought, four, two. He made a note. But what's this? Three years ago, in the September drawing, it was number nine, nought, four, two that took the first prize. Most remarkable. There was a hint there of a definite rule! ... What could it be? And for half an hour he would remain dead still, bent low over the desk, without twitching a muscle."

But not all lottery addicts turn like Conrad's fictional hero to mathematics for help; many place their faith in mysticism. Prophetic "dream books" (and other works of do-it-yourself divination) have wide sales wherever lotteries are held. These books are allegedly the compilations of numerologists, soothsayers with the blood of ancient prophets in their veins, palmists, chronologists, astrologers, psychologists, clairvoyants, and so on. The dreams in the dream books are classified into numbered subject sections; and each section has numerous subsections

Left, a British "Bingo Special" train, (arranged by a bingo organization) on its way from London to Brighton in 1962. The 300 women and 50 men on the train played bingo incessantly through the round trip. Numbers were called over loudspeakers from a central control point on the train; stewards in each compartment relayed cries of "bingo" by telephones.

A bingo operator, or caller, can cheat by simply calling out a false number for the ball he has drawn: Above right, his thumb obscures the actual number. For checking purposes the balls are put in a corresponding numbered hole; but if the caller puts a ball in upside down (right) the switch is unlikely to be spotted during the game. Such subterfuges are usually used to end a game quickly or to assist an accomplice (who signals the numbers he needs).

that, by cross-indexing, can be made to cover an almost endless variety of dreams. By juggling with the numbers attached to the interpretation of your dream, you are supposed to be able to find the right number to choose in a lottery.

Naturally the large prizes offered in lotteries encourage attempts at cheating. For instance, a numbers game that flourished in Belgium in 1945 was completely ruined by 12 of the agents who sold the tickets. This game was linked with the five daily balances of the Bourse (the Paris Stock Exchange) that were published in the newspapers. If a number on a holder's ticket corresponded with the final five digits of the balance figure at any time during the week, he could draw a prize through the agent. Tickets were sold tightly sealed, in order to prevent the agents from perpetrating the very swindle they did perpetrate. Obviously, if they could see the numbers on any of their unsold sealed tickets and these turned out to be winning numbers, they could draw additional prizes for themselves. In this case the agents discovered that if the sealed ticket were soaked in carbon tetrachloride the paper became temporarily transparent and revealed the number; and that, when dry again, the paper showed no sign of its soaking. The agents played havoc with the laws of probability and before long put the promoters out of business.

In bingo too, cheating from the players' side is not unknown. And where successful, of course, it is not the operator who loses but the other players. The *New York Sun* reported that in 1960 a rich elderly woman, then using a pseudonym, had admitted to fraudulently capturing $250,000 during her bingo sessions in halls all over America. Her method (which she said she would only fully reveal in her memoirs) had needed two assistants and complete sets of the various cards used in particular halls—as well as a photographic memory and the ability to substitute cards under the eyes of people sitting around her. (She did, however, admit that her method no longer worked once operators began fixing serial numbers to both cards and markers.) But cheating on this scale is confined to countries like America, where the large prizes make the effort and the considerable risks involved worthwhile.

Football (and baseball) pools have already been discussed in Chapter 4, as forms of gambling on spectator sports. But, being pools, they are also a form of sweepstakes; i.e., the winners' prizes vary according to the amount of money in the pool and according to the number of winners. The prizes for winners of sports pools are often extremely large, and therefore elaborate precautions are taken to prevent cheating. The organizers of one of the biggest British football pools have security measures that are apparently foolproof. And they need to be, when you consider the company's 10,000 employees (most of whom are concerned with checking coupons) as well as the many thousands of post-office employees who, in theory, have opportunities to plant coupons in the mail after the results of the football games are known.

The routine precautions include the following: snap searches of employees; four separate code stampings of every coupon received; codes changed at

Right, a lottery ticket from Macao, (the Portuguese colony in China) that might have won a first prize worth $300,000. The sale of these tickets is illegal outside Macao.

Dream books are used by many superstitious gamblers to predict winners in pools and lotteries. Below, a modern Chinese dream book from Hong Kong. The gambler looks up the key image of his dream and bets on the corresponding number.

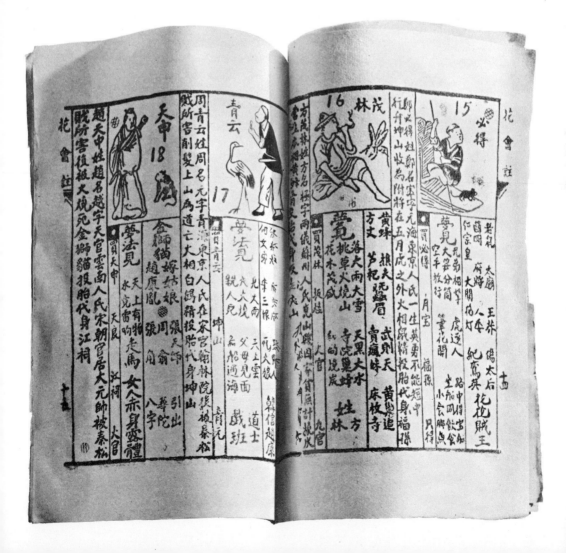

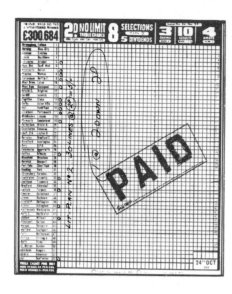

Left, a British football-pools coupon that won a bettor the equivalent of $560,000 for 70 cents staked (in 1959). Sports pools are a thriving gamble almost everywhere. In Britain one of the biggest football-pools companies employs over 10,000 people. Right, girls sort bettors' postal orders, according to value, to be counted on high speed machines. Far right, an electronic computer double-checks all coupons. Below right, the large checking room where employees carefully examine and record details of each football coupon entered, to find winners and to prevent errors or cheating.

unpredictable intervals; personal watch by ex-police security men on all mail deliveries and collections; locking and sealing of every door and window in the many checking buildings as soon as the kick-offs of the week's games are signaled; interruption by security men of any incoming or outgoing telephone calls after kick-off time; secret checking of the security men themselves by another group of unknown security men; and complete banning of all kinds of radio receivers within the building at all times.

In addition, the entire collection of the week's coupons is kept in sealed bags in a guarded strongroom; there is a thorough investigation of any and every coupon arriving after the normal deliveries of mail on the day of the matches, whether or not a claim is subsequently made; and special watches are kept on the coupons of those who win prizes in two or more consecutive weeks. All genuine winning coupons are carefully screened; additional investigations are made if the winner has sent in a coupon for the first time, or has apparently changed any "system" he may previously have been using, or has posted his coupon later in the week than has been customary with him.

A whole season's envelopes and coupons are filed, and there are constant probes into any peculiarities that may be revealed in the coupons of consistent winners; and all prizes are independently checked by an accountant from the local government. Such full-scale precautions against cheating are a feature of practically every big legal lottery—the Irish Sweep, the state lotteries, and so on. Thus the ordinary gambler is reassured that chance and chance alone dictates the fate of his bet.

This "safety" factor is a major reason for the popularity of the world's lotteries: But consider also that gambling on lotteries involves no skill or special knowledge, can produce huge wins for small stakes, and can be done almost anywhere by anyone at any time. It's hardly surprising, then, that lotteries in their various forms can today rival horse racing (in practically every country except America) as man's favorite gamble.

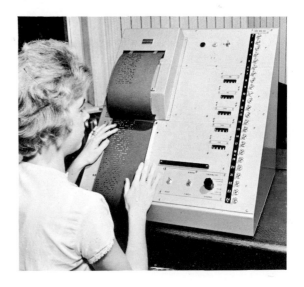

11 The profession of gambling

The professional gambler is a person whose sole source of income is gambling. If he doesn't depend on gambling for his living, then he is an amateur—no matter how expert he is at cards nor how informed he is about horse racing, and no matter how often he plays or bets. Most members of the profession of gambling can be fitted into one of three categories: They can be skilled and experienced gamblers who manage to stay ahead of the game honestly (by knowing the odds and percentages, among other things, and betting accordingly); they can be professional cheats or confidence men; or they can be businessmen who own and run gambling premises and facilities (and who themselves may never gamble).

A great deal of romance—and some infamy—has long been attached to the character of the professional gambler. Popular fiction is full of romantic idealizations of the gambler as a devil-may-care rogue (though not a villain), a footloose and self-sufficient wanderer who drifts from adventure to adventure and from woman to woman. Folk songs (like the American "blues" "Roving Gambler") describe the restless, nomadic life of the gambling man; romantic fiction (like the American musical *Showboat*) stresses his invariable fascination for women. Of the more recent versions of this fictional image of the professional gambler, the American television series *Maverick* is the best example. Even the hero's name is appropriate: In the American West, a "maverick" is

Nick the Greek, America's most famous professional gambler, in action at the faro tables. Like all "straight" professionals, he always prefers games with low house percentages in which he can make full use of his skill and experience.

specifically an animal that hasn't been branded with a mark of ownership; generally, the term is applied to an independent, wild, and irresponsible person. Both as a hero and as a gambler Maverick is representative of a stock fictional character—though a very popular one, especially in America.

Professional gamblers probably enjoy this public image of themselves as much as anyone. But their enjoyment is likely to be tinged with irony, for real professionals may not be very colorful or romantic. And, if they stay on the straight and narrow, they are often unlikely to be very rich. For example, an American professional named Jeremiah Preedy, who ran card games on Mississippi river-boats in the early 19th century, is supposed never to have made a dishonest bet in his life. He was pursued everywhere by parasite tipsters, whose advice he generously bought because he knew they were desperate for money; but this kindness of heart soon ran his fortunes down to nothing and he died in poverty. (Later he was made the hero of a melodrama called *The Gambler* that, together with *The Drunkard* and *The Sinner*, had record runs in the mid-19th century with traveling theatre companies.)

Another American professional, Jackie Swire, made $100,000 profit a year during three years spent in the same river-boats. He invested the money in government stocks, went on playing poker with the interest, and eventually became a millionaire. But according to his autobiography he could never sleep peacefully: "It was the thought of the morrow, the hideous valley of prophecy

Left, the professional approach to gambling. Dedicated card players hide their emotions behind dead-pan "poker faces," so as not to reveal the strength or weakness of the cards they hold. But amateurs display a far more happy-go-lucky attitude—like the lady, right, playing the five-cent slot machines at Harold's Club, Las Vegas.

in which my bills might have to be met, that robbed me of my rest. For I was forever in the hands of fortune and skill, and forever putting on a plain face that was not mine but the face of one more confident than ever I could be of success."

Anxiety, insecurity, the ever-present fear of financial ruin—these are the full-time companions of the professional gambler. A far cry from the reckless and fancy-free gambling man of fiction, but a truer picture. And another part of that picture is the immense amount of hard work that is necessary for a professional gambler's success. Though chance is an unbeatable factor, its effects can be minimized in a number of ways; and the professional must learn these methods and use them to his advantage if he is to stay in action for any length of time against the stiff competition he will meet.

If his game is cards, he must learn (for instance) all the odds against his drawing specific hands; he must have a computer-like ability to remember all the cards that have been played so that he can (with mental mathematics) adjust the odds and his betting; and he must develop an ability to gauge the psychology of his opponents, to read the strength of the others' hands from, say, the smallest change of expression. This last ability may come largely from the professional's instinct or intuition, but the intuition itself will have been sharpened by experience. Patrick Herne, a professional who made enough money out of poker to start his own saloon on Broadway, New York, in 1840, wrote: "I spent 14 hours at a stretch overlooking four poker games and never embroiling myself in any of them, but only studying the faces and cards of the players and deciding what I would have done in their stead had I been in the position of any one of them without the knowledge I had of their opponents' hands."

But the would-be professional's accumulation of experience while he is learning his trade is always hazardous, for he is completely at the mercy of chance and of more skilled players. "I was for ever assembling capital," wrote Minnie Matruh, a Midwest madam who turned her brothel into a gambling saloon when she found she had an almost uncanny gift for remembering cards. "My jewels went first and my house next; then my clothes—even those I stood in, so that I had to resort to borrowed finery—merely so that I could practice and lose and lose again until the way of it was that I made of my skill something worth while."

An 18th-century English country parson, William Wiley, mentions in his diary that "a certain gambler has come into the village to live, now retired, as he says, from his obnoxious trade and prepared to live a life of good work. It is galling to me to accept his ill-gotten gains for the work of the parish, but I do so ne'er the less. And in truth I have found him a most Proper Person in all his manners. I ventured to ask him if he ever regretted his trade and he told me that he had found it monstrous hard and that if life came his way again he would as lief be a peasant in the fields."

The parson was also assured by his gambler acquaintance that gambling can be an honest profession as well as a difficult one. "He shocked me with tales of

Left, an illegal three-card monte (find-the-lady) game being played in a London street. The operator has already switched the three cards and is accepting a player's bet. Right, the final stage in the game: The operator is about to turn up the bettor's card. Professional "street cheats" of this kind generally use accomplices who act as stooges and watch for police.

gamblers who have wasted their own substance and the substance of others for greed, but told me too that he himself had always played his Faro and Whist as a business, producing to himself a Balance at each year's end and learning from his Ventures what might not be done and what might, for Profit. Many a year he has subsisted on the charity of others but promises me he has robbed none. It is the goats that give the stink to the sheep, he says with some truth, and a gambler can be an honest man, as any can, but it is not in the eyes of Others to behold him thus."

A professional gambler can indeed be an honest man. Probably the best living example of the professional who is both skilled and straight, who knows from experience the hardships of the gambler's life, and yet who has become almost as legendary a character as any gambling man of romantic fiction, is America's most famous gambler, known everywhere by his nickname—Nick the Greek.

Born in 1893 in Rethymnon, Crete, and educated at the Greek Evangelical College in Smyrna, Nick (whose real name is Nicholas Andrea Dandolos) is the son of a rug merchant and the godson of a wealthy shipowner. When he was 18 years old, his grandfather sent him to America, giving him an allowance of $150 a week. In Chicago he met and fell in love with a girl, but they quarreled and Nick moved on to Montreal. There he became friendly with a leading jockey of the day, Phil Musgrave; assisted by the jockey's advice and his own natural ability for working out odds, Nick won $500,000 in six months' betting on horse races.

Nick then went back to Chicago and promptly lost the entire amount playing card and dice games that were unfamiliar to him. But he was not at all deterred from continuing in his chosen profession. He began to study these games assiduously and in a few years had become so well known as a freelance gambler that casino proprietors were offering him large salaries to work for them. He usually refused, but became an enormous attraction at the casinos nevertheless merely by playing—partly because he would seldom stop gambling even after losing (as he frequently has done) as much as $100,000 in a single session at the tables.

Nick the Greek follows one basic gambling principle: to give himself as near an even chance as possible, so that his skill and his insight into his opponents' character may be given a fair contest. Thus he usually avoids games like roulette where he considers the house percentage to be too great. He enjoys playing *craps*, though his real genius is for cards—*faro* and particularly *stud poker*, at which he has won, throughout his career, over $6,400,000. But, whatever the game, he always draws crowds of people anxious to witness one of the huge side bets that have made him famous. When playing a game like craps (which often has comparatively low house limits) he has been known to make side bets of $5000 and more.

Although Nick the Greek is a relentless, calculating gambler, he seems to enjoy losing as much as winning. With him the gamble seems to count more than the money; once away from the tables he treats his money as casually as the ash of his famous cigars. He has often carelessly left huge sums in his hatbands or in suits sent to cleaners. It has been estimated that $500,000,000 has passed through his hands, and on his own admission he has swung from the extremes of poverty to the extremes of wealth 73 times. Yet he always plays on credit, pays all debts punctually, and is scrupulously honest.

Naturally this unpredictable gambler with a degree in philosophy and a passion for Aristotle and Plato is the source of endless speculation and rumor. It is widely believed that he once won a city block in Los Angeles, that he challenged an arrogant opponent to draw one card for $550,000 (the other man backed down), that he played faro for 10 days and nights without sleep. These stories may or may not be true. But one thing is certain: Nick the Greek has been gambling honestly for many years on an unprecedented scale, and he is still in business. Which shows that, given the necessary skill and capital, you don't have to cheat at gambling to make it pay.

Some professional gamblers, of course, hold a different view. They prefer to ensure their winnings by resorting to various forms of crookedness. Consequently they never participate in the competition with chance that is the dedicated gambler's chief source of pleasure (although the cheat may gain similar thrills from backing his skill at cheating against detection and punishment). This urge to cheat at gambling is by no means new: Evidence of it can be found in the early history of most nations.

In Britain the first recorded mention of dishonesty in gambling dates back to the reign of Cymbeline (a first-century A.D. king of Britain, if we accept his self-styled kingship on his coinage). Because London was not then established, the seat of power was variously at St. Albans and Colchester; and in the histories of both towns are references to punishments inflicted for what (freely translated) was "the unlawful defacing of the coinage in the cause of deceit and false victory."

Over a thousand years later the records, in this case of the City of London, contain innumerable reports of prosecutions and punishments. For example:

"Elmer de Multon was attached, for that he was indicted in the Ward of Chepe for being a common night walker; and in the day is wont to entice strangers to a tavern and there deceive them by using false dice."

In 18th-century England it was common practice for competent cheats to take on apprentices for substantial fees and teach them the tricks of the trade. The indenture often included a guarantee that the apprentice would not be allowed to practice until the chances of his getting caught were reduced to a minimum. Fees were sometimes as high as the equivalent of $1500, and one master of trickery took on four pupils a year, advertising in the press for "apprentices to highly fortunate banker." The cheats operating these "schools" would take their pupils with them into the gambling houses as assistants or decoys.

America, too, has had its share of professional cheats who made fortunes from the gambling activities of others. Typical of these were the cardsharps who flourished on the plush steamboats that began to ply the Mississippi and Ohio rivers in the early 1880s. The first of these steam-powered paddleboats appeared in 1811. By 1820 there were 60 of them in regular service: By 1833 there were around 500. And the number gradually increased as the small frontier towns of Louisville, Cincinnati, Memphis, and St. Louis blossomed into large cities. The people who traveled up and down the river in this way were an odd, cosmopolitan band. But they generally had two things in common: They were nearly always extremely wealthy, and they were nearly always easy prey for the professional cardsharp.

At first the cardsharp was an outcast on these boats. He was tolerated, but only so long as he remained discreet; if he was caught, he could expect no mercy. But as the boats grew in size and the passenger lists started to swell, the status of the cardsharp changed. Suddenly the boats' officers became aware of the large potential income that lay at the tips of the cardsharp's fingers— and they became his accomplices. (Many captains even considered it bad luck to leave shore without at least one cardsharp aboard.) When a victim complained, he was ignored. If he continued to complain, he was silenced with a knife or a pistol.

By the 1830s as many as 1500 professional gamblers had been attracted to the steamboats that ran between New Orleans and Louisville. Most of them were experts with almost every kind of cheating device—marked cards, reflectors,

loaded dice, and so on. And they seemed to have little difficulty in fleecing the wealthy slave owners and planters who welcomed the chance to enliven a dreary journey with a game of poker, *brag*, *whist*, or faro.

The river gamblers generally worked in teams, adopting different disguises, and pretending not to know one another. Thus, when one of them had succeeded in tempting a few "suckers" into a card game, his colleagues would always be at hand to make up the required number. This teamwork was also useful when a sharper found himself in an honest game with experienced players —for then it would be too risky to try the usual tricks. On these occasions the cardsharp's accomplices would watch the game casually and signal (or "item") to the sharper the strength of his opponents hands.

Some cardsharps made a speciality of signaling, and were known as "itemers." The most celebrated of these Mississippi itemers was James Ashby, who used to disguise himself as an eccentric old violinist. During the journey Ashby would walk around the boat, talk wildly, play tunes on his violin, and watch the gambling. The tunes he played were in fact signals to his accomplice who would be playing at one of the tables in the guise of a country simpleton. But Ashby wasn't content to fool the ordinary passengers. He often pulled the trick against other cardsharps—and his act was so polished that he succeeded in fooling them for several years.

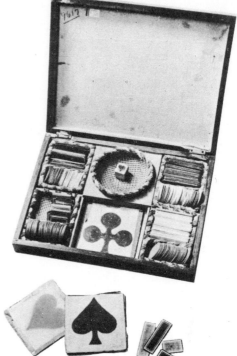

Left, a game of faro—the American "Old West's" favorite gamble—at the Orient Saloon, Arizona (1903). Above and right, portable backgammon and crown-and-anchor sets used by an American riverboat gambler (at the turn of the 19th century) who plied his trade up and down the Mississippi River on the famous *Natchez*.

The crooked professional gamblers of most Hollywood Western films are modeled on the stock image of these river-boat sharpers: Generally they are villainous-looking characters who wear black frock coats, black string ties, black moustaches, and long sideburns. Of course, the modern cheat projects a different *persona* (though his methods are just as professional and effective, and the menace to the gullible amateur remains the same). One modern version of these moustachioed originals is the race-track confidence man. Usually, he works in the most exclusive enclosures, is impeccably dressed and beautifully spoken. His all-too-simple technique was described to me by the chief security officer of a British racecourse:

"The con man often begins by asking a 'mug' if he'd be so kind as to lend him a pencil. He then marks his racecard with the borrowed pencil and starts up a flow of easy conversation. Presently his confederate appears and hands him a wad of notes, remarking that he's off to see one of the 'heads' to gain information for the next race. The con man gives a satisfied smile, pockets the notes, and continues to talk affably to his victim. Invariably the victim congratulates him on his good fortune, and displays an eagerness to be 'in the know.' At this the con man plays hard to get and politely tries to steer the conversation onto a more general topic, whereupon the victim naturally becomes more eager than ever.

Crooked card players often work in pairs, signaling to one another by means of a series of prearranged hand gestures. When one of the pair is dealer, his partner may signal the card or cards he wants to be dealt or, depending on the game, the card he wants his partner to discard. These signals are often made by sweeping the hand across a particular part of the face or body. The "division" of the body for a typical system of signals is shown on the left. Right-hand page, the signaler in action. By moving a hand across his hairline, for example (right), he signals "I need a king"; by moving a hand across his eyes (far right) he signals "I need a queen"; and so on.

"Soon the confederate reappears and whispers to his colleague. By this time the victim is begging for information. The first con man turns hesitantly to his confederate and asks, 'I wonder if we might let our friend here in on this one? He seems most anxious to have a bet and hasn't much reliable information of his own.' There is a show of reluctance on the second con man's part. He doesn't know whether they ought to. What would the source of their information say if he discovered they were leaking confidential tips to strangers? And so on. 'You see,' the first con man explains, 'we have a very private source of information—as a matter of fact the trainer of one of the leading stables—and of course it plays havoc with the betting if there's a sudden rush. However, I daresay you weren't thinking of putting on more than a fiver, were you?'

"Until this encounter, the victim probably hadn't intended putting on more than a few shillings. But now he's all eagerness. Diffidently he says that he'd very much like to put £20 on—or even more if it could be arranged. Suddenly he's overcome by the thought of a certain win and begs to be allowed to bet every penny in his pocket.

"The con men begin to shake their heads. 'Awfully sorry, it's too big a risk—a breach of confidence. I'm sure you'll understand.' They begin to move away, raising their hats politely. At this point the victim is practically in tears. 'But surely,' he says, 'you could add my money to yours.' The con men look rather pained at this, as if they don't relish the thought of acting as errand boys to a casual acquaintance. But at last they succumb. They take the victim's money and disappear—for good. Often they use the money to lay their own bets. And win or lose, it's never unprofitable to bet with other people's money."

This is one method of cheating the racing public. Another, known as the "ticket method," is equally successful. The "ticketers" who work this trick are forgers rather than con men. Ticketers usually work in pairs and their method takes advantage of the fact that British racecourse bookies issue numbered tickets as receipts to bettors. This is how they work:

On the last race of the day the ticketers select a bookmaker, place a small bet, and take away the ticket as a specimen. Then they print a series of tickets numbered from 1 to 1000, identical in every respect to the bookmaker's own tickets. Armed with these, they attend the next day's meeting. They watch the bookmaker closely, making a note of any substantial bets that are placed—and of the numbers issued to the bettors. When one of these "large" bettors backs a winner, the ticketers rush in, present the forged ticket, and run off with the winings. (If necessary, one of the ticketers delays or obstructs the bettor until his partner has had time to collect.) As can be imagined, this swindle often proves very lucrative indeed—though it can only be worked a limited number of times at each meeting.

But crooked professional gamblers have never confined their activities only to the race tracks or gaming rooms. You can find them on sidewalks or in back rooms hoodwinking the innocent in games of *three-card monte*. Or, at the other extreme, you can find them, like Ivar Kreuger, on the fringes of respectable investment and finance circles. In the latter field, the swindlers can come up with the most fantastic schemes; and the more fantastic they are, the more readily they seem to succeed—for a while. The "casino investment concern" (which I will discuss later) is one of the most recent creations of this type; but probably one of the most infamous was the swindle that has gone down in history as the "South Sea Bubble."

The South Sea Bubble was a giant speculative scheme that rocked England at the beginning of the 18th century. No professional gambler, as such, originated or operated the scheme; but many were to thrive beneath its respectable cloak. For at the beginning the scheme *was* perfectly honest and respectable.

It was originated in 1711 by Robert Harley, Earl of Oxford, the Lord High Treasurer of Britain. He formed a company (the South Sea Company) with the

Above, a set of marked cards. Cards may be marked in a great number of ways—by adding spots or lines to the design on the back, by thickening lines, by shading, and so on. In this instance each card has been marked with a shaded square on the top and bottom.

Cheating at baccarat usually requires the croupier's co-operation—particularly in small gambling clubs where players are given an opportunity to shuffle the cards before the croupier stacks them in the sabot (dealing box). Far left, a batch of prearranged cards (here with red backs for identification) is introduced into the game by a cheat. Left, the croupier places all the cards into the sabot, taking care not to disturb the order of the inserted batch. The cheat waits for his sequence of cards to appear (right), then plays and bets accordingly.

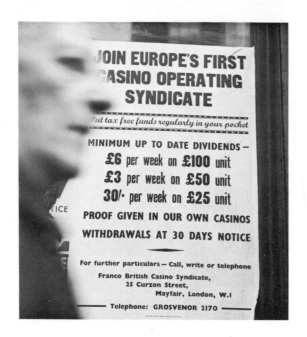

Left, one of the many posters advertising the fraudulent casino investment scheme that appeared in Britain in 1962. The posters promised £6 ($16.80) a week income for every £100 ($280) invested. Police were called in when confidential records of investors were found in an ash can outside the firm's London office (right). Far right, an investor quizzes a policeman about her money.

object of exploiting trade in the South Seas, and was granted a monopoly of British trade with South America and the Pacific Islands. At first all went well. In 1718 the king became governor of the company, and the directors declared that they would take over the National Debt (worth about $260,000,000) in return for further trade concessions—and that they would pay $17,500,000 for this privilege. When their offer was accepted by the government in 1720, the company's shares rocketed overnight.

The extraordinary success of the South Sea Company encouraged imitators, anxious to cash in on the sudden boom. Soon a host of ludicrous ventures were being advertised, and thousands of gullible people rushed to throw their money into the hands of the professional swindlers who promoted them. The prospectus for one of these ventures announced that a company was being formed "for the carrying on of an undertaking of great advantage, but nobody to know what it is"; another was to finance a firm for the melting down of wood shavings that were to be "cast into planks"; and another had plans for especially bottling South American sunlight "for release in less salubrious climes in times of inclement weather."

These "fringe" companies were condemned bitterly by the parent concern, but it was too late. By August 1720 the bubble had burst, and the price of South Sea stock began to topple. Thousands of people who had invested their money in both the real and bogus companies suddenly found themselves penniless. Many fled the country, many committed suicide. (Over 800 suicides were directly attributable to the calamity.) The government set up a court of inquiry and discovered that even the South Sea Company itself had been swindling the public: For by bribing certain ministers, the directors had managed to get the company's share value raised to an artificial level. Robert Walpole, the prime minister, immediately confiscated and sold the property of the directors (who

included several senior government ministers) and allocated the money to the victims. But he was unable to check the wide-spread disaster.

The recent "casino investment" concern to which I referred earlier is really a small-scale repeat of the South Sea Bubble. It was heralded by a number of posters that began to appear in the windows of empty shops in London, Liverpool, and Manchester in 1962. The advertisement offered a weekly income of $17 for every $280 invested (an interest rate of 260 per cent). Investors were invited to apply for pamphlets that explained the system in full detail: "Our organization operates at continental casinos, using operators who have expert knowledge and practical experience in playing the game of roulette. Our system is infallible subject to sufficient funds being available. . . . The proof of the soundness of this system is the fact that no investor has ever lost a penny of his capital. We publicly challenge any mathematicians or so-called 'experts' to disprove our claim."

Many Britons invested sums of up to $280 in the scheme, and for a number of weeks received dividend checks at the proper interest rate. These were accompanied by a letter saying that the capital sum could be withdrawn at 30 days' notice. Then, suddenly, the checks stopped arriving. The office of one firm was found to be abandoned; the staff of another claimed to have had a burglary in which the assets had been stolen from a safe; another lost its managing director, who had "gone to the continent in connection with the casinos" and forgotten to sign checks before going. The police discovered that none of the 20,000 small investors had ever got more than a fifth of their capital back in "dividend" checks. They also found that the men responsible for the "casino enterprises" had made a profit of about $280,000.

So much for the professional cheat, whose activities are outside the pale to both honest gamblers and anti-gamblers. The next character to be looked at in our story of professional gambling—the bookmaker—holds a much more ambiguous position. In countries like America, where his profession is illegal, he is considered a not-so-petty criminal. But in countries where bookmaking is legal, he is an above-board business man who usually adopts a businesslike approach to gambling. We have already looked at the bookie in action (both legally and illegally) in earlier chapters; here we can detail some of the mechanics of his highly professional activities. Of course, like all business, bookmaking has its ups and down; but (as one British bookmaker told me) it can be the "most pleasant and bother-free" of occupations—once the business has been set up. But to get established a bookie needs amounts of money and persistence "that would make the non-gambling mind boggle like a seismograph." This was my informant's personal story:

"You can't imagine what a job I had getting started. Nowadays it's relatively easy. Under the new Act [i.e., the Betting and Gaming Act of 1960 that legalized off-course bookmaking] you've got to have a license from the Watch Committee [a town's official guardian of public morals] to start a betting shop, and they never object so long as nothing's known against you and you can find somewhere to open up. As far as they're concerned you can start tomorrow— unless there are objections from the other bookies about taking their business. But you fix that first if you've any sense.

"It wasn't that easy when I started in 1929. I had been working as a plumber's mate and I was getting nowhere fast. Then I had a real stroke of luck: A relative died and left me a small legacy. I say 'small,' but it was a fortune then— £500 [about $1400]. I'd always been keen on horse racing and seized the chance to start my own bookie business.

"But in those days you had to be really careful. You were allowed on the courses, but the only way to get the back-street business was to have 'runners' bringing it in on the quiet. You had to pay them a percentage, win or lose, and you had to pay their fines when they got caught. What with that and my losses I was down to my last pound within two weeks of starting—and I had to go out of business for a week until I'd turned that one pound into 20. And the same thing happened to me at least two dozen times during the next couple of years. It was always the same problem—shortage of capital. For in addition to the running expenses (which included clerks' fees and their fares) there was the protection money you had to pay too if you didn't want to be beaten up and have your stand wrecked.

"Apart from the capital, a bookie must have a feeling for odds: I don't mean just the ability to work things out mathematically as an accountant would, but rather a feeling *inside* that tells him when to shorten or lengthen odds. And, believe me, this takes a long time to develop. I know one chap who ruined a good business simply because he didn't have the flair for odds. You must have them working on your side. For that's how you make a profit. A couple of big mistakes and you can be out of business for ever.

"Another bookie I know had really bad luck—not with his bets but just with circumstances. First of all he made an enemy of the police because his runners kept getting caught; then he got beaten up for not going into a protection racket; and finally he lost and lost until he was unable to pay his debts. After that he got warned off all courses and was finished. I tell you, it's a tricky game. But I wouldn't have changed it. You get plenty of excitement, and once you are in the money you can extend operations—operate a football-pool syndicate, take bets on other events like tennis matches or prize fights. Or you can build up a postal betting business, like William Hill, or start in the manufacturing business, like Littlewoods.

"I've personally done what most of the boys I know have done: As soon as the 1960 Act came in I opened a small betting shop, put a manager in, and kept the course work for myself. There's nothing like it. The shop's all right— easy money rolling in all day long—but the track's where you want to be. Plenty of noise and people, and your tic-tac signaling when you're packing too much in your book. It's exciting. But I could have gone down as easily as I've come up. For getting to be a bookie is just as much a gamble as staying one."

Since the Betting and Gaming Act, life has been made considerably easier for the British bookmaker. To set up shop he has only to procure a bookmaker's permit and license. This he does by making an application to the appropriate authorities and sending a copy within seven days to the local chief of police. Then he must publish "by means of advertisement in a newspaper a notice of the making of his application." This notice must state that "anyone objecting to the granting of this permit must within 14 days after the publication of the notice, send to the appropriate clerk of the authorities two copies of the statement of the grounds of his objections." Provided there are no valid objections, the bookie receives his license in a few weeks after paying a fee equaling $280. (These licenses, incidentally, do not automatically allow a bookmaker to operate on a racecourse or dog track. The right of entry to these is still controlled by the individual managements.)

The larger a bookmaker's business is, of course, the more complex it becomes. The William Hill Organization in Britain, which claims to serve over 2,000,000 racing and football-pools customers, has over 300 highly trained telephonists on its huge staff. (The Organization trains its own telephonists and settlers.) Their job is to take the bets down as they come in, recording the time at which they were taken, and place them on conveyor belts that carry them to the field tables where they are entered into the field books.

The new $5,600,000 Hill building in London has its own up-to-date printing plant, an underground parking area with special delivery bays for the armored vans that collect and deliver the postal bets, an air-conditioning plant, and a staff restaurant that accomodates 450 people—a far cry from the small second-floor room where William Hill started his bookmaking business. Hill's business is an example of professional gambling at its most efficient—and its most

Punt				Gold Aura				Lomond				Portlet				Ships Biscuit			
	50	7	*(ht*		6	1	34		9	2	1		90	20	48		50	8	62
114	50	7	*(Mc*		12	2	35		4 –	1	2				*CHN*	77	25	4	63
	25	3 –	27		6	1	36		9	2	3	240	90	20	*CNB*				*Moch*
158	14	2	28	144	100	16	*Joe*		45 –10		4						50	8	
	7	1	29		18	3	37		4 –	1	5		4 –	1	49		6	1	64
182	14	2	30		12	2	38		9	2	6		9	2	50	156	12	2 25	65
	7	1	31	214	30	5	*Joe*	121	18	4	*H.T.*		9	2	51				
	3 –	–	30		25	4	*HT*		9	2	7		18	4	52	272	100 16 39		*HN*
202	7	1	33		12	2	39		27	6	*Johns*		22 –	5	53				*Mc*
316	100	14	39	264	6	1	40		9	2	8	350	27	6	54	301	25	4	
					12	2	41		4 –	1	9		9	2	55		12	2	66
					18	3	42		90	20	*HN*		4 –	1	56	379	12	2	67
					6	1	43		9	2	10		4 –	1	57		6	1	68
					12	2	44		4 –	1	11		9	2	58		9	1 –	69
				334	12	2	45		13 –	3	12	438	45	10	*Johns*	357	9	1 –	70
					6	1	46		9	2	13						6	1 52	71
				358	12	2 50	47	341	4 –	1	1	493	45	10 86	*Gee*	378	12	2	72
									4 –	1	63 15					436	50	8 62	*Henne*
									9	2	16		36	8 94	*Ellie*				
									18	4	17	548	9	2 96	*HN*				
									45	10	*HT*		4 –	1	59				
									9	2	18		4 –	1	60				
									13 –	3	19	570	9	2 100	61				
									4 –	1	20								
									4 –	1	21	625	45	10 100					
									18	4	22								
									18	4	23								
									9	2	24								
									4 –	1	24								
								550	13	3 100	26								
		7/1				*6/1*				*9/2*				*9/2*				*6/1*	

Left, the receiving room for off-track bets at the William Hill Organization in London. Regular clients may phone to find out the latest odds (written on the blackboard at the end of the room) and to place bets on a credit basis.

Bottom left, the kind of book kept by on-track bookmakers' clerks in Britain. The book gives a complete record of bets made, the odds given for each bet, and the number of the bettor's ticket for each bet. Right, an example of the numbered tickets that bookies give as receipts. Bettors must produce these tickets when collecting their winnings.

affluent, for Hill is sometimes called upon to pay out over $2,800,000 a week to winning bettors. In 1961 he paid out $3,133,144 *in one day* to football-pools winners.

Today, with the appearance of schools providing comprehensive courses in bookmaking, the aspiring British bookmaker can get his experience in a comparatively easy way. The London School of Turf Accountancy, for example, runs both evening and correspondence courses on every aspect of bookmaking; from "control and co-ordination of staff" to "hedging" and "tote odds." It costs from $56 to enroll for such a course.

A glance at some of the section headings in the School's "Complete Course for Manager and Bookmaker" shows how involved and technical a bookmaker's job can be. Some of the headings for the chapter on settling bets provide a good example: "Using all three systems to calculate Mixed Doubles, Trebles, and Accumulators"; "Using the Pyramid Block System to calculate the number of Doubles, Trebles, and Accumulators in a given number of selections when two or more of them are in the same race"; "Using either the Pyramid Block or Crash Block to settle mixed E.W. Doubles, Trebles, and Accumulators, when two or three selections are placed in the same race."

We needn't complicate our story by going into the art of settling. Another chapter, entitled "The Field Book," gives a less technical but equally enlightening glance into the bookmaker's world. Here are the opening paragraphs:

"Let us visualize a large bookmaking organization with, say, 100 or more telephones which are continually in use during the course of a racing day. It stands to reason that the bookmaker needs to have some idea of his liabilities on each race. To get this information he refers to his field book, where he sees at a glance the amount of money he has taken on a particular race and also the amount he will win or lose on each runner.

"As each bet is received over the telephone, it is conveyed to a second person (generally the boss or his manager) for perusal. He in turn calls out this amount to the man in control of the field book and it is duly entered against the name of a runner. The bet is then given to a settler for his attention when the race is over. It is essential for the field book operator to be fully abreast of his work, as the onus or responsibility for correctly assessing the amount of money on each runner rests entirely with him. The bookmaker may enquire at any time for the stakes he is holding for a particular horse, and that figure must be given to him immediately. He compares this figure with the odds quoted at the time, and decides whether he may accept or refuse further commissions. . . ."

The 1960 legislation financially destroyed the street bookmakers in Britain. The street bookies were never legal, but their professional association (The Street Bookmakers' Federation) had always paid their fines in the past if they were arrested and they had prospered in a small way. Many could no longer afford the money needed to legalize themselves, nor the heavy overheads of shop

furniture and staff hire. Neither could they afford to pay the stinging new fines (up to $280 for the first offense, up to $560 for the second, and an additional three months' imprisonment for the third) to which street bookies became liable after the Act.

But it would be wrong to leave the impression that there are absolutely no restrictions on the professional bookmaker in Britain. There are several. Bookmakers by law may not advertise a shop's whereabouts and the facilities it offers. They may not encourage bets, offer waiting clients the pleasures of television or radio, serve refreshments, or offer inducements of any kind to remain on the premises. But providing they observe these restrictions, they have nothing to worry about legally.

In the few other countries where off-track bookmaking is legal the story is often very similar, though naturally slight variations occur from place to place. In New Zealand (where off-track betting has been legal since 1950) bets must be placed with the bookie at least 90 minutes before a race, and are then transmitted to a central office. In Western Australia and Tasmania, where most of Australia's off-track bookmakers are centered, bets may be placed (as in Britain) right up to the start of the race: But the minimum bet allowed is five shillings. (In Britain the minimum is usually two shillings.)

In Western Germany bookmakers are legal on and off the course, but by far the greater percentage of the betting is done through totalizators. Bookmakers

Left, an evening session at the London School of Turf Accountancy, where students receive detailed instruction and training in all aspects of the bookmaker's profession. Within a few weeks of its opening in 1963, about 450 students had enrolled at the school.

Right, after a successful police raid on the headquarters of a New York betting ring, a detective answers calls from unsuspecting clients and records their bets as evidence.

277

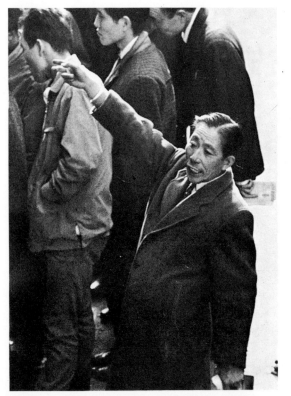

Tipsters (or touts) add color and excitement to race tracks the world over. Above, the Maori Prince Ras Monolulu, Britain's best-known tipster, suggests a likely winner to a bettor at Epsom. Left, a Japanese tipster in action. Right, American tipsters offer their "tip sheets" to passers-by at the Hialeah race track, Florida.

and the organizers of totalizators must each pay a tax of $16\frac{2}{3}\%$ of their income. Bookmakers are illegal in Italy, though there is a certain amount of tote betting. Most of the money bet on horse racing in Italy goes on pools controlled by the Italian National Olympic Committee. In 1962 the equivalent of over $6,000,000 was spent in this way.

Bookmakers are illegal in France (which doesn't mean they don't exist) and most betting on horse races is done via the tote. Since 1933 a pari-mutuel system (see page 195) has been operating that permits off-track betting through authorized agents—but these are not bookmakers. Since off-track bettors in France have to pay a government tax from $1\frac{1}{5}$ to $1\frac{4}{5}\%$ on all bets over 10 francs (about two dollars), it is hardly surprising that more than two thirds of the total betting on races is done at the tracks.

The mechanics of betting legally in America were discussed at length in Chapter 8. Bookies (on- or off-track) are strictly illegal, except in Nevada. Nevertheless they continue to flourish in many states—partly because (according to the U.S. Attorney General Robert Kennedy) they pay "protection money" to local politicians and policemen. An American bookmaker's business can be carried on discreetly behind the public's back: Since most of the betting is on credit, and over the telephone, all the bookie really needs is a room with a phone. And generally the amount he pays in protection money is in proportion to the number of telephones he has. (In recent years bookies were paying as much as $450 per week per telephone in New York City.)

François Blanc (left), creator of Monte Carlo's casino, and his twin brother Louis, who in 1842 together started 19th-century Europe's most fashionable casino, at Homburg.

All in all, American bookmaking seems practically as big-time as in Britain, in spite of the law. Some figures quoted by Mr. Kennedy indicate the extent of its success: An Indiana bookie once received a total of $1,156,000 in bets over a period of three days; a Los Angeles bookie took in $4,511,000 in a year; and a Chicago bookie's annual income was about $6,400,000.

The bookmaker is probably the most prominent of the professional gamblers who make their living by providing gambling facilities for others—prominent because he is the one with whom the general public has most contact. But equally important is the professional gambler whom the general public is least likely to meet—the owner of a gambling casino. The workings of casinos will be examined in the next chapter; here we can round off our survey of professional gambling with a brief look at the early career of the most famous of all casino owners, François Blanc—the man who created Monte Carlo.

Blanc's career was unusual from start to finish. He was born in 1806 near Avignon in the South of France, and by the time he was 28 had made enough money from his speculations on the stock exchange to open a small bank in Bordeaux together with his twin brother Louis. Once the bank was safely launched, the Blanc brothers settled down to speculating on the stock exchange on a grand scale.

At that time the monopoly of the *télégraphe aérien* (a primitive system of signaling from town to town by means of telescopes and heliographs) was held by the state. When the Blanc brothers attempted to set up their own telegraphic system, they were blocked by this state monopoly. However, this didn't deter them; they knew one of the operators at the existing telegraph station personally and with his help planned to adapt it for their own use. A series of code signals was arranged between them, and in this manner the Blancs were able to get advance information concerning fluctuations on the stock exchange, and thus to get the jump on their rival bankers.

Unfortunately for the Blancs their scheme was given away by a telegraph official on his deathbed. Of course, there was an uproar—even though similar systems had been employed by rival bankers. (The Rothschilds, for example, had had great success with a pigeon-post news service.) The Blanc brothers were immediately prosecuted for using state secrets; it was discovered that they had made the equivalent of more than $500,000. But their counsel proved to the satisfaction of the president of the court that their activities were completely above-board, and they were acquitted and allowed to keep their profits.

After this the Blanc brothers moved to Paris. Gambling was about to be suppressed in France at any moment, but the casinos were clearly making vast profits. So the Blancs looked around for a less conspicuous place than Paris where they could finance a casino and cash in on the gambling boom. They found the perfect place in the semi-bankrupt area of Hesse-Homburg where the landgrave (a German count having territorial jurisdiction) was only too pleased to sell them a concession for the building of a casino.

Once the casino was built, the brothers began to advertise it widely. They made great play of the curative values of the local waters, and of the fact that they were adventurously going to lessen the bank's advantage by reducing the number of zeros on the roulette wheels from two to one, and by halving the bank's advantage in *trente-et-quarante*. They were wise enough to realize that so long as they retained even a small percentage they could never lose, and that in time they would gain more customers by this policy. They were proved right by the fact that six years after the casino had opened they were said to be making a *net* profit of more than $100,000 a year.

Even when Prince Charles Bonaparte won nearly $15,000 in six days play and brought the casino's reserves down to rock bottom, François Blanc (who had assumed sole charge because of the illness of Louis) was quick to see that he could benefit from advertising the fact. Blanc's public relations were masterly. He produced lavish posters and pamphlets and distributed them throughout Europe. He managed to talk the railway authorities into running a line to the casino, and persuaded the French national theatre company (the *Comédie Française*) to come and give performances. Always he concentrated his attention on people rich and famous enough to be an attraction in themselves.

But his most triumphant moment as a casino entrepreneur was in 1863, when he obtained the apparently useless gambling concession of the principality of Monaco. The result of that *coup* will be seen in the next chapter.

12 Famous gambling centers

Of all the great gambling centers in Europe, Monte Carlo is without doubt the most famous—though its casino has been operating for only just over 100 years. Considering the size of the principality of Monaco in which Monte Carlo is situated (it covers a total area of 368 acres on the Côte d'Azur of the South of France), it is remarkable that it should have risen to fame so quickly. That it has is due to the efforts of one man, François Blanc.

Monaco's history, prior to its fame as a gambling center, was a stormy one. Its geographical position made it a natural base from which successive invaders, with their eyes on Western Europe, could conveniently launch their fleets and armies. These invaders included the Phoenicians, the Greeks (who called Monaco "Hercules Monoecus" because it was supposed to have been the scene of one of Hercules' twelve labors), the Romans (who used it as a strategic base and erected a statue of Augustus to commemorate his victory over the Gauls), the Vandals, Goths, Lombards, and Saracens.

Since the 13th century the reigning princes of the principality of Monaco have been Grimaldis—a family that fled from Italy to Monaco, later to become rich landlords, and later still (1793) to become dispossessed by the national convention during the French Revolution.

Monaco's throne was restored in 1814 but the family fortune had been lost. Honoré V struggled valiantly but unsuccessfully to rebuild it; and when he died

The ornate main casino at Monaco's Monte Carlo, most famous of Europe's gambling centers, where hardened professionals, hopeful amateurs, and casual tourists from all over the world come to mix with the famous and gamble in high style.

Left, a game of chemin-de-fer in the main gambling hall at Monte Carlo in 1874. Today it is forbidden to take photographs of the casino's layout, or of a game in progress, due to stringent security precautions.

Right, Monte Carlo casino in the 1860s, shortly after its completion. Less than 10 years later, luxurious gardens surrounded the casino, a railway linked Monaco with Nice, sea communications had been improved, a large hotel had been built, and Monte Carlo was well on the way to becoming the gamblers' Mecca that it is today.

his successor, Florentine, made a desperate effort to remind people of Monaco's existence by turning it into a health resort.

At that time health resorts were becoming extremely fashionable throughout Europe, and in many cases extremely profitable. One in particular—Germany's Baden-Baden—was flourishing, largely because a new casino had been opened there. It was said that the holder of this casino concession was taking in as much as 50,000 francs ($10,000) a day. In places like Homburg and Pyrmont, casinos were having similar successes.

The Grimaldis were quick to perceive the revenue possibilities in this casino boom. So in 1856, when two French entrepreneurs named Albert Aubert and Léon Langlois expressed a desire to start a "Société de Jeux" in Monaco for the promotion of sea-bathing facilities, they were immediately granted a 35-year monopoly. They planned to provide a theatre, a restaurant, a new hotel, beaches, and gambling rooms, and to start a regular steamer service between Monaco and Nice. In return for the monopoly, they agreed to pay a quarter of their profits to the principality.

But these ambitious plans failed to materialize. The partners evidently lacked the capital needed to transform their dreams into a reality; they had to sell the casino concession. The concession changed hands several more times during the next few years. Then, in 1861, the Grimaldis suffered a near-fatal blow. In that year the Turin Peace Treaty was signed between France and Austria, bringing to an end the war that France and Sardinia had been waging jointly against

Austria. In the negotiations that followed, Monaco's two leading townships, Roquebrune and Menton, were annexed by France. This took away four fifths of Monaco's territory and reduced it to its present size. To soften the blow, France agreed to pay Prince Charles of Monaco the equivalent of $600,000 and to build a new highway and a railway connecting Monaco and Nice.

It was, surprisingly, at this juncture that Monaco's fortunes began to take a turn for the better. Prince Charles had heard that a casino was flourishing at Homburg, and that it was being run by a brilliant Parisian financier named François Blanc. In a moment of inspiration Charles suggested to the harassed owners of Monte Carlo's apparently useless casino concession that they approach Blanc and ask him to take it over. The offer was accepted. Once again (in 1863) the concession changed hands—for the equivalent of $366,000.

When Blanc took over the casino, communications by both land and sea were incredibly bad. The only way to reach Monaco by land was by carriage over a narrow mountain road that led over the Corniche (known today as the Grand Corniche) from Nice to La Tourbie, and the rest of the way by foot. The carriage ride from Nice to La Tourbie cost 50 francs ($10) and took three hours; the descent from there on foot to Monaco took another hour. On fine days a steamship (under the command of the Monégasque captain Imbert) crossed from Nice to Monaco, but the service was extremely erratic.

When travelers did finally arrive at Monaco, there were no hotels to stay at, and no restaurants to eat in. The casino itself (a temporary building in the Rue

Lorraine) was shabbily decorated, and play on its few tables was frequently stopped because the casino had run out of funds. It is hardly surprising that there was a dearth of customers. "From an existence of dreaming inaction," Blanc wrote in the *Journal de Monaco*, "Monaco must rouse itself to one of courage and activity. A whole town remains to be built!"

Blanc brought to Monaco exactly what was needed—experience, energy, and capital. In next to no time he had built a new casino (it was inaugurated in May 1865) and beside it a new hotel, the Hôtel de Paris. He then spent the equivalent of $400,000 on roads, gardens, and the harbor, and gradually a new town (occupying more than half of Monaco) was built up round the casino. In 1866 the reigning prince, Charles III, decreed that the area (which was dominated by a mountain) should be called Monte Carlo.

Within five years of Blanc's arrival in Monaco, the proposed railway line between Nice and Monaco was in operation; and in 1870 a new road between the two towns was completed. Once the communications had been improved, visitors began pouring into Monaco, and Blanc did everything possible to encourage them to stay. For instance, he reduced (as he had at Homburg) the number of zeros on the roulette wheel from two to one, lessening the bank's advantage. Nevertheless, he was still able to show a profit of 800,000 francs ($160,000) at the end of the casino's first year of business.

Blanc's success naturally provoked a certain amount of envy—particularly among the neighboring towns. The Nice newspapers opened a violent campaign against the new casino, claiming that it was responsible for a sudden rise in the suicide rate. In one story they declared that bodies of broken gamblers were piling up in the grottoes below the casino's rock; in another, that bodies were being taken out to sea and dumped. These fanciful stories spread abroad, and in the 1870s diatribes against the new casino often appeared in the newspapers of America and England.

But despite the rumors and the bad publicity (which began to subside when Blanc put a number of editors on his payroll) the casino continued to prosper. When Blanc died in 1877 he left a fortune worth about $14,400,000.

François Blanc's able son Camille took over the direction of the casino on his father's death, and under him it continued to prosper and expand. The original, rather modest, structure was redesigned and extended. A new west wing housed the Monte Carlo Opera House and Theatre (opened in 1879 in the presence of Prince Charles III of Monaco and Sarah Bernhardt) and a new east wing housed the *salle privée* (a select gaming room where only the extremely wealthy could afford to play).

In 1898, an exclusive club known as the International Sporting Club was opened in François Blanc's old house. Here gamblers could play roulette, *trente-et-quarante, chemin-de-fer,* and *baccarat* right through the night. In 1900 a tunnel leading directly from Monte Carlo station to the casino and Hôtel de Paris was built. And in 1932 (just 10 years after the death of Camille Blanc)

Above, a croupier at the Monte Carlo casino goes through each of the six packs of cards to be used in trente-et-quarante, verifying that all are there, and that they are unmarked. Right, a croupier and his team sort the "plaques"—rectangular counters used for placing big bets at baccarat.

the International Sporting Club was removed to a large palace adjacent to the casino and the Hôtel de Paris.

As for the physical appearance of Monte Carlo today : Though a second casino (the Summer Casino) has been built in recent years, Blanc's original building (now known as the Winter Casino) continues to dominate the town. The main casino is entered by a flight of marble steps. On the left of these steps is the "Commissariat," open from 10 A.M. to 2 A.M., where tickets for the public and private rooms are issued and identities checked. The entrance leads into a long oblong hall overlooked by the Atrium, a gallery designed by the French architect Dumoulin. Off the hall to the left is the casino's theatre, and at the end the gaming rooms. These are extravagantly decorated by fashionable artists of the late 19th and early 20th centuries. In the *salle blanche* a big decorative panel representing the Florentine Graces was painted by Gervais, while the arched ceiling of the *salle vert* is the work of the painter Galleli. The salle vert was originally designed as a smoking room (which explains why Galleli put cigars between the fingers of the nude women he painted on the ceiling); but it has since been converted into an elegant bar.

The old Winter Casino has 11 rooms. The smallest (i.e., the ones where the stakes are smallest) are known collectively as "the Kitchen": This is where the majority of Monte Carlo's "amateur" gamblers play, and in summer months it is overrun by tourists in slacks. (The *New York Times* recently described the Kitchen as "the third class waiting-room of a railway station.") It costs two and a half new francs to enter the Kitchen; and gambling on the roulette, trente-et-quarante, chemin-de-fer, and baccarat tables stops at midnight.

But the Kitchen accounts for only about a quarter of the casino's revenue. The really serious gambling takes place in the salles privées, where play on the roulette, chemin-de-fer, trente-et-quarante, *craps,* and baccarat tables goes on until the early hours of the morning. (Suits, incidentally, are obligatory in these rooms.) Admission to the salles privées costs five new francs ($1), and in them it is rare to see a bet of under 10,000 new francs (the equivalent of about $2000). The greatest concentration of cash is usually found at the baccarat table known as the *banque à tout va* (anything goes) where a baccarat hand may be worth 200,000 new francs ($40,000).

The big bets are placed with rectangular colored chips, called plaques: The orange ones represent 1000 new francs, the pink 2000 francs, the yellow 5000 francs, the white 10,000 francs, and the green 20,000 francs. But it wasn't always so. Before the First World War, gamblers often used gold pieces instead of chips. Because of this an Englishman, Sir Frederick Johnston, once won 25,000 francs ($5000) with a gold button from the sleeve of his jacket. The button in question had come off and rolled onto the floor. When the croupier spotted it he called out "Don't disturb yourself, Monsieur, where is the louis going? On the red?" At this Sir Frederick, who had not noticed the loss of his button, replied laughingly to what he thought was a joke: "Always red." He then left the room and forgot about the incident, until a croupier came running up, and handed him his winnings. Sir Frederick tried to refuse the money, saying that he hadn't played, but was finally persuaded to accept it. Only later did he discover the loss of his button and realize what had happened.

The gamblers at Monte Carlo are as miscellaneous a collection as at any other casino. But the atmosphere in the Winter Casino is different: It has the unmistakable overtones of the well-bred, and one has to go back to 1950 to find the last recorded occasion when there was a fracas in the salles privées. It occurred when a Greek roulette player decided to bet on the number Five. He covered it in every possible way—en plein, à cheval, carré, and transversale—and in every case with the maximum stake. Though Five didn't turn up, he won some of his bets through the combinations. He bet again and again, always on these combinations, and won each time on one of the alternative numbers. The level of excitement was raised to such a degree that the croupier accidentally rolled the ball in the same direction as the wheel. Observing the mistake the *chef de partie* (who is in charge of the table) stopped the wheel, whereupon the gambler became abusive, swept his chips off the table and, in picking them up, missed

A practice session at Baden-Baden casino, Germany. In most casinos croupiers are not only given full-scale training but also practice constantly to keep themselves in top form. Above left, a croupier goes through the ritual of throwing the ball around the roulette wheel. Above, a mock roulette game is staged : The head croupier supervises, others act as players ; they often feign cheating to teach trainees the art of detection. Left, a dealer practices shuffling the baccarat cards, and below, another dealer practices fanning out the packs.

the next turn of the wheel: Five came up. The gambler's abuse cost him the equivalent of $40,000.

The casino is open throughout the year. And recently a special summer casino was built along the beach to help absorb the heavy influx of visitors that occurs during the summer months. These visitors to Monte Carlo never lack entertainment. Near the casino is the International Sporting Club, now used mainly for banquets and Friday-night galas, which has more gaming tables; there is the casino restaurant, with its pale green walls, water-lily chandeliers, and a resident prophetess (known as *La Bohémienne*) who specializes in palmistry, astrology, and graphology. There is the Hôtel de Paris (adjoining the Sporting Club) a glowing edifice replete with marble and stained glass, *boutiques* full of expensive jewelry; and for the more down-to-earth there is a theatre and an open-air cinema.

Today, of course, Prince Rainier III is the reigning monarch of Monaco. But the controlling shares in the casino are held by the multimillionaire Greek shipowner and businessman extraordinary, Aristotle Onassis. Onassis's 17,000-ton ocean-going yacht *Christina* is now one of Monte Carlo sightseers' principal sights. On it he entertains many of the world-famous celebrities who visit Monte Carlo—film stars, statesmen, royalty, and industrialists alike. In recent years his guests have included Sir Winston Churchill, Frank Sinatra, the king of Greece, Greta Garbo, Maria Callas, and Cary Grant—to name just a few. Onassis's presence in Monte Carlo can be said to be largely responsible for the casino's continuing success; like Blanc before him, he seems to add to and attract the glamor that makes Monte Carlo unique among gambling centers.

For the most part the casino is a model of efficiency. From the office of the eight directors (one of whom is Prince Rainier's personal representative) on the first floor, to the basement workshops where the tables and wheels are serviced and adjusted, the enterprise is run with clockwork precision. All possible precautions are taken to ensure that both player and casino are given an absolutely fair deal. Each day before the first play begins (at 10 A.M.) the roulette wheels are checked for balance with a spirit level, the balls are measured, the croupiers' rakes are examined, and each table is issued with its half-a-million francs' worth of chips. (These have been exclusively designed for the casino, and are said to be virtually impossible to counterfeit.) In addition the equipment on the card tables is carefully checked.

The croupiers themselves are carefully trained and disciplined at the casino's own school: Their course takes between six and eight months. A good croupier must possess a knowledge of at least one language other than French, must have an impeccable record and, above all, must have the natural facility to keep a cool head in moments of excitement and crisis. Croupiers also must have memories that can infallibly record the ownership of any of thousands of francs' worth of chips or plaques placed on any section of the table, and the mathematical ability to work out the odds instantly on any payoff.

Security naturally heads the casino's list of priorities. The finance offices on the first floor, for example, are situated at the end of a corridor so narrow that only one person can approach at a time. Players must leave hats, brief cases, and similar articles in the cloakrooms. (This rule was made in the 1920s after a gang smuggled a smoke bomb into the casino and escaped with several cash boxes during the panic that followed its explosion.) The casino also has its own independent electricity system, which is kept as a reserve. Thus, if there should be a breakdown in the normal system (or if a thief should cut the wires), the casino would not be plunged into complete darkness. And at the slightest sign of trouble croupiers have only to press a button for the contents of their cash boxes to drop through pneumatic tubes into a vault in the basement.

The croupiers must observe a strict code of conduct. They are not allowed to accept social invitations or gifts, must have no contact with patrons outside the casino, and must not talk to strangers in the street. Each table is under the supervision of a chef de partie who keeps a sharp watch on both patrons and employees. The chefs de partie are watched, in their turn, by the casino's force of 50 plain-clothes detectives, who are double-checked by another special force of security men.

The casino's police force is completely independent from Monaco's police, though the two forces work in close harmony. Each day the names of all visitors to the casino are sent to the Sûreté Publique to be checked against the files of "wanted" and "convicted" men. If a gambler who was once caught cheating should return to the casino, the local force is notified and the visitor is tracked down and expelled from the principality.

In addition to its police force, the casino employs security men who are expert physiognomists. Their job is simply to watch the people. Should anyone on the casino's black list (for cheating, welshing on debts, etc.) try to get into the casino, one of these remarkable men will undoubtedly spot him. For many years the chief physiognomist at Monte Carlo was a Monsieur le Broq. Le Broq claimed to "know" at least 60,000 faces and could attach names to more than half that number. Unlike the police, his method was not to study the eyes or nose of his "victim," nor (particularly in the case of women) the hair. He maintained that the most identifiable characteristic of all was gait: And in thousands of cases he proved himself to be right.

Public gaming was made illegal in France in 1857. But once Monte Carlo's success became evident, the French people began to urge the government to change the law. In 1907 the government gave way: Public baccarat and chemin-de-fer games (but not roulette until 1933) were once again made legal. Immediately casinos began to spring up around the French coast—in particular at Le Touquet, Biarritz, Cannes, Nice, and Deauville. Of these, the casinos at Deauville and Cannes were probably the biggest threats to Monte Carlo's supremacy—and remain so.

Modern Deauville (like modern Monaco) was really created by its casino—which is an extremely large, lavish building, containing a cinema, a theatre, a restaurant seating more than 800 people, and an abundance of roulette, baccarat, and chemin-de-fer tables. The casino dominates the town: It controls the racecourse, subsidizes (among other things) regattas, tennis matches, pigeon shooting, and an air service.

The casino's size can be gauged, for example, by the fact that in one room alone there are 40 chemin-de-fer tables. (One of these has a *minimum* stake of the equivalent of $250.) Incidentally, the French government claims 65 per cent of the casino's gross takings, and the local principality takes 10 per cent.

Deauville's casino was founded in 1912 by Eugene Cornuché. Credit for its success, however, must be shared by three very different but very remarkable men: the French novelist Alexandre Dumas who lived and wrote at Deauville during the 1840s (he finished *The Count of Monte Cristo* there), and helped to make the resort fashionable; François André, a cooper's son who became Cornuché's partner; and Nico Zographos, a member of the legendary Greek Syndicate whose presence at Deauville attracted many of the world's top gamblers. (André and Zographos will be discussed in Chapter 13.) Incidentally, one of these distinguished visiting gamblers is supposed to have created a custom at Deauville. This was the Polish pianist Paderewski who sat down one night and played Chopin's Funeral March after losing heavily at roulette. Evidently this appealed to the management's imagination, and continuous music has been the rule ever since.

Cannes was a small seaside village before 1834—when a British minister of state, Lord Brougham, was held up there by an outbreak of cholera. He found the place enchanting, built a villa, and suggested to Napoleon III that Cannes would be an ideal place to build a harbor (an enterprise that Napoleon undertook). Once Lord Brougham's villa was ready, many of his friends began to visit him there. Soon it became fashionable to spend the winter in Cannes.

Each day before a casino opens, every single piece of equipment in the gaming rooms is carefully checked—the croupiers' rakes, the chemin-de-fer shoes, and the roulette balls are inspected, and (far left) the roulette wheels are tested for balance with a spirit level. Croupiers then lay out the chips ceremonially (left) to ensure that none is missing, that they are all clean, and that no counterfeits were used the day before. The shape and color of chips vary with the value—for example, white chips are generally used for placing high bets. Right, a Baden-Baden croupier checks the silver chips. Below, a chemin-de-fer table at Brighton casino, England, showing the positions of players and employees.

Valet   Chip changer   Croupier   Valet   Supervisor

| Faro | On "last turn"=$16\frac{1}{4}$% | Trente et Quarante | On a *refait* at 31 |

On "splits"=2%

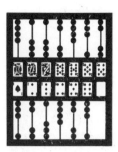

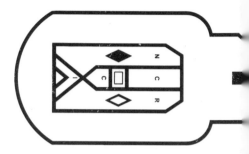

| Craps | From about $\frac{3}{5}$% to $27\frac{3}{11}$% | Roulette | American wheels
=from $5\frac{5}{19}$% to $7\frac{17}{19}$%
European wheels
=from $1\frac{13}{37}$% to $2\frac{16}{37}$% |

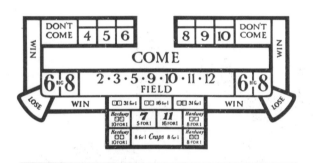

| Blackjack | From about 6%
to about $21\frac{1}{2}$% | Baccarat | From about $\frac{1}{5}$%
to about $6\frac{1}{4}$% |

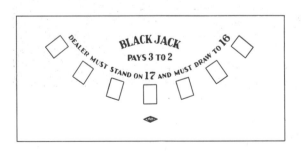

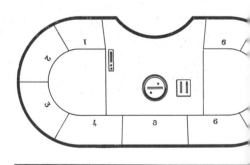

Casino operators cannot depend on luck for their profits; they must have a better chance than the players of winning each bet, to be sure of making a profit in the long run. Therefore casinos usually take "house percentages"—by paying winners at less than the true odds. Of course, percentages vary from casino to casino and from game to game. These diagrams show the range of percentages on seven popular casino games. Faro seems most favorable for players, since it is only on two kinds of bet—"last turn" and "splits" (see p. 169)—that the house takes a percentage. In other games the house has an edge on every bet—sometimes a very large one at that.

Carnival wheel   From about 40% to about 95%

Slowly the town began to expand. In 1900 Grand Duke Michael of Russia financed the building of a large hotel (the Carlton) and two casinos (the Municipal and the Palm Beach). In addition, he built himself an enormous house (which has since been turned into an apartment block), established a Russian Church, and planned a golf course. Today Cannes is particularly popular as a holiday resort. But its casino remains a very important one: When the Greek Syndicate took over the control of Cannes casino, they ensured its pre-eminent position—alongside their creations at Le Touquet and Deauville.

The French casinos are among the most fashionable and well known in Europe, but their prominence is rivaled by similar gambling centers in other countries. Portugal, for example, has a number of flourishing casinos (there is a particularly fine one at Estoril), as has Italy (notably at San Remo, Venice, and Rome); and there is an exceptional casino open all the year at Salzburg in Austria. And, of course, Germany has long been the home of major gambling centers; it was at Homburg that François Blanc made his first fortune.

Today, Baden-Baden has become the most fashionable casino in Germany, for Homburg (as will be seen in a moment) ceased to exist as an important gambling center at midnight on December 31, 1872. Baden-Baden's casino is also the oldest in Germany (it has been in existence for more than 200 years), though the present buildings were designed only 100 years ago at the instigation of the French holder of the gambling concession, Edouard Bénazet. Of course, more gaming rooms, bars, and so on have been added in recent years.

Like many of Europe's gambling centers, Baden-Baden was initially famous as a health resort. (Its waters were as popular with the Romans 2000 years ago as they are with visitors today.) But the casino was really responsible for making the town fashionable and for attracting such diverse personalities as Kaiser William I, Bismarck, Dostoevski, Alfred de Musset, Berlioz, and Brahms. Today Baden-Baden is a necessary stop for Europe's peripatetic casino gamblers—especially during the festivities of the International Racing Week.

Homburg's story (as I intimated earlier) is less happy. Before 1872, Homburg was pre-eminent among German resorts: Louis and François Blanc had succeeded in transforming it from an obscure and dirty village into a splendid town with a *Kursaal* (casino) that had inlaid floors, mirrored walls, and a fine bas-relief ceiling.

Contemporary accounts suggest that Homburg was the most serene of all 19th-century European gambling centers. One Englishman who visited the Kursaal in 1868 wrote: "He who goes to Homburg expecting to see some melodramatic manifestations of rage, disappointment, and despair in the losing players reckons without his host. Winners or losers seldom speak above a whisper; and the only sounds to be heard above the suppressed buzz of conversation, the muffled jingle of the money, the sweep of the croupiers' rakes, and the ticking of the very ornate French clocks, are the impassively metallic voices of the banker. People are too genteel at Homburg to scream, to yell, or to fall into fainting fits."

But, respectable or not, Homburg didn't escape the Prussian government's edict that all gaming houses should be suppressed on January 1, 1873. Ems and Wissbaden (the two German gambling centers most nearly approaching Homburg in fame and style) closed in October 1872; Homburg closed in December. Tourists from all over Europe came to witness the town's last days. Dostoevski, who was one of the tourists, wrote: "The façade was still bright, and the town affected a lighthearted appearance which revealed none of the sadness of the approaching end. Neither the company nor the populace appeared ready to admit defeat. One would have supposed that they knew full well they could deal with the government of Bismarck as easily as they had with that of the Landgrave. But it was not possible—it could never be possible. Homburg must sink again into its former torpor."

An excessively cruel winter did nothing to deter the hordes of visitors who flowed into the town. Theatre and concert halls were packed and players in the casino were betting on an unparalleled scale. On the last night (December 31, 1872) crowds lined the gaming rooms from wall to wall. At 11.55 P.M. the

croupier on the big roulette table announced dramatically "Messieurs, à la dernière." The table was immediately covered with chips, gold, and bank notes for the last turn.

The croupier spun the wheel and then, as it slowed to a standstill, called out "Vingt, noir, pair, et passe." There was no more play.

Blanc, of course, was present. He found the occasion poignant, and refused to hand the keys of the Kursaal over to the authorities until the superintendent of police had been sent for. But by midnight he had ceded his creation—except for the theatre, the waxworks, the gasworks, the restaurant, and the railway. He sold these a few days later, and added another million to his fortune.

London's fame as a gambling center dates back to the mid-18th century when gaming clubs like Almacks, White's, Brooks's, and the Cocoa Tree first became fashionable. But the peak of this fame was not reached until some 50 years later, with the founding of a new club (in 1827) by a one-time fishmonger and free-lance gambler named William Crockford. And though many of the old clubs still enjoy wide reputations among gamblers today, Crockford's remains the most internationally famous.

William Crockford's career was a remarkable one from start to finish. He had been a fishmonger of Fleet Street with a sideline in bookmaking and such small-scale swindles as the three-card trick. In 1816 he bought a quarter-share in a gambling tavern in St. James's. But Crockford realized that this tavern could only have a limited success. He knew that the most popular clubs (like White's and Brooks's) were popular because they were selective, and that if he wanted to compete with them he would have to plan on a much grander scale, and go all out to get the top people as members. And William Crockford certainly wanted to compete.

Accordingly, he bought four adjoining houses around the corner in St. James's Street (a very fashionable area of London), decorated them lavishly, offered the finest foods and wines at very reasonable prices, and enrolled a number of distinguished members. Among the first of these were the Duke of Wellington

Inside Crockford's Gaming Club, London. Far left, the grand spiral staircase that leads to the roulette, chemin-de-fer, bridge, and poker rooms on the first and second floors. Left, croupiers take up positions for the start of an evening's roulette session. (Play starts at 5 P.M.) Far right, one of the high-stake chemin-de-fer tables. The seat charge on this particular table is £5 ($14) per shoe.

and Lord Chesterfield (who gained the place early notoriety by losing the equivalent of $115,000 in a single seven-hour *hazard* session). Not long after, Lord Rivers, Lord Sefton, and Lord Grenville joined and added to the club's reputation by losing the equivalent of nearly $500,000 each in an evening.

Big stakes were common in London games, but there was something about Crockford himself (apart from the splendor of his club, the titled company, and the fascination of watching big-time gambling) that attracted members, and gained their confidence. He allowed heavy debts (he is said to have been owed the equivalent of $1,000,000 at one time) and was scrupulously attentive to the demands of secrecy. This was made quite clear when (in the early 1840s) he was called before the House of Commons Committee on Gaming Houses, for he adamantly refused to answer questions about his members, saying: "I do not feel myself at liberty to divulge the pursuits of private gentlemen." But apparently his stout defense of his members (many of whom were important members of parliament, including Disraeli, the prime minister) was of no avail. The Committee legalized entry by the police into "any gaming house on a request being presented by any two householders." This clearly meant the end of the kind of privacy that members had previously enjoyed.

Four days after the decision (on May 25, 1844) William Crockford died, at the age of 69. He left behind a fortune estimated at the equivalent of $5,000,000. After his death, the club faded into obscurity. But it was resuscitated nearly 100 years later as a bridge club; and more recently (as we will see shortly) it rose to fame again as an opulent, high-class gaming club.

London's fame as a gambling center diminished after the middle of the 19th century; but despite the new laws, the two great clubs of the 18th century, White's and Brooks's struggled on. At White's, especially, bets had always been made on every conceivable event. Members bet on births, deaths, marriages, on the length of individual lives, the duration of ministries, the name of a mistress, and most natural phenomena. In one of his letters, the English writer Horace Walpole wrote of a member of White's staff who, "on coming into the club on the morning of the earthquake [in 1750] and hearing bets laid whether shock was caused by an earthquake or the blowing up of the powder-mills, went away in horror, protesting they were such an impious set that he believed if the last trump were to sound they would bet puppet-show against Judgement."

The fact that, in White's, piety played second fiddle to enthusiasm is underlined in another letter of Walpole's: "A man dropped down at the door of White's; he was carried into the house. Was he dead or not? The odds were immediately given and taken for and against. It was proposed to bleed him. Those who had taken odds that the man was dead protested that the use of a lancet would affect the fairness of the bet; he was therefore left to himself and presently died—to the great satisfaction of those who had bet for that event."

Since the 1960 Betting and Gaming Act (which legalized many continental games that had previously been banned in Britain) a great number of gambling clubs have sprung up in modern Britain—particularly in London. (The *Sunday Mirror* recently estimated that the equivalent of about $750,000 changed hands nightly in London's West End alone.) These clubs vary considerably in size and intention: Some are small combined drinking and gaming clubs (drab but usually honest); a few, though they make a pretense at luxury, are completely crooked (with rigged roulette and loaded dice); others are thoroughly reputable high-class clubs, run with all the strict propriety and meticulous attention to detail that characterizes the big French casinos. Into this last category come clubs like Aspinall's, Les Ambassadeurs, Quents, the River Club, Almack's, White's, Brooks's and, of course, the new Crockford's (now removed to premises in Carlton House Terrace).

Today, Crockford's has nearly 2500 members. It is estimated that approximately $75,000,000 is staked annually at the tables and that the nightly profit to the proprietors is about $4500. (Under the new Act, proprietors may not take a percentage of the money staked at their tables. But they can charge seat money.) Two very successful innovations at Crockford's are the new chemin-de-fer tables (which earned the club a gross profit of about $500,000 in their first four months) and the even newer roulette table (used for the first time in October 1963). The introduction of roulette at Crockford's raised some tricky legal questions: Roulette played in the continental manner (i.e., with the zero giving the bank a favorable percentage) contravenes the 1960 Act, which states that roulette is only legal providing that the game is so conducted that the chances therein are equally favorable to all players.

Many clubs have avoided the problem by employing roulette wheels without zeros, relying mainly on seat money for their profits. This often proves extremely costly, for there is nothing to stop players with unlimited capital from doubling up their stakes indefinitely. (Some clubs have imposed low house limits, but this drives away the big-time gamblers.) Crockford's, however, has found another way of presenting roulette legally. To get into the roulette room, members must pay an entrance fee equaling $2.80 for which they are given a ticket that has printed on it the words, "This portion has to be handed to the croupier if participation in the draw for the bank is desired." This gives players the opportunity to hold the bank if they so wish (they rarely do) and offers each player a completely equal chance. And to ensure that the game is run with a maximum of efficiency, seven croupiers have been imported from France at a cost of over $1800 a week in wages.

New Orleans was America's first big gambling center: It was in New Orleans that the famous gamblers who flourished before the American Civil War learned the tricks of their trade, and it was New Orleans that started the gambling fever that swept like wildfire throughout the United States after the war. New Orleans, in fact, was a gambling town from its earliest beginnings in 1718, with all its coffee houses and taverns providing rooms and tables for private gaming.

As the town prospered and grew, the number of gambling houses grew accordingly, despite attempts by provincial governors to check the "corruption." Eventually (in 1811) a law was passed prohibiting gambling anywhere in the state; but gambling houses continued to flourish underground. In 1823, the municipal authorities, desperate for money, persuaded the legislature to compromise and pass a law permitting New Orleans to license six gambling houses at $5000 a year each—the money to go toward a hospital and a college.

This led to the establishment of the earliest of the large gambling houses that were to dominate the American gambling scene. The first (and most famous) of these houses was started in 1827 by an entrepreneur named John Davis. Davis's extremely lavish gambling house was open day and night (there was even a branch house open at week ends); he supplied gamblers with the finest food and wine free of charge, provided expert croupiers and private rooms for "aristocratic" gamblers. The games played were *faro*, roulette, *vingt-et-un*, *brag*, *écarte*, *boston*, and *blackjack*.

Davis's virtual monopoly of New Orleans gambling came to an end in 1832, with the removal of the restriction on the number of gambling licenses that could be issued. Very soon there was a great number of flourishing rival establishments. Gambling, in fact, so dominated life in New Orleans that a few years later, in an attempt to restore some sense of moral conduct to the city, the state of Louisiana revoked all the gambling license laws and made gambling of every kind illegal.

But the war that broke out between the United States and Mexico in 1846 brought troops in thousands through New Orleans and, though gambling was still officially forbidden, it was soon flourishing throughout the city. Wholesale bribery and blackmail of politicians and police kept the saloons open, and by the end of 1850 there were over 500 "sawdust joints" where card and craps games could be played 24 hours a day. Most of these water-front shacks (they

In Las Vegas, America's gambling capital, most hotels are glorified casinos, almost every store (even the airport) has a bank of slot machines, and gambling goes on for 24 hours a day. The favorite games are craps, blackjack, and "slots." Far left, the dealer hands the dice to the shooter in a craps game; left, the slot machines (different models take anything from a cent to a dollar). Right, cards are dealt in a game of blackjack. Below, Fermont Street, with its myriad of casinos and gambling rooms where owners use any advertising technique to draw clients—even offering winners take-away slot machines.

Las Vegas promoters dream up every conceivable gimmick to keep people gambling. Several casinos have slot machines designed like actual "one-armed bandits" (left), with masks and guns. Such relatively inexpensive pleasures as swimming or sun bathing might keep gamblers away from the tables, so one hotel has instituted a poolside craps table (right) and roulette on the terrace (far right).

could hardly be called casinos) were completely corrupt, and honest games of craps could be found only in private homes.

New Orleans was the precursor of many of America's other notorious early gambling centers. Of those other towns, Chicago (which by 1840 had become just as unhealthy as New Orleans) was typical. In 10 years it had grown from a shanty town into a minor city, and its gambling activities were growing at the same rate. The historian John Quinn gives this picture of early Chicago: "Its particular fame as a gambling center rested on the fact that it was filled with a set of sharpers drawn from all quarters of the United States, comprising as motley, disreputable, and dishonest a class as ever cursed any city under the face of heaven. Wealthy suckers were found in abundance, and 'brace' dealers, 'bunko' men, and rogues of every description carried off money in bundles. It is not surprising that the characteristically excitable, speculative, and eager people of America descended on the city from thousands of miles distance in order to satisfy their addiction to gambling. Theirs was the thrill and the misery, the city's was the fame."

It seems a long step from the seedy water-front gambling houses of early New Orleans and Chicago to Las Vegas, the glittering show-place of modern American gambling. But in fact Las Vegas too (for all its present magnificence) was created by hoodlums and underworld gangsters who remained deeply entrenched there until as recently as 1947. But more of this in a moment.

Today, Las Vegas is the world's biggest gambling center. Most of its gambling activities are carried on in "The Strip," the six-lane highway that extends outside the city's limits past lines of neon-lit hotels, casinos, and restaurants. Unlike the casinos of Europe, Las Vegas's big casinos are always parts of hotels: And these hotels are the height of luxury. They contain magnificent bars, night clubs, swimming pools, restaurants, gift shops, and gaming rooms. (You can eat and drink at your table and even, at some hotels, telephone directly from your table

to your stockbroker or banker.) There is everything, in fact, to encourage visitors to stay and gamble. For gambling is the be-all and end-all of life in Las Vegas, and play at the tables stops only for one half-minute in the whole year—at the first stroke of midnight on New Year's Eve.

Las Vegas (the name is Spanish for "the meadows") was originally a camping ground for travelers making their way across the desert from Santa Fe to California. There was no real settlement until 1885, when 30 young men were sent by the government to Las Vegas to "build a fort there to protect immigrants and Indians and teach the latter how to raise corn, wheat, and potatoes." But the young men didn't stay long, and the area remained uninhabited until it was announced that a new railroad was to be built through Las Vegas to the southwest. On May 15, 1905, a land auction was held and in two days 2000 lots of land were sold at a total price of $265,000. Soon a huge tent city had grown up, and these tents provided Las Vegas's first saloons and gambling houses.

In 1931 the state of Nevada legalized gambling, but though Las Vegas had its share of small gambling houses (and still does) there were no luxury hotels or casinos until 1946. In that year the notorious New York gang leader and speculator Benjamin "Bugsy" Siegel opened a club called the Flamingo on what was then a three-mile desert strip between Las Vegas and McCarren airport. (The desert didn't worry Siegel, who filled 40 acres of it with imported lawns, cork trees, live flamingos, and artificial ponds.) Siegel had already made one unsuccessful attempt to beat the existing gambling laws by opening casinos on luxury ships at anchor just over three miles off the coast of Southern California. He reasoned that because the ships were floating in international waters they were not bound to obey the gambling laws. But California's governor Earl Warren tightened the laws so that they unquestionably covered ships at sea too, and Siegel was forced to plan his gambling haven elsewhere. He turned to Las Vegas, on the assumption that if wealthy patrons were prepared to go out to sea to gamble, they wouldn't be put off by a journey into the desert—providing legality was assured, and transport and accommodation were comfortable. And as it turned out, he was absolutely right.

Siegel's reign in Las Vegas was short-lived. A year after the opening of the Flamingo he was murdered (presumably by a rival gang) and it wasn't long before his successor, Gus Greenbaum, suffered the same fate. Alarmed by evidence of the underworld's power in Las Vegas, the Gaming Control Board decided that it was high time they took firmer control. They made it a law that all casino owners must apply to the State Tax Commission for a license.

But Las Vegas had been launched, and nothing could check its progress. Once the Flamingo had proved itself a success, other hotels began to spring up. In 1950 the Desert Inn was opened, in 1952 the Sahara and the Sands, and by 1956 there were 12 luxury hotels with casinos along the Strip. All of these have large gambling rooms with a generous number of craps, blackjack, roulette, and faro tables. In 1961 the *Saturday Evening Post* estimated that Las Vegas has over 9,000,000 visitors each year. It gave the area's annual profits (as reported for tax purposes) as $107,000,000—compared to $50,000,000 in 1954; and it concluded that "you could live like a prince in Venice and gamble every night for a month for the price of a week in Las Vegas."

To the Las Vegas casino men, gambling is an industry, and they treat it as such. (To pay running expenses alone, the big casinos must win $25,000 daily—

Under-cover gambling may go on in many jails, but in Nevada State Prison (U.S.A.) an officially approved gambling center flourishes. The hours of play are carefully regulated, guards supervise, and prisoners with good records are appointed dealers. Left, a poker game in progress. Players draw "brass" (specially minted octagonal coins, below) from their prison accounts, which they redeem for real money when their sentences are up. Right, a craps game in the "bull-pen"—the long, low hall where all prison gambling takes place.

which means that approximately $130,000 must be gambled at their tables each day.) Money is spent to bring money in on a scale that François Blanc would have never thought possible. Some hotels run free air flights, some have their own fleet of planes, others (like the Tropicana) place a Rolls Royce car at the disposal of special guests. (At the Flamingo, you can even get married in the front-lawn chapel.) And all the top hotels spend fortunes to get the world's biggest stars to perform at their night clubs.

Should you want a break from gambling, or from watching other people gamble, Las Vegas has a great deal more to offer in the way of entertainment. At all the top hotels you can move from lounge to lounge, drinking and listening to music, you can eat a porterhouse steak in a restaurant and be entertained by top stars like Peggy Lee, Frank Sinatra, Sammy Davis Jr., and Lena Horne; you can swim in the hotel pools or walk around the two miles of town or along the Strip. And when you feel like gambling again you will be made more than welcome at any one of 40 casinos, all in the Monte Carlo class as far as the stakes are concerned—or at any of the more than 100 smaller, less expensive ones in the town.

For Las Vegas's casino proprietors have learned one thing: Gamblers like to be recognized as important, and they like to have their money taken from them in style. And this is exactly what happens to the majority of Las Vegas's over-optimistic visitors.

13 Famous gamblers

Of the hundreds of famous names who could be included in this chapter because of their gambling activities, I can make only an arbitrary choice. So, like most anthologists, I am presenting the ones that seem to me particularly interesting because of both their fame and their gambles. Most of the names to be mentioned here are famous for reasons other than gambling; they are, to be precise, the names of famous people who gambled.   There have been few full-time professional gamblers who have gained fame (or, for that matter, notoriety) outside their gambling circles. Nick the Greek, whose professional activities were described in Chapter 11, is an exception: Many non-professional or even non-gambler Americans know of him. But there are a number of other men in the gambling fraternities of Las Vegas who are as well known to other professionals as Nick the Greek, but whose names would mean nothing to the rest of the world.

There have been plenty of people, however, whose names are practically household words in most corners of the world and who were avid gamblers. Some of these names take us back centuries into antiquity: For example, thanks to a great many novels, plays, films, and potted histories, very few people can have escaped hearing about Julius Caesar and his young friend Mark Antony. Not only were they Roman rulers and important historical figures; they were also gamblers who (according to the ancient historian Plutarch) spent much of their leisure time playing dice or sortilege games, betting on cockfights, and so on.

Many of the heroes of the historic American West were not only gunfighters and adventurers, but professional gamblers as well. Luke Short, a renowned dandy and ladies' man, was a top gunman in the rough days of Tombstone, Arizona, and a dealer in saloon gambling hells.

Left, Wyatt Earp (photographed in 1885). Modern film and television programs have immortalized his exploits as a marshal and gunfighter in the American West during the 1870s and 80s. But Earp was almost as famous for his skill with cards and dice as for his skill with a gun.

Dodge City, Kansas (where Earp was marshal), was one of the most notorious of the wide-open cattle towns and gambling "hells" of the Old West. Right, customers pose during a quiet moment in the Long Branch Saloon—scene of many killings.

As I have indicated throughout this book, Roman history contains countless stories of the gambling activities of important Romans, including emperors. The emperor Claudius was so obsessed with dice games that he had the interior of his carriage altered to enable him to throw dice while traveling. A skit on the death of Claudius, by the Roman dramatist Seneca, represented the late emperor in hell, condemned for ever to pick up dice and try to shake them in a cup without a bottom.

Nero, who succeeded Claudius, was equally obsessed with dice; He often staked sums up to 400,000 *sestertii* (the equivalent of about $50,000) on one throw. The mad emperor Caligula gambled constantly, and had the nasty habit of replenishing his losses by arresting or executing wealthy citizens (on trumped-up charges or none at all) and confiscating their wealth.

A considerable number of monarchs in later history managed nearly to rival the Roman emperors in their addiction to gambling. Henry VIII of England was mentioned back in Chapter 1 as having gambled for and lost some immense church bells from the City of London. And gambling was one of the principal pastimes in the court of France's Louis XIV (thanks largely to Cardinal Mazarin, who introduced a great many games, including *hoca*).

Heavy gambling would seem to have an obvious place in the pleasure-filled lives that we attribute (rightly or wrongly) to the wealthy, leisured kings and aristocrats of the past. But a roster of famous gambling names can draw from other walks of life as well: from the ranks of great and dedicated writers, for instance, such as Dostoevski or Montaigne; or from the ranks of equally great

and dedicated scientists such as Cardan or Descartes. And famous gamblers can also be found among legendary folk heroes—especially the heroes of America's Old West, like the famous gunfighter and marshal Wyatt Earp.

Earp's exploits as a defender of law and order have been embellished over the years with fiction, but his skill as a gambler was certainly fact. His salary as a marshal was only a fraction of the income he made from his ability as a card player—and from an "Oriental Saloon and Gambling House" in Tombstone, Arizona, which he partly owned. (One of the dealers in that same saloon was Earp's friend, the gunfighter and card sharp Doc Holliday).

Another Western gunman whose activities in the 1860s and 1870s have become legendary was Wild Bill Hickok. Like Wyatt Earp, Wild Bill was a sheriff for some time, and his exploits have also received a lot of fictional exaggeration. And he, too, was a prolific gambler. In fact, he died while playing *poker* in a saloon at Deadwood, Dakota, when (for probably the first time in his career) he was seated with his back to the door. About halfway through the game a "tin-horn" gambler named Jack McCall came into the saloon, drew a gun, and shot Hickok in the back of the head. (McCall, it turned out, had been hired as an assassin by a group of crooked gamblers who were afraid that Hickok was going to be appointed marshal of Deadwood—which would apparently have been hard on their business.) Hickok had just drawn cards when he was shot, and friends who picked up the cards found that he had drawn a pair of aces and a pair of eights. Ever since then, aces and eights have been called, by poker players, the "dead man's hand."

For contrast we can leave the wild and woolly American frontier saloons for the elegant and fashionable *salons* of European society. Through these sophisticated circles, taking full advantage of the 18th century's gambling frenzy, moved one of the most famous gamblers of any time and place: the Italian adventurer, rogue, and great lover Casanova.

His full name was Giacomo Jacopo Casanova de Seingalt; he was a wanderer who traveled from city to city (Venice, Greece, Paris, Berlin, London, Madrid, etc.) as the mood took him—or as discretion warranted. And everywhere he went (as he says in his *Memoirs*) "pleasure, gaming, and idleness were my usual companions."

It is remarkable, considering the extent of his travels and adventures (amorous and otherwise), that Casanova ever found time to sit down at a gaming table. But, in fact, gambling was his living. At the age of 20, he writes, "I had to earn my living in one way or another, and I decided on the profession of gamester." Within a week he was completely penniless; but by some judicious borrowing he managed to retrieve his fortunes. This sudden plunge from affluence into poverty was a regular occurrence throughout Casanova's gambling life. Still, he was both ingenious and unscrupulous enough to find invariably some way to get back on his feet. All in all, he won more often than he lost—a fact that makes one of his recent biographers hint that he seemed "a little too lucky at the gaming tables."

Faro was his favorite game; but then it was the favorite of practically all society gamblers and pleasure-seekers of the time. Around 1750, for instance, according to the *Memoirs*, a faro bank at Lyons took in about 300,000 francs during a few days. When Casanova was holding the bank, he was usually successful. But once in Venice, in a gambling house where only noblemen had the privilege of holding the bank, he lost 5000 sequins (gold pieces) in a day or two. As usual, of course, he recouped his losses—or, rather, his mistress of the day, gambling with her own money, recouped them for him.

Left, gambling in the 1880s at one of the rougher saloons in Pecos, Texas. The seated man wearing a white hat was a small-time cardsharp and gunman; apparently he was oblivious to the fact that the term then used by cheating gamblers for the victim they intended to fleece was "the man in the white hat."

Right, a portrait of the 18th-century Italian adventurer, gambler, and author Casanova de Seingalt, which appeared after his death on the cover of new editions of his novel *Edoardo ed Elizabetta*. Far right, a contemporary caricature of Casanova (entitled "Casanova the card player"), from the 11th volume of his famous *Memoirs*.

Another time, when Casanova's luck had temporarily run out, a lady came to his aid in a different way:

"I played on the martingale [the doubling-up system described on page 221], but with such bad luck that I was soon left without a sequin. I was obliged to tell [the lady] of my losses, and it was at her request that I sold all her diamonds, losing what I got for them. . . . I still gamed, but for small stakes, waiting for the slow return of good luck."

As an adventurer, Casanova's most notable exploit was his swashbuckling escape from a Venice prison after he had been arrested as a spy. But the high point of his career as a gambler was his role in organizing a government lottery in Paris in the 1760s. A French nobleman wanted 20,000,000 francs from the king for a military school. The king favored the idea of the school, but wanted to avoid either emptying the treasury or increasing taxes. Casanova heard about the need, and presented an idea for a lottery. (The idea was not original with him; he had taken it from an acquaintance, who became his partner.)

At first the authorities doubted whether such a scheme would work. But Casanova insisted that, not only would the people gamble heavily on such a lottery, but the king would be sure to make a profit. (The lottery had to be the king's rather than privately owned, to forestall any possible doubt of its honesty.) The idea was finally accepted, and Casanova and his associates were hired as officers of the crown to organize the lottery. Several ticket-selling offices were set up, and Casanova ran one of these himself:

"With the idea of drawing custom to my office, I gave notice that all winning tickets bearing my signature would be paid at my office in twenty-four hours after the drawing. This drew crowds to my office and considerably increased my profits. . . . A number of the clerks in the other offices were foolish enough to complain to Calsabigi [his partner] that I had spoilt their gains, but he sent them about their business telling them that to get the better of me they had only to do as I did—if they had the money.

Left, an engraving of George "Beau" Brummell, the 19th-century British society dandy and gambler. Right, the crowded gaming room of Brooks's Club, London, where Brummell gambled regularly (depicted in a satirical cartoon by his contemporary, the artist George Cruikshank).

"My first taking amounted to forty thousand francs. An hour after the drawing my clerk brought me the numbers, and showed me that we had from seventeen to eighteen thousand francs to pay, for which I gave him the necessary funds.

"The total receipts [from the first day, throughout France] amounted to two millions, and the administration made a profit of six hundred thousand francs, of which Paris alone had contributed a hundred thousand francs. This was well enough for a first attempt."

Since Casanova's time, his name has become (like Don Juan's) a synonym for a successful seducer of women. In the 19th century, Britain produced a man who might have rivaled Casanova both as a social lion and as a gambler, and whose name has also become invariably associated with a particular field of interest—not women this time, but clothing. His name was Beau Brummell.

George Bryan Brummell was the son of a rich man who had been private secretary to a British peer. He had a top-grade education at Eton and Oxford and later went into the army, in which he befriended the Prince Regent. With his lively wit and fine taste in clothes, and the private fortune he inherited from his father, he soon established himself as an important figure in early 19th-century high society. Among other things, he was the one man permitted to treat the Prince Regent with disdain and rudeness in public.

Brummell belonged to White's and Brooks's Clubs and regularly gambled there for high stakes, careless of whether he won or lost so long as the company was good and he could enjoy the conversation—which meant, for the most part, his own. But there were occasions when his companions got in the last word. One evening, for instance, when he was playing *hazard* at Brooks's Club, his opponent was a brewer named Alderman Combe, a great gambler who was said to make as much money at gambling as he did at brewing. Brummell was casting the dice and said to Combe: "Come, Mash-tub, what do you set?"

"I'll have a pony," Combe said. (A "pony" in the gambling slang of the time was 25 guineas—the equivalent of $70.)

"I'll drive your ponies home twenty-five times running," Brummell said. And, according to the story, he proceeded to make 25 consecutive winning throws of the dice. When he pocketed his winnings he bowed low to Combe and said, "Thank you, Alderman. For the future I shall never drink any porter but yours."

"I wish," Combe replied, "that every blackguard in London would tell me the same."

At White's Club was a member named Bligh, who was believed to be mad; he had periods of suicidal depression alternating with states of euphoria. But he was an excellent gambler and very good company in his happier moments (though a somewhat disturbing companion in his black moods). Brummell, playing at the same table as Bligh one night, lost 1000 guineas and, pretending to be tragically affected, called to the waiter: "Waiter, bring me a flat candlestick and a pistol. I'll light my way to death." Whereupon Bligh, who was sitting opposite to him, calmly produced two loaded pistols from his coat pocket and laid them on the table.

"Mr. Brummell," he said, "if you are really desirous to put a period to your existence, I am happy to offer you the means without troubling the waiter."

Brummell's popularity as a socialite at one time seemed inexhaustible. But the gambling that helped to keep him in the public eye ruined him financially. He was at last completely beggared, though for some time he managed to hold on with the help of funds raised on the mutual security of himself and his friends. Some of them were in no more flourishing condition than he was; but their names and expectations helped them to raise loans—at exorbitant interest. Brummell quarreled with the Prince Regent (no one has yet established the cause of the row); and finally he was forced to leave England because of other quarrels connected with the repayment of the interest on the loans he and his friends had raised. He went to France, where for a time he was British Consul in Caen, was imprisoned for debt for a short term in 1835, and lingered pitifully on till 1840 when he died in a madhouse at the age of 62.

During his spell in prison, when one of the few friends to take the trouble to visit him asked how he had come to such a state, Brummell gave a true gambler's answer. He referred to a "lucky charm" that he had once had—a coin with a hole in it, which he had been given as a schoolboy at Eton. "An old woman for whom I performed some trifling service gave it to me with the injunction to take good care of it, for as long as I did good fortune would attend me. Good fortune did in fact attend me, until the evil hour when I gave the coin in error to a hackney-coachman; after that—a complete reverse."

Turning now to a few famous names that were prominent in the 20th century's gambling world:

André Citroen, the French automobile manufacturer, seemed to use gambling as a spectacular form of publicity stunt. He was an unquestionably brilliant designer and a staunch believer in the future of the automobile even in the early days of this century (when only a few farsighted people saw anything but comedy in the internal combustion engine). Yet it might be said that his fame and reputation rested as much on his flair for publicity as on anything else.

His career was crowded with elaborate and dramatic *coups* of publicity: Once he managed to persuade the authorities to let him light up the Eiffel Tower with his name; he often got kings, actors, famous bands, and even clergy to attend the previews of his motor shows; he gained world-wide attention by sending Citroen cars on expeditions across the Sahara; and one night in 1926 he went on playing *baccarat* for the sole purpose of being able to have it published that he had achieved one of the biggest single-session losses in the history of the game. The loss was 13,000,000 francs (the equivalent then of about $500,000); and as a consequence it became necessary for Citroen to call in the banks to take over his firm. But a man with his energy and resilience couldn't stay down for long. He immediately raised the output of his factory, planned a new sales campaign that included America, and was quickly back on his feet again financially.

Throughout his life Citroen dearly loved to mix with the rich and famous—or perhaps I should say with other rich and famous. It was for this reason that he gambled, for the casino at Deauville was always packed with the sort of people that he delighted to rub shoulders with. "I am not the least interested in the game," he once said, "nor in whether I win or lose. I am only interested in whether or not the amount is large enough to be noticed." Everything he did was to attract attention. He even managed to get Deauville to change the rule that only men should be allowed in the private baccarat room. He did this by arranging for his wife to gate-crash the saloon and to plead with Nico Zographos, the banker in the game, to stop her husband from going on after the ruinous losses he had suffered that evening.

In Citroen's heyday, his gambling activities made headline news. He had only to enter a casino with Paderewski or the Aga Khan to have the length of his baccarat session and the amount of his winnings or losses written about in every newspaper and glossy magazine in Europe. He was photographed and featured as one of the few men in Europe who could raise the bank to any limit he cared to set (it wasn't true, but it was good publicity); and his fabulous successes at the tables (which were many) were associated, by way of clever gossip writing, with the success of his products. He was often presented as a man who translated his gambling acumen into terms of motoring for the millions.

Perhaps because he had had so much publicity when he was alive, Citroen got little when he died in 1935. His business had crashed and been taken over by Michelin. One obituary gave him less than one column inch of space and attributed his business defeat to "gambling on the success of that most foolish of all inventions, the front-wheel drive." (He didn't invent the front-wheel drive, but he tried to popularize it in his 1934 models.) It was the only gamble that ever brought him bad publicity.

The wealthy British businessman and store owner Gordon Selfridge gambled widely and apparently enjoyed it greatly, though (like Citroen) he seems to have gambled because it was the socially correct thing for rich men to do, rather than

Far left, the French motor car tycoon André Citroen, a prodigious gambler (and loser) and a habitué of the Greek Syndicate's baccarat table at Deauville. Left, the French racing driver François Secot is greeted in Paris (in 1934) after his triumphant 3125-mile drive through France and Belgium in a Citroen car. He covered the distance in a record 77 hours.

Right, the British department-store owner and gambler Gordon Selfridge, with the Dolly Sisters (in white) and his daughter in 1926.

because he was addicted to gambling. But Selfridge's protégées, who were known everywhere as the Dolly Sisters, were gamblers to the heart—mostly on Selfridge's money. The sisters (whose real names were Janzieska and Roszieska Deutsch) were Hungarian vaudeville and cabaret artists who had been spotted by the American impresario Flo Ziegfeld in 1911 and had been given a chance in his *Follies* of that year. Later they came to London and were seen in cabaret by Selfridge, who invited them to visit him at his villa at Deauville.

They paid their visit, which lasted nearly a quarter of a century, and during that time they gambled away the equivalent of nearly $8,000,000. They often won as well, of course, and put their winnings into jewelry, villas, and a boutique in the Champs Elysées; but most of these had to be sold at one time or another when they were suffering a losing streak.

Of the Dolly sisters, Selfridge's particular devotion went to Jenny; but when he bought sizeable interests in the casinos at Le Touquet and Deauville he allowed both of them unlimited credit. And not only that: When they had lost the equivalent of $10,000 or $15,000 at a single sitting of baccarat (they often lost that much in the first few minutes' play) he would send them diamonds "to compensate for your losses, my darlings."

Eventually, Selfridge's personal losses at the casinos, plus the losses of the Dolly Sisters (and of another of his girl friends, the actress Gaby Deslys) ruined him and his business. At the age of 83 he went bankrupt, though he claimed that his failure was due to the slump of 1930. He was a considerable showman who knew how to apply publicity methods to his business and make them work; but in his personal relationships he was on less safe ground.

Jenny also went bankrupt after Selfridge reached the financial stage when he could no longer pay her gambling debts. Her biggest win had been the equivalent of nearly $400,000 in a single session of baccarat; but her biggest loss was physical rather than financial. She was in a car accident that left her disfigured; and later she was the victim of an attack by a violent burglar who blinded her with pepper when she discovered him robbing her Chicago home. She was brought to such a state of despair by all these tragedies that she killed herself.

In the last years of the 19th century and the early years of the 20th, American gambling was dominated by men who were usually as rich, or richer, than Selfridge or Citroen, and whose exploits at the gaming tables of New York, Chicago, New Orleans, and elsewhere have never been rivaled since. Losses of $25,000 on a single hand of cards or roll of dice were considered fairly commonplace in the gambling houses of these cities; many of the tycoons who frequented these houses uncomplainingly lost hundreds of thousands a year. These men were top industrialists, financiers, stock marketeers, and multimillionaires; among them were such internationally famous names as the young heir to a fortune Reginald Vanderbilt, the industrialist Henry C. Frick, and the judge (later, the steel magnate) Elbert H. Gary.

One figure seems to have been especially predominant in this world of tycoon gambling—a man whose name was respectably associated with Wall Street and the high echelons of the steel industry, but whose nickname proved his eminence among gamblers: John W. "Bet-a-million" Gates.

Gates was unquestionably one of the great gamblers of all time. He would quite literally bet any amount on anything against anybody. He would play poker with an upward limit on bets of $50,000 as readily as with a limit of one dollar; he would play *bridge* for $1000 a point. Once he was invited to play poker with some overconfident gamblers who felt that their purse of $35,000 was quite a considerable basis for a protracted session of play. Gates shocked them by suggesting that they toss a coin for the whole amount. If no cards, dice, *roulette* wheels, etc., were available, Gates would happily toss coins for practically any sum; or he would bet on raindrops sliding down a window. (Once on a train in 1897 he won $22,000 backing the right raindrops.)

Before Gates achieved his industrial wealth and gambling glory, he had been a simple barbed-wire salesman in Texas. But he rose rapidly as a businessman and stock-market operator; and at the height of his career he was several times a millionaire, thanks to his role in the organization of the American Steel and Wire Company and U.S. Steel, and his interests in copper mines and railroads. He also had interests in circuses—appropriately, since his gambling fame was sufficient to make him almost a one-man circus. What Bet-a-million Gates had won or lost the night before was considered important news not only throughout America but in Britain and Europe as well.

There are various stories and legends describing the way Gates got his nickname. One of these concerns a racing exploit in 1900: Gates had entered a horse of his own in a race, and had backed it with a total of $70,000 in bets. The horse won, and Gates collected $600,000. The rumor of this win spread, and (as such rumors will) became exaggerated: Eventually, according to this legend, it was being said that Gates had "bet a million" and had won over $2,000,000.

Another version (which I find somewhat more enjoyable, and which seems to fit with Gates' expansive personality) also involves a race-track bet. An official at a track supposedly asked Gates to limit his bets to $10,000 a time. According to this story, Gates resented this attempt to inhibit his enjoyment, and circulated through the crowd offering to bet anyone a million dollars on any one horse. He didn't get anyone to take the bet; but he did get a nickname.

Such dramatic gestures ascribed to Gates (whether or not they happened) helped to earn him a reputation for reckless, hot-headed gambling. And later stories, when New York was blazing with the exploits of its millionaire gamblers, increased his reputation. Gates had one day in the summer of 1902 visited the Saratoga race track and had lost around $375,000. (Racing was one of his favorite gambles, but he lost at the track more often than he won.) After dinner he went to the Club House (which was a gambling casino owned by Richard Canfield, New York's leading gambling impressario) and began playing faro.

The American gambling "king" of the 1900s, John "Bet-a-Million" Gates, holds up a grandchild in an expansive pose during a public tour of the Gates barbed wire factory—from which he made most of his huge fortune.

At first Gates played under the usual house limits of $500 for bets on single cards and $1000 for "doubles." He lost a few times, then suggested that the game be made private and the limits raised to $2500 and $5000. He continued to lose under these conditions, and in a few hours had dropped $150,000 in the game (making a total of $525,000 lost, including his racing defeats, that day).

But he didn't give up. Instead, he pushed the limits up to $5000 and $10,000 and continued to bet furiously. Then his luck changed: He shortly won back the $150,000 and had won an additional $150,000 by the time the game ended —thus having cut his losses for the day to the relatively small figure of $225,000.

Gates enjoyed poker as much as faro, and in this game also maintained his name as an impetuous gambler. A pot in a Gates poker game might reach anywhere from $50,000 to $200,000; Gates himself lost nearly $1,000,000 in about one year's poker playing (1899-1900). But, according to most authorities, in spite of these gargantuan figures, Gates was not just a devil-may-care millionaire who threw his money away for the sake of gambling's excitement. He was shrewd, cool, and analytical both at business and at the gaming table; all his risks were well calculated, the odds against winning well assessed. He didn't plunge without taking a long, hard look at his chances; but when he felt they were favorable, he plunged wholeheartedly. Of course, he often suffered immense losses; but he also often won heavily, and generally stayed ahead of the game.

Like any skilful gambler, Gates would try to gain the advantage however he could. He was quite capable of such deceptions as betting astronomical sums on a weak poker hand to frighten opponents out of the game; and sometimes he used slightly more dubious tricks, such as inviting a group of jockeys to dinner, wining and dining them, and picking up enough tips from their unguarded conversations to win more than $200,000 at the next day's races. But such sharp practice is far from cheating; and it can be quite safely said that Gates was never a cheat.

That Gates stayed ahead of the game in every respect is proved by the fact that he remained a multimillionaire all his life. But he didn't always remain a gambler. One of the last stories told of him described a visit he paid in 1909 (when he was 54) to a Church conference in Texas, where he addressed the gathering on the evils of gambling. He warned them not to play cards or dice, not to bet on horses, and not to speculate on the stock exchange. But one warning he offered them seems rather a paradoxical statement for a man to make who had apparently given up gambling: He told the conference: "Don't be a gambler; once a gambler, always a gambler."

If Gates did give up gambling before 1910, then he got out just in time. Because by then a man named Arnold Rothstein was beginning to become prominent in the American gambling world—and in several less attractive worlds. Rothstein's prominence, as a gambler or otherwise, was notoriety, not fame: He was a gambling cheat and a racketeer, a major figure in the underworld that practically ran New York in the two decades from 1910 to 1930.

Rothstein was born in New York in 1882, the second son of orthodox and respectable Jewish parents. He had a chip on his shoulder from the first, for he believed himself to be unloved and unwanted; at the age of three he is said to have tried to kill his brother Harry with a knife because he believed Harry to be a favorite with his parents. Whether this was true or not is impossible to say; but, just or unjust, his resentment had the effect of turning him into a brooding, misanthropic child, with little to recommend him except a grasp of figures and a natural ability in all games requiring some skill.

As one example of that skill, in later life he once played *billiards* against a champion player named Jack Conway. The game lasted for 34 hours continuously, and Rothstein finished the series of matches the winner of $10,000. (Later he developed a facility for fixing games of pure chance so that he won those as well.)

He began his professional career at school by becoming a moneylender. He earned a little money by such extracurricular activities as selling newspapers and running errands; when he had accumulated a small amount of capital he

Arnold Rothstein (left) was pre-eminent among the gangsters and crooked professional gamblers who terrorized New York during the 1920s and 30s. Rothstein's gambling skill was great, but his facility for fixing games of pure chance (and hoodwinking the police) was even greater. Above, members of the Chicago White Sox baseball team (and their lawyers) in court. The players were accused of conspiring with Rothstein to fix the World Series. (He was alleged to have paid them $10,000 each.) Although eight of the players were indicted, Rothstein was acquitted. Nine years later (in 1928) he was shot down after refusing to pay a gambling debt. Right, Rothstein's body is removed from the Polytechnic hospital, New York, where he died.

lent it out, charging $1 interest on every $5 he lent. In this way his capital increased to $500 by the time he was 17, when he left home for good. He was ruthless with anyone who tried to avoid debts, finding it profitable to invest a certain percentage of his capital in hiring thugs, who beat up anyone who didn't repay IOUs at the scheduled time.

He maintained this ruthlessness into his racketeering adulthood. Such things were part of the business, and it was a strict business—since Rothstein was interested only in money and power. And it quickly became a big business. At one time it seemed as if all New York was in his control. Mayors, police chiefs, judges, businessmen, sportsmen, brothel keepers, dope peddlers, and petty criminals of all kinds were on the Rothstein shopping list. He bought and sold them and used the profits to establish himself as a property owner. The hotels and stores he owned were used as collateral to borrow money from the banks to finance the underworld—under the nose of the law.

Rothstein appears in F. Scott Fitzgerald's novel *The Great Gatsby*, only slightly disguised as a character named Meyer Wolfsheim, and a particular passage in that book refers to one of Rothstein's most notorious *coups*. Nick Carraway, the narrator of the novel, is asking Gatsby who Wolfsheim is.

" 'Meyer Wolfsheim? He's a gambler.' Gatsby hesitated, then added coolly: 'He's the man who fixed the World's Series in 1919.'

" 'Fixed the World's Series?' I repeated.

"The idea staggered me. I remembered, of course, that the World's Series had been fixed in 1919, but if I had thought of it at all I would have thought of it as a thing that merely happened, the end of some inevitable chain. It never occurred to me that one man could start to play with the faith of fifty million people—with the singlemindedness of a burglar blowing a safe.

" 'How did he happen to do that?' I asked after a minute.

" 'He just saw the opportunity.'

" 'Why isn't he in jail?'

" 'They can't get him, old sport. He's a smart man.' "

After this particular exploit Rothstein was in fact smart enough to be able to convince a Grand Jury that he was innocent. The facts as known were these (telescoped for brevity):

The Chicago White Sox were a star baseball team owned by a man named Charles Comiskey. They were under contract to him and won a great deal of money for him; but he underpaid them. When they asked for more money, he refused. Naturally resentful, several of them plotted to lose matches deliberately —both to get back at Comiskey and to make extra money themselves. They looked around for a big-time gambler who would pay $10,000 to each of the 10 players to lose a match against the champions, Cincinnati. There were several big men who were willing to conspire in the fixing but none who had the necessary $100,000. Undoubtedly some of them suggested Arnold Rothstein.

According to Rothstein's evidence at the trial, he was approached but refused. Nevertheless, his bookkeeper, a Mrs. Brown, was later found to have records of a number of huge bets that Rothstein and his associates put on Cincinnati to win. (Mrs. Brown and eight of the White Sox players were indicted.) But although Cincinnati won—and although Rothstein was shown to have won $350,000 betting on them—no conclusive evidence that could lead to a conviction could be obtained. The ludicrous result of the trial was that, in spite of signed confessions by some of the players, it was never even conclusively proved that the series was fixed, let alone that Rothstein had anything to do with the fixing.

But Rothstein could not shake himself free of the opprobrium that attached itself to his name during the following year. The scandal (now ironically called "the Black Sox" story) was bad for business, and he announced that he would retire from gambling and concentrate on Wall Street and real estate in future. But he didn't. He continued to concentrate on anything that would make money, including high-stake *craps* games. One of these games brought the police on a raid only to get themselves shot at by Rothstein, who was subsequently indicted on a charge of felonious assault—and acquitted.

Naturally, this crooked gambler could not go on indefinitely building up his fortune without making enemies. But it is remarkable that he should apparently have made his deadliest enemies by accusing his fellow players in a poker game of cheating. This is what he did in 1928. His skill at poker had been met by skill, and luck had left him. He quit the game owing nearly a third of a million dollars; and he refused to pay it because, he said, "the game was rigged." For weeks he stalled his debtors: Sometimes he pretended that he was merely keeping them waiting for their own good and because he wanted to demonstrate his own power; at other times he returned to the original explanation, that he would never pay at all because he had been cheated.

But, according to the harsh underworld code, welshers had to be punished. Rothstein was fatally shot in the abdomen in the Park Central Hotel on November 4, 1928. Although he was still alive and conscious for some time after the shooting, he never revealed the name of his killer.

The day Rothstein died Herbert Hoover was elected president and the book-makers with whom Rothstein had bet on Hoover's success were jubilant because they would never have to pay him. The amount of his winnings would have been about $500,000—which would have been only a small percentage of the fortune that he acquired during his life. Yet 10 years after his death, his brother filed a plea of bankruptcy in the estate. Millions of dollars of the assets had been in narcotics, which the federal authorities seized soon after his death. Millions more had been in corporations that vanished into thin air without the continued ministrations of the man who, as the New York *Herald Tribune* said, "was a unique figure in the life of the city. . . . No one need be much surprised that the fruits of his life and works have turned out to be no more substantial than a structure he might have built out of a deck of his own well-riffled cards."

The final place in this anthology of famous gamblers has been reserved for one of the best-known names in 20th-century European casino gambling. It is, however, not the name of a person but of a group: the Greek Syndicate.

The name seems to belong in tales of international crime and intrigue, in cloak-and-dagger thrillers—as the name of the sinister, anonymous villains. But in fact the members of the Greek Syndicate were far from villainous or sinister, and were never anonymous. Nor, for that matter, were they all Greek. There were five in the Syndicate. Taken in alphabetical order, their names were: François André (French), Zaret Couyoumdjian (Armenian), Eli Eliopulo (Greek), Athanase Vagliano (Greek), and Nicolas Zographos (Greek).

The Syndicate was initially formed in Paris about 1919. Zographos and Eliopulo had left Greece for Paris to exploit their gambling skills, and had set up as bookmakers as well as playing baccarat regularly in Parisian clubs. In one of these clubs they met Couyoumdjian, who was also living as a professional gambler. Because the three found themselves taking the bank regularly, they decided to pool their resources—and the Greek Syndicate was born. Later Vagliano joined them, bringing with him the fortune he had made in shipping, and André became the fifth member soon afterward.

All through the 1920s and 1930s the Greek Syndicate dominated the highest gambling echelons of Deauville, Cannes, and Monte Carlo. They constantly played against some of the richest men and women of the world—including such famous names as the then Aga Khan, ex-king Farouk of Egypt, and Baron Henri de Rothschild. Yet the Syndicate managed over the years not only to remain solvent but actually to make a profit: Each of its members ended his career far richer than he had begun. And much of the credit for this success must be given to the gambling abilities and instincts of Nico Zographos.

When Zographos was in his twenties he had put his mathematical aptitude to work to master the mathematics of gambling—and especially of the game of baccarat. He studied and he practiced in baccarat games with friends, among whom was Eliopulo; soon he was almost incredibly expert.

Much of his skill was due to his incredible memory. Zographos could remember every card that was played throughout a game (or "shoe") of baccarat—and 312 cards are used. He invariably knew what the last few cards were before they were drawn. Thus he could usually gauge the fluctuations in the odds favoring the bank (which he worked out mathematically beforehand); to put it simply, he would usually know what his chances were of drawing a card he needed, and so could adjust his betting.

In baccarat the bank usually has a small but definite favorable percentage: Throughout a shoe it may average about .8 per cent. Of course, the advantage will alter in every individual hand, depending on what cards have been used. The bank is held by the man who bids highest for it (who, at Deauville or Cannes, was generally Zographos backed by his partners). The banker has also another valuable advantage: He can stop play whenever he likes, avoiding bankruptcy in a losing streak by giving up the bank.

At the height of his career Zographos also had a considerable psychological advantage over opponents because of his impressive reputation as a consistent winner. Also, his memory helped him psychologically as well: He always knew exactly how much each of his opponents had won or lost during the evening (as well as how much they could afford to lose). This knowledge, and his almost infallible gambling instincts, enabled him to predict how certain players would bet—and, conversely, enabled him to guess from the betting what cards his opponents were holding. Of course, as I pointed out in Chapter 11, such abilities are prerequisites for any would-be professional gambler; but few professionals have developed these abilities to the degree of expertise that Zographos achieved. (Incidentally, there has never been the slightest hint that the Greek Syndicate's games were anything but honest and aboveboard.)

It was partly due to the collective skill of the Syndicate members (they each held the bank frequently, though Zographos held it most often) and partly to their collective wealth that they were able to startle the gambling world of 1922 by taking an almost unheard-of step. They decided no longer to impose a betting limit on baccarat when the Syndicate was in charge.

The idea originated with Zographos; the bulk of the necessary capital to back the venture was put up by Vagliano (the equivalent of nearly $2,000,000). At the beginning of the Deauville season Zographos, taking the banker's chair for the initial baccarat game, simply announced: "Tout va." The sky was the limit. As the Syndicate expected, big-time gamblers came from all over the world to play for immense sums, hoping to break the Syndicate. But gamblers who wanted to win heavily had to bet heavily; and Zographos managed to win just often enough to keep replenishing the Syndicate's capital—and to deplete that of many of his opponents.

According to an article that appeared in the British newspaper the *Sunday Dispatch* after Zographos's death in 1953, an American gambler once challenged him to play one hand for 1,000,000 francs (then about $168,000). Zographos

Above, the British financier Solly Joel at the wheel of his yacht *Eileen* in 1931. Joel was a frequent visitor to the high-stake gambling tables at Deauville, Cannes, and Monte Carlo. Right, the Aga Khan at Deauville in 1926. He visited regularly—to watch his horses race and to play baccarat. Both men gambled regularly against the Greek Syndicate.

agreed—but with the proviso that they played the best of three hands. Zographos lost the first hand, calmly won the second, and then the third.

But Zographos didn't always win. At Cannes in 1926, for example, he lost the equivalent of $672,000 in a week's play. On the last night, after losing several coups, Zographos left the table and returned a few moments later with another 1,000,000 francs—apparently his last—and risked the whole sum. Sensing his danger, his opponents bet heavily. Zographos (as unruffled and expressionless as ever) dealt the cards. His opponents received an eight and a seven. It was Zographos's turn. His first two cards were court cards, and therefore worthless; he drew a third.

It was a nine of diamonds—an unbeatable nine. He had won. And he continued to win that night and the following nights. The nine of diamonds afterward became his insignia, appearing on his cigarette case, on his cuff links, and even on the flag of his yacht.

That moment was the turning point for the Syndicate. They never came close to the brink again in spite of frequent challenges. They reigned supreme until the Second World War put a temporary stop to gambling in Europe and to the Syndicate's activities. But, afterward, the gamblers returned to the casinos, and the Syndicate (with some new faces) took up where it had left off. Today, all the original members are dead. But the Syndicate still exists, and still can be said to achieve more consistent success than any comparable group in Europe.

Appendix 1 Glossary of gambling terms

Accumulator: In British horse racing, a cumulative bet. The bettor designates a horse in each of several races and bets on the first one; if he wins, his winnings become his bet on the next; and so on.

A cheval: A roulette bet on two numbers adjacent on the layout.

Across the board: An American racing bet on a horse's finishing either first, second, or third.

Active player: In baccarat, a player who represents a combined group of players in play against the bank.

Any raffle: In hazard, a player's bet that with three dice he will throw any three of a specific number.

Ante: A poker bet, placed by the first player before cards are dealt.

Backgammon: A "triple win" in the game of the same name.

Banco: A baccarat player's call, announcing that he will bet against the bank.

Banco suivi: A baccarat player's call after he has lost a coup, when he wishes to bet against the bank again.

Bank: The operators of a game (like faro, roulette, or baccarat) in which the players gamble against the operator rather than among themselves. Also, the money reserves held and used by the operators.

Bingo: Winner's cry in the game of the same name.

Blackjack: The combination of an ace and a card that counts 10—a winning hand in the game of the same name.

Blind bet: A bet made by a race-track bookmaker to draw other bookmakers' attention away from his sizeable betting on another horse—and thus to avoid a shortening of the odds on the other horse.

Bluff: To bet heavily in poker while holding a weak hand—in order to frighten the other players into folding.

Bookmaker (or **bookie**): A person who accepts bets from the public, usually on racing or sports events.

Bust: Term sometimes used for a player's exceeding a count of 21 in blackjack.

Call (or **see**): To end betting on a hand of poker by covering the last player's bet without raising it.

Caller: The operator of a bingo game, who draws the numbers and calls them out.

Carpet joint: An American slang term for a luxury gambling casino.

Carré (or **square**): A roulette bet on four numbers forming a square on the layout.

Chance: In hazard, a number thrown instead of the main. To win, the thrower must repeat it before throwing the main.

Chuck number: In hazard, a bet on the numbers one to six.

Cognotte: In baccarat, a slot in the table reserved for the bank's winnings: Also, in chemin-de-fer, a slot in the table reserved for the bank's cut from the winnings on each coup.

Colonne (or **column**): A roulette bet on a complete line of 12 numbers running the length of the layout.

Come bet: In craps, a bet that the dice will win on the come-out.

Come-out: In craps, the thrower's first throw of the dice.

Come-out bet: In craps, a bet that a specified number will be made by the thrower on his come-out.

Coup: Term used in European casinos for a complete round of play in such games as baccarat or roulette.

Crap: A losing throw in craps—either a Two, Three, or Twelve made on the first throw, or a Seven thrown when trying for a point.

Croupier: A casino employee who operates a roulette game.

Daily double: In American horse racing, a combination bet on two horses in two races. If the bettor wins on the first race, his winnings become his stake on the second.

Doubling-up: The basis of some widely used systems. After a loss the player doubles the size of his previous bet hoping to win back the money lost and make a profit.

Douzaine (or **dozen**): A roulette bet on the numbers 1-12, or 13-24, or 25-36.

Draw: One of the two basic forms of poker. A player is dealt five cards and can discard up to four and draw replacements.

Each way: A racing bet on a horse's finishing first or second.

En plein (or **straight**): A roulette bet on an individual number.

Even chances: Equality between the unfavorable and favorable chances. In tossing a coin each side has an even chance of coming up in one toss.

Fade: To accept a bet in craps.

Faites vos jeux: A European croupier's call to players to place their bets.

Favorable percentage: The amount by which the chances of winning a bet are mathematically better than even.

Favorite: The horse generally considered most likely to win a race.

Fix: To influence the result of a game or sports event (e.g., by bribing players) in order to win a bet.

Floating game: An illegal craps game that is moved from place to place to avoid police.

Flush: In poker, any five cards of one suit.

Fold: In poker, to drop out of the betting on a particular hand.

Forecast: In British racing, a combination bet in which the bettor predicts the horses that will finish first and second.

Four of a kind: Four cards of the same numerical value.

Full house: In poker, a hand containing three cards of one value and two of another.

Gammon: A "double win" in backgammon.

Gin: A hand in gin rummy in which all 10 cards are melded, with no leftovers.

Go down: In gin rummy, when a player ends the play by showing his hand.

Handicap: Term for a horse race in which the horses carry different weights, assigned by racing officials, to even out the chances of winning.

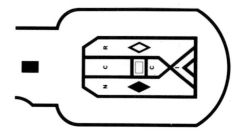

High: In hazard, a player's bet that with three dice he will throw a total of 11 or more.

Hit: A blackjack term for the player's drawing another card after the deal. Also, a single win in backgammon.

Hole card: In stud poker, the first card dealt (face down) to a player.

Hot: A craps term for a thower (or the dice) during a winning streak.

House: A casino or gambling center; also the operators of a gambling game.

House advantage (or **edge**): A gambling house's means of ensuring a profit—usually by paying winners at less than the mathematically correct odds.

Impair: A roulette bet that the winning number will be odd.

In the money: Term used to describe the horses that finish first, second, and third (and sometimes fourth) in a race—the horses on which money will be paid to bettors.

Itemer: A cardsharp's accomplice, who watches the game and signals the nature of the other hands to his partner.

Jackpot: The largest payout that can be won on a slot machine.

Kip: In two-up, the flat stick on which two coins are placed to be tossed.

Last turn: In faro, the last three remaining undealt cards.

Lay-off bet (or **hedging**): A bet made by a cautious bookmaker on a horse on which he has accepted large bets—in order to cut his losses if the horse wins.

Layout: In games like roulette or bank craps, a diagram (often on cloth) with spaces indicated for different bets.

Loaded dice: Dice containing some kind of weight that will cause certain sides to come up regularly.

Long odds: In racing, odds (such as 100 to 1) offered against a horse unlikely to win.

Long shot: A horse against which long odds have been offered.

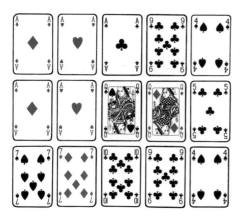

Low: In hazard, a player's bet that with three dice he will throw a total count of 10 or under.

Main: In hazard, a number that the thrower chooses to try to make on his first throw.

Manque: A roulette bet on numbers from one to 18.

Martingale: The name of a "doubling-up" system mostly used in roulette.

Meld: In rummy games, three or four cards of consecutive value and the same suit, or a set of three or four cards of the same value.

Miss-out: A craps term for a Two, Three, or Twelve made on the first throw.

Morning line: A statement (usually issued by officials in the morning before a day's racing) of approximate odds likely to be offered for horses running that day.

Natural: In craps, a Seven or Eleven made on the first throw.

Nick: In hazard, the successful throwing of the main.

Noir: A roulette bet that the winning number will be black.

No-throw: In two-up, a throw of one head and one tail.

Numbers bet: In hazard, a bet in which the player tries to forecast the total count of the three dice.

Odds: A statement of comparison between unfavorable and favorable chances. E.g., in throwing a six-sided die the odds against a specified side's coming up are 5 to 1.

Odds on: Odds offered for a horse that is almost sure to win. At odds of 100 to 1 on, a winning bet of $100 would bring in $101.

One-armed bandit: A slot machine.

Pair: In poker, two cards of the same value. Also, a roulette bet on an even number.

Pari-mutuel: A means of gambling on races in which all bets are pooled and winners are paid according to the size of the pool and the number of other winners.

Parlay: The American term for an accumulator bet in horse racing.

Pass: A craps term for a Seven or Eleven made on the first throw, or for the successful making of a point.

Passe: A roulette bet on numbers 19 to 36.

Pitch: A British on-course bookmaker's betting stand.

Place: A racing term for a horse's finishing in second place.

Place bet: In craps, a bet on the result of a throw when the thrower is trying for a point.

Point: In craps, any of the numbers Four, Five, Six, Eight, Nine, and Ten—which, when thrown on the first throw, must be repeated before throwing a Seven.

Pot: In poker, the total sum of money bet on a hand.

Pulling: Term for a jockey's holding his horse back to prevent it from finishing among the winners.

Quiniela (or **quinella**): In American racing, a bet in which the bettor predicts the horses that will finish first and second.

Raffles: In hazard, a player's bet that with three dice he will throw three of a specific number.

Raise: In poker, to bet a larger sum than any other player's previous bet.

Reel timing: Cheating the slot machines by timing the spin of the reels and setting them in motion in a way that will make them come to rest in desired positions.

Rien ne va plus: A roulette croupier's call that ends betting on one spin of the wheel.

Ringer: A horse (or greyhound) entered in a race under another's name—usually a good runner replacing a poorer one.

Rouge: A roulette bet on a red number.

Royal flush: The highest poker hand—ace, king, queen, jack, 10 of one suit.

Runner: In racing, a bookmaker's employee who gathers information on the progress of betting elsewhere on the course. Also, an agent for the American numbers game.

Sabot (or **shoe**): The open-topped, open-sided box from which cards are dealt in baccarat and chemin-de-fer.

Saliva test: A chemical means of determining whether a horse has been doped.

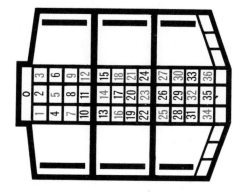

Sawdust joint: An American slang term for a non-luxury gambling club.

Settler: A British bookmaker's expert who calculates payouts.

Shortening the odds: A bookmaker's reduction of the odds offered for a horse in the face of heavy betting.

Show: A racing term for a horse's finishing in third place.

Side bet: A bet made between craps players (or onlookers) on the results of a particular throw of the dice.

Sixaine (or **transversale simple,** or **line**): A roulette bet on two horizontal rows, with three numbers each, on the layout.

Six-dollar combine: An across-the-board bet in American racing.

Spinner: The persons who tosses the coins in two-up.

Splits: In faro, a bet divided between two cards.

Stacked deck: A pack of cards that a cheat has prearranged, for his own benefit.

Starting price: The final odds offered for a horse as the race begins.

Stay: Term used to refuse extra cards from a blackjack dealer.

Straddle: In poker, the term sometimes used for the bet (twice the ante) placed by the second player before the deal.

Straight: In poker, five numerically consecutive cards of different units.

Straight flush: In poker, five numerically consecutive cards of one suit.

Stud: One of the two basic forms of poker. Players receive some cards face up and may not draw replacements.

Sure thing: Any bet that has very little chance of losing.

System: A method of betting (usually mathematically based) used by a player to try to get an advantage.

Three of a kind: Three cards of the same numerical value.

Ticketer: A forger of bookmakers' tickets.

Tic-tac: The code of hand signals by which, in British racing, bookmakers' employees relay information on current odds and betting around the course.

Tiercé: A French combination bet. The bettor predicts the horses that will finish first, second, and third.

Tipster (or **tout**): A person who sells to bettors his estimate of likely winners of a race (sometimes of a lottery).

Totalizator (or **tote**): The computer that records the amount of money bet on races in pari-mutuel betting, and that calculates the size of payouts on winners.

Tote board: A race-track information board that displays approximate odds, betting totals, payout prices, and other information necessary to the bettor.

Transversale pleine (or **street**): A roulette bet on a horizontal row (on the layout) of three numbers.

Trick: Four cards, one from each player's hand, put down in one round of play in games like whist and bridge.

Trump: In games like whist or bridge, a suit that is given (by prearrangement) a higher value than any other.

Turf accountant: A British euphemism for a bookmaker.

Two pairs: Two cards of one value and two of another (in poker).

Welsh: To fail to pay a gambling bet.

Wheeling (or **locking**): An American racing system devised for the daily double bet. The bettor backs one horse in the first race and every horse in the second.

Wild cards: Cards that can be substituted (by prearrangement) for any other card.

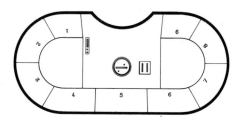

Appendix 2 Gambling around the world

The following survey provides a look at the state of gambling in 44 of the world's major countries—wherever facts and figures were available. It includes information on the legality of gambling in each country, and on the money spent on the principal gambles.

Afghanistan

All forms of gambling are illegal. The law is strictly enforced and anyone caught gambling is prosecuted according to Islamic laws.

Argentina

The government has practically a monopoly on all forms of gambling. Horse racing is extremely popular in Buenos Aires, and the government operates a state lottery. Illegal gambling activities are punishable by prison sentences of up to six months.

Australia

Betting on horse races is the most popular gambling activity, with lotteries and betting on dog races close behind. In 1955, the equivalent of $65,000,000 was bet on horses and dogs through totalizators, and a total of $461,000,000 was bet with licensed bookmakers (on the course) in all states except Queensland. (Bookmakers will also take bets on special sporting events like professional boxing matches and even sailing-skiff races, though this kind of betting is illegal.) Every town of importance has at least one racecourse, and the attendances are high: In the Melbourne area, for example, the average attendance for a race meeting is 35,000.

Lotteries are operated in all states. In New South Wales, Queensland, and Western Australia the state governments run them; in Victoria and Tasmania the organizers operate under government licenses. In 1955, country-wide lottery ticket sales amounted to $62,000,000. Ticket prices range from the equivalent of 25 cents to $2, though $10 tickets can be bought in special lotteries (such as those held on the Melbourne Cup horse race).

Gambling legislation, expenditure, and organization vary greatly from state to state. In New South Wales, $168,000,000 were bet with about 2,000,000 licensed bookmakers. About $26,000,000 were spent on government lotteries. Most gambling in this state is done through totalizators at horse, pony, and greyhound race meetings. But gamblers also managed to spend about $1,500,000 on "poker machines" (a kind of slot machine that bears card symbols). The only illegal gambling games in New South Wales are *fan-tan*, another Chinese game called *pak-a-p*, and *two-up*.

In Victoria the Tattersall lottery (run to provide an additional income for hospitals and charities) draws most gambling money (in 1959, $17,700,000). Under the Police Offences Act *bingo* is illegal in Victoria, as are *baccarat*, *hazard*, fan-tan, and two-up.

Queensland's most distinctive lottery is called the "Golden Casket." It was inaugurated in 1916 and now attracts an average of about $3,000,000 a year. In Southern Australia (according to a report from the Betting Control Board in 1958) $53,000,000 were gambled with on-course bookmakers at 446 race meetings. At 350 meetings $4,000,000 were bet through totalizators. The Royal Commission on betting in Western Australia for the same year (1958) recorded a total turnover of $25,000,000 for all bookmakers.

Austria

The State Gambling Monopoly now controls the state lottery, the totalizators, and the football pools, and supervises the organization of all other lotteries, casinos, and small-scale gambles. (In 1961, 489 lottery agencies and 3949 football and horse-racing pools agencies came under its control.) There are two state lottery drawings each week; winners receive 14 to 4800 times their original stake. In 1961, the equivalent of approximately $1,300,000 was spent on the various lotteries. From this total the government made a gross profit of approximately $766,000.

In the same year, 44 football pools and nine horse-racing pools were held, giving the government a profit of $260,000 and $3500 respectively. Sweepstakes, raffles, and bazaars are also legal, as long as the proceeds are used for charitable or social purposes. In 1961, the total turnover from 27 small-scale lotteries was $1,075,000.

Austria has seven casinos, four of which are open throughout the year. All are run under state supervision. In 1961 the gross government revenue from taxes on casinos was $1,900,000. The government uses a percentage of its income from gambling to finance amateur sports and horse breeding; most of the rest goes toward social and educational services.

Belgium

Casinos were made illegal in 1902, but the eight casinos already in existence at the time were allowed to remain—at Knocke, Blankenberghe, Ostend, Middelkerke, Spa, Chaudfontaine, Namur, and Dinant. Anyone setting up a casino now is liable to be fined the equivalent of $100 or to be given a six-month prison sentence.

It is also illegal to organize a lottery without state permission: Anyone who does so may be fined up to $60 or imprisoned for up to three months. Anyone gambling in the street is liable to have the money and objects of the game confiscated. The law affords no redress for unpaid gambling debts.

Gambling on horse races, athletic events, cockfights, and pigeon races is legal, but agents must obtain authorization from the Minister of Finance. Every licensed betting agency is required to pay a quarterly tax—which usually amounts to a minimum of $196. In 1960, the equivalent of about $13,626,000 was gambled on horse races.

Bolivia

All forms of public gambling were made illegal in the mining regions in 1930, and in 1938 this law was extended to cover the rest of the Republic. The government, however, runs a successful state lottery, which is an official source of government revenue.

Brazil

Gambling on games of chance is prohibited. Off-course betting on any sporting event other than horse racing is also forbidden. Penalties for breaking these laws range from three months to a year's imprisonment, accompanied by fines and even, on occasions, the confiscation of property.

Horse racing takes place on Saturdays, Sundays, and holidays at the Gavea track in Guanabara, and on Saturdays and Sundays at the main track in Sao Paulo. (There is also mid-week racing at three other courses in Sao Paulo.) The numbers game (known as *bicho*), though illegal, is a favorite form of gambling in Brazil.

There are several state-controlled lotteries whose profits go mainly to charity. A federal lottery is held on Wednesdays and Saturdays and pays out a first prize that is the equivalent of about $20,000. On certain occasions during the year (for example on Christmas Day and St. John the Baptist's Day) prizes are much larger—often as much as $100,000.

Bulgaria

All forms of private gambling and betting are prohibited. The new holiday resorts on the Black Sea, however, have gambling casinos; and the state-controlled lottery (which offers prizes of such scarce commodities as cars, apartments, and television sets, as well as large cash prizes) attracts wide participation.

Cambodia

There is a state lottery and a single casino—which is open to foreigners only. All other forms of gambling are prohibited.

Canada

By an Act of Parliament passed in 1954 all gambling houses, casinos, clubs, betting shops, and so on were made illegal. Violators of this law are liable to two years' imprisonment. Bookmaking, the organizing of pools, and private betting between more than 10 people are all forbidden. (Exceptions to this ruling are made for pools or betting enterprises set up before 1912, or for gambling ventures incorporated after that day by special act of parliament.) Small-scale lotteries for charitable purposes, however, are permitted.

Pari-mutuel betting on horse races through totalizators is permitted, though it must be supervised by an official of the Ministry of Agriculture. Five per cent of the total amount of money bet on any race must be paid to the Receiver

General of Canada; the organizers are allowed to keep nine per cent of the total amount, and the rest is paid out as winnings. Any violation of the pari-mutuel gambling laws can lead to a fine of up to $500.

During 1960, the Federal Department of Agriculture supervised pari-mutuel betting at the tracks of 100 racing associations. The total amount bet for the whole of Canada that year was $141,419,679. Of this amount the racing associations kept $13,648,410, and the provincial governments collected $9,578,474 in taxes. The largest single amount taken in from betting was in 1960 at the 14-day meeting at Greenwood Racing Club (at Toronto, Ontario): The sum of $7,755,356 passed through the tote machines, a daily average of $553,954.

In March 1963, a report from the Ontario Royal Commission on crime made it clear that the law has not deterred all of Canada's gambling enthusiasts. Anti-gambling squads uncovered evidence of the misuse of social clubs for gambling games, of the illegal operating of pinball machines, and of imports of foreign lottery tickets.

Chile

Lotteries, casinos, and horse races are all popular in Chile. A law of 1925 authorized the University of Concepción to operate a lottery, and a further law (of 1930) authorized the creation of a national lottery, the proceeds of which go to public welfare. In 1959, 1,248,000 tickets were sold in the Concepción University lottery, which brought in the equivalent of nearly $5,500,000. Profits go toward the university's operating expenses and provide grants for students. In the same year (1959) more than 1,000,000 national lottery tickets were sold in 26 drawings, giving the government a net profit of nearly $1,300,000.

Public gambling was legalized at the summer resort of Vina del Mar, near Santiago, in 1928 and Chile's first casino was opened there. Two years later, the creation of further casinos in various other fashionable resorts was authorized: *Roulette,* baccarat, and *chemin-de-fer* are the usual games played. In 1959 the turnover at the casino of Viña del Mar was about $1,430,000.

Chile has seven race tracks, the biggest at Santiago and Valparaiso. On Sundays and popular feast days, clubs organize gambling on horse races and give all the proceeds to charity. Betting on horse races is authorized only through on-track totalizators: In 1959, about $17,000,000 were gambled in this way. Bookmaking on horse pools, as well as private tipping or the taking of bets, is illegal. According to the Department of Juridical Statistics, there were only two convictions under the gambling laws in 1961, and none at all in the first five months of 1962.

Czechoslovakia

Private gambling is illegal, but a state-controlled lottery exists, along with a state-sponsored pools system that covers a great variety of sports including soccer, horse racing, and ice hockey. The national lottery began in 1954. There are two annual drawings for 25 prizes, and winnings are tax free. The two existing sports pools (*sazka* and *sportka*) began in 1957 and the turnover in their first four years was the equivalent of about $210,000,000. The state takes a large share of this to subsidize sports.

Denmark

Bookmaking and gambling houses are illegal. The state runs football pools and a lottery; the profits from these help to finance cultural and sporting activities. The only legal way of betting on horses is through on-track totalizators. (The Copenhagen race track takes in the equivalent of about $1,450,000 in bets each season.)

Private dice games are often played in wine and beer restaurants, but for drinks rather than for money. There are also a few gambling halls with slot machines and roulette wheels, but the stakes are always minimal (usually about seven cents).

Finland

All forms of privately organized gambling are forbidden. Lotteries and football pools are allowed, and betting on horse races is legal; but all these activities are run by the government, or by government-sponsored societies. Both the state lotteries and the football pools are extremely popular: In 1962, the income from the football pools was the equivalent of about $18,000,000.

Half of the proceeds is distributed to the winners; about 20 per cent is kept for administrative expenses; and of the rest, 60 per cent goes to sports organizations and 40 per cent to scientific and youth organizations. Proceeds from the state lottery are distributed in much the same way, the only difference being that profits are given to artistic rather than to scientific organizations.

As for gambling on horse races: 75 per cent of the proceeds is distributed as winnings, and the state takes from between eight and 17 per cent of the remainder (according to a graduated scale). The rest goes to horse-breeding societies.

France

Football pools, dice games, privately organized lotteries, and gambling on sports or athletic events are all illegal. Bookmakers are also illegal: Gambling on horse and dog races is almost wholly on-track and pari-mutuel (through totalizators), and is controlled by the Ministry of Agriculture. But betting at registered off-track *Pari-Mutuel Urbain* (P.M.U.) offices is permitted, though bets must be placed before the start of the day's races. Bets are then transmitted to the race track, for these offices are really extensions of the on-track totalizators.

The equivalent of $520,000,000 was placed in bets through the P.M.U. in 1962. (One of the most popular kinds of bet on horses is the *tiercé*, that involves the selection of three horses to finish first, second, and third in specified races run on Sundays and special holidays. The stake—60 cents—must be placed at a P.M.U. office before the morning of the race. The better wins if his selected horses finish in the first three, though his winnings are much larger if the exact order is forecast.) Altogether 300,000 people (stable boys, trainers, jockeys, saddlers, shoesmiths, and so on) are employed in the horse-racing "industry" in France. They are paid from taxes derived from the totalizators.

Two kinds of gambling house are permitted in France: casinos and *cercles*. Casinos are open to the public on proof of identity and payment of an entrance fee. Roulette is played in most casinos, as (in the larger casinos) are *boule*, baccarat, and *poker*. Cercles are clubs open only to members (incidentally, in most cases only men can become members). Baccarat and poker are the principal gambles in cercles. France has around 150 casinos and 80 cercles; 30 of the latter are in Paris.

The only lotteries allowed in France are the *Loterie Nationale* (which is drawn at least once a week) and certain specially authorized charity lotteries. These are all controlled by the Ministry of Finance. In 1962, $132,295,800 were spent on tickets for the Loterie Nationale. About 20 per cent of the sales money is kept by the Ministry of Finance: The rest is paid out in prizes.

Ghana

A national lottery, overseas sports pools, betting on horse races, sweepstakes, cards, and dice are all popular gambles (though many card games are illegal). In June 1960, Ghana's first casino (the Casino Africa) opened at the Ambassador Hotel in Accra, under American management.

Great Britain

Most British gamblers put their money on horse races, greyhound races, and various forms of numbers games. The weekly football pools dominate the last category, which would also include bingo and premium bonds. (The latter are government-issued bonds: The interest goes into a fund from which prizes or "premiums" are drawn.)

Gambling activities are controlled by the 1960 Betting and Gaming Act. Briefly, the act authorizes the issuing of permits to bookmakers and the granting of betting-office licenses at the discretion of the local authorities. (Totalizator betting was made legal in 1928.)

The act also legalized gambling for profit in clubs, provided that the gambling is carried out as an activity of the club; that apart from any annual subscription for membership, the only other payment is a fixed sum paid and determined before gambling begins; that the club is not of a temporary nature, and that all gamblers are members or *bona fide* guests; that the chances in the game are equally favorable to all players and/or that the game is conducted in such a way as to be equally favorable to all players; and that no toll or cut is levied on the stakes for the benefit of the promoters. The act mentions no game by name, so promoters must look to the general provisions to define the terms of the games they organize.

Under the 1960 act, gambling machines are legal provided that no person under 18 has any access to them (this keeps the machines out of shops, restaurants, and so on); that not more than two machines are available for play in any one building; that the stake is no more than the equivalent of seven cents; and that the stakes are disposed of as winnings to a player or for purposes other than for private gain.

In 1962 betting on the horses (through totalizators and bookmakers on and off the course) amounted to the equivalent of $1,512,000,000; on football pools to $239,120,000; on greyhounds to $322,000,000; on bingo to $84,000,000; on premium bonds to $43,120,000. Twelve million people fill in football coupons each week; after the 1960 act was passed, bookmakers' betting shops opened at the rate of 100 a week. The total turnover on all forms of legal gambling at present has been estimated at about $2,400,000,000—about $50 a year per adult member of the population of Great Britain.

At present only money spent on football pools and bets at greyhound tracks is liable to be taxed: The revenue from the existing betting duties (33 per cent of the money staked on football pools, 11 per cent of the greyhound totalizator stakes, license fees from bookmakers on greyhound tracks) is not more than $112,000,000.

The 1960 act led to the opening of several casinos: The largest of these is the Metropole, at Brighton. Chemin-de-fer is the main game played. The only clubs to operate roulette on the continental style (i.e., with a zero) are Quents and Crockford's in London. (Roulette is only legal if the chances are equally favorable to all players: To comply with the law, Quents and Crockford's give every player a chance to hold the bank.) A recent innovation at Crockford's is chemin-de-fer: In the club's first four months of operation, the "chemmy" tables produced a gross profit of $494,400.

Greece

A committee of five government-appointed officials has the responsibility of supervising gambling. This committee divides all gambling games into three categories:

Mechanical: This includes all automatic games of the amusement-arcade type, like pinball machines. Once permission has been obtained, these games can be played for money in any café or club.

Mixed: Most card games are included in this category together with a few mechanical games. These games can be played only in special gambling rooms.

Games of chance: These are strictly forbidden, except in licensed casinos and clubs. All these games come under the jurisdiction of the Minister of the Interior and clubs must apply to him for permission to run them. The Minister makes his decision after consultation with a specialist committee of five.

A state-sponsored football pool has been running since December 1958. Gambling is on football matches played on Sunday afternoons. Of the money paid by participants, five per cent goes to the coupon sellers, 45 per cent to prizes and running costs, and 50 per cent to sporting organizations.

Greece also has a national lottery with five drawings each year. And horse racing is a popular gamble: At Athens there are races on Wednesdays and Saturdays, and betting can be done through the totalizator or off the course with bookmakers. Greyhound racing and private lotteries are illegal.

Haiti

There are *maisons de jeux* in most towns, and a large casino in Port-au-Prince. The national lottery attracts a good deal of betting, and private lotteries flourish in many towns, with ticket sellers touting at street corners. In these private lotteries, almost anything can become a prize—sometimes a hen, a goat, a pig, or a cow. Cockfighting, and gambling on it, is widely popular.

Hungary

The State Bank and the National Savings Bank run two kinds of gambling activities—football pools (*toto*) and a lottery (*lotto*). Toto was first organized in 1947, and during the past 15 years some 500,000,000 tickets have been sold. Lotto is even more popular: Since its introduction in 1957, more than 4,000,000 tickets have been sold every week at the equivalent of about 28 cents each. (The state takes 50 per cent of the price of all lotto and toto tickets.)

Apartments are popular prizes: At a lotto drawing on October 7, 1960, the first prizes were two two-roomed apartments, a one-roomed apartment, a two-roomed family house, and a car. There are also various types of lotteries using bank deposit accounts, and investors may win money or prizes instead of gaining interest on their money. The most popular of these (gambling on savings books) allots 25 prizes per quarter per 1000 books.

Individuals are not permitted to organize gambling activities and even in the case of authorized lotteries (to serve the public interest) money prizes may not be offered. Card games are very popular and in some cafés cards may be played for money, subject to safeguards (i.e., betting limits) that eliminate the possibility of heavy gambling.

India

Betting on horse racing is the main gambling activity of India, and race tracks are found in all the main cities. Card and dice games and betting on dog races are also popular. Gambling houses are illegal, and anyone caught running one is liable to a fine of the equivalent of $21, or to one month's imprisonment. Police can arrest (without a warrant) anyone found playing for money with cards, dice, or counters, or anyone found setting any birds or animals to fight in a public street.

Irish Republic

Gambling is controlled by the gaming and lotteries act of 1956. All games in which the odds between the banker and the player are unequal, and all slot machines, are forbidden. Side-show games (costing the players the equivalent of seven cents) at circuses and fairs are permitted provided that no player can win more than the equivalent of $1.40. Gambling games can only be played on licensed premises.

There are no football pools or casinos. Lotteries can be organized, providing it can be proved that they are for charitable or philanthropic purposes. The total value of prizes must not exceed $1400.

The Irish Hospitals Sweepstakes is the main gambling enterprise, and its tickets are sold (often illegally) throughout the world. (The Irish Sweepstakes was first held in 1930 to improve the financial situation of the hospitals.) Two thirds of the profit goes to the hospitals, one third to the Ministry for Local Government and Public Health. In 1962, 7099 prizes were awarded, totaling about $6,000,000. Winnings are tax free.

Bookmaking on horse and dog races is legal in Ireland: 540 bookmakers' licenses were issued in 1960.

Israel

There is some pool betting on football matches, though not a great deal. Lotteries are banned in principle, but (with state permission) may be held for charity. There is no legal prohibition of private betting, though legislation concerning this is under discussion at the time of writing (1963). Gambling houses are not allowed.

Gambling activities are controlled by the Criminal Code Ordinance of 1936, which states that anyone setting up a casino, a gaming house, or a lottery is liable to prosecution. Three organizations are permitted to hold regular lotteries: They are the "Mif'al Hapayis," the "Red Shield of David" (which corresponds to the Red Cross), and the "Committee for the Soldier." The most important of these is the Mif'al Hapayis, a non-profit-making company sponsored by the government and local authorities: It runs a weekly lottery, and the net proceeds are allotted to local authorities for building hospitals, dispensaries, and schools. Disabled people are employed to sell lottery tickets.

Italy

In general, gambling is forbidden in any public place, or in any club or private house. But in places like San Remo, Campione, Venice, and St. Vincent (in the Aosta valley) casinos are permitted. These are subject to strict controls—and to an annual ·governmental tax that is the equivalent of about $96,000. Roulette, *trente-et-quarante,* and baccarat are played.

A state-controlled lottery is drawn each week. Winning numbers are published by the press and announced over the wireless. In 1962, a total of about

$81,000,000 was gambled on the lottery, and of this about $37,000,000 were paid out in prizes. Four other lotteries are organized and administered directly by the state. (These are controlled by a decree of August 4, 1955.) In 1962 about $4,500,000 was spent on these lotteries and $1,500,000 were given out in prizes.

Betting in pools on football and horse racing is controlled by a legislative decree of April 1948. These pools are organized by the state. The only exceptions are for those connected with sports—such as *Totocalcio* and *Totip*—which are controlled, respectively, by the Italian National Olympic Committee and by the National Union for the improvement of the breeding of horses.

Italian law permits totalizator betting on horse and dog racing, which is controlled by the authority of Public Safety, according to a law passed in May 1940.

Japan

Most forms of private gambling are forbidden, though the sale of government-sponsored lottery tickets and betting on race and cycle tracks has been legalized. (There is also legal gambling on motorboat racing, and on motorcycle racing.) More money is bet on bicycle racing (the equivalent of about $165,000,000 annually) than on any other type of officially sanctioned racing, and authorized cycle tracks are found in all major cities. (Sometimes as many as 12 races take place daily on every track.) Local government authorities sponsor these races to raise money for the construction of houses and schools. Income derived from gambling on horse races is spent on the improvement of horse breeding and the importing of thoroughbreds.

It has been estimated that bookmakers earn more than $16,500,000 a year, despite the fact that private bookmaking was banned in 1955. The total amount of money gambled in 1961 on horse racing was about $93,300,800; of this, about $76,729,000 was paid out in prizes.

The game *pachinko* was introduced to Japan in 1950: Soon after, authorized pachinko gambling houses began to attract many gamblers.

Kenya

According to the 1954 Report on Betting, Gaming, and Lotteries, gambling in Kenya is not excessive. Betting is principally on horse racing, but since there are only 23 days of horse racing in Kenya each year (apart from some small-scale meetings) the volume of betting is usually no more than the equivalent of about $180,000 a year. (Money is also bet, however, on overseas racing.) Bookmakers must be licensed by the Betting Control Board.

Football pools and dog racing are both illegal. Lotteries, though legal, are run on a comparatively small scale. In 1949, for example, the total expenditure on lotteries was only about $150,000. The main lotteries are organized by a social service league and a youth league. Tickets for several overseas lotteries (such as the Irish Hospitals Sweepstakes) are also sold.

Luxembourg

All kinds of gambling were forbidden by a law of 1903, which is still in force. It is also illegal to operate a gambling premises, to permit gambling on your premises, or to advertise gambling in any way (which includes advertising overseas gambling).

Malaya

Betting on horse racing, lotteries, and numbers games, slot machines, poker and *canasta,* dominoes and dice, are all popular forms of gambling—though many of them are illegal. In 1952 all lotteries were declared illegal (except when run for charitable purposes and authorized by the Financial Secretary). In 1953 an act was passed banning common gambling houses and other forms of public gambling. Police officers were authorized to arrest anyone found in a suspected gambling place.

It was also made an offense to bet with a bookmaker or to act as a bookmaker on the premises of any club. Betting on horse races now takes place at the turf clubs of Singapore, Kuala Lumpur, Ipoh, and Penang, and members of these clubs may bet legally through totalizators.

Chap ji kee is a very popular gambling game in Singapore; one estimate gives the daily expenditure as the equivalent of about $250,000. In this game the promoter chooses a name or a number (which the bettor must guess) from a list and places it in a locked box. He then gives the bettors a riddle, which is supposed to serve as a clue. Winners are paid at 100 to 1. The numbers game is also extremely popular and results are published in the daily press. Players can win 700 times their original stake (of 20 cents).

Mexico

An act of 1947 made public gambling a federal offense. This law has been rigidly enforced, and penalties for infringing it include prison sentences from one month to three years, and fines from the equivalent of about $40 to $800. Raffles and state lotteries are permitted, as is betting on races and sports events (when carried out under official supervision). Most horse racing takes place on tracks in and around Mexico City.

New Zealand

Off-track betting on horse racing has been legal since 1950. Official figures for 1957 show that whereas the on-track betting turnover was the equivalent of $64,680,000, off-track betting brought in $65,240,000. The only legal way to make an off-track bet is through the Totalization Agency Board. (There are over 300 of these agents throughout the country.) Five per cent of the gross totalizator off-track takings goes to the state.

Lotteries may be run providing they are licensed by the Ministry of Internal Affairs (and providing they are for educational or welfare purposes). All casinos and common gaming houses are illegal, and police are entitled to search suspected premises. Betting on sports or athletic events is also illegal, as is private betting in public : Offenders are liable to be imprisoned for three months, or to be fined $280. In 1959, gambling on bingo was made legal, and is now one of the country's most popular gambles.

Nigeria

Lotteries, sweepstakes, cards, dice, and other gambling games are all widely played in Nigeria without any legislative control. Football-pool promoters, however, must obtain licenses. Betting at the race tracks is common in the west of Nigeria, but not in the east. The western region also runs a state-controlled lottery of its own.

Norway

Football pools, horse races, and the state-sponsored lottery draw the major amount of gambling money. In 1952 the equivalent of about $6,850,000 was gambled on the state lottery : In 1962 the sum had almost trebled—to approximately $18,000,000.

Peru

Gambling is mainly on horse races (held on Saturdays and Sundays throughout the year at the *Hipodromo de Monterrico*), cockfighting (held on Sundays and holidays in various local arenas), and on lotteries. A sweepstake, called *La Polla*, is also run every Sunday by the Jockey Club.

The Lima lottery is drawn every month, and the first prize is usually the equivalent of about $40,000. Special drawings are also held at Christmas and on the national holidays (July 28-30), when the first prize is greatly increased. The lottery is government-controlled, and proceeds go to hospitals and national charities. In addition there are the Arequipa, Cuzco, Trujillo, and Huancayo lotteries. All these pay weekly prizes of about $4000. The amount invested weekly on horse racing is about $262,500.

Most private gambling games are illegal, though dice games are played in many private clubs. Bingo is organized legally by public welfare institutions.

Poland

The *Totalizator Sportowy* is the main gambling enterprise : It has 17 main branches, and 1733 sub-branches. This organization controls the *Toto Lotek* (the national lottery) and the football pools. The total income from bets on the toto lotek in 1962 was the equivalent of about $40,000,000. Fifty per cent of the total amount staked goes in prizes. The rest (after deduction of working costs, management expenses, etc.) goes into a sports fund.

Organizations, institutions, and commercial enterprises also run small lotteries. (These require a state permit.) There is also a lottery system organized on bank savings accounts; prizes take the place of regular interest. The depositor chooses the size of the account he wishes to have according to the prize he wishes to' gamble for. A form of the numbers game has also gained a national following.

All horse racing is state-controlled.

Portugal

Gambling is controlled by the Games Inspection Council, which supervises the running of casinos and submits proposals to the Minister of the Interior for the regulation of gambling.

A law passed in 1956 legalized on-track totalizator gambling at horse races, and a law of 1958 permitted the operation of casinos in specific localities. (There is a particularly large casino, open all the year, at Estoril.) Football pools and sports pools are controlled by the Santa Casa de Misericordia, which also holds the monopoly on the national lottery.

South Africa

The only legalized form of gambling is on horse races, and this is regulated by different "ordinances" in the various provinces. All bets must be made through totalizators on licensed race courses.

Despite their illegality, most card and dice games are popular. A gambling act of 1939 declared pin-tables, slot machines, and lotteries to be illegal. And the Sports Pools Act of 1949 laid down that "nobody should begin or have any financial interest in any organization conducting a sports pool."

All colored people are forbidden to gamble in any way.

Sweden

Gambling is chiefly on horse races, football matches, and the national lottery. Horse pools are run by the organizers of a number of horse and trotting tracks. The most popular of these pools is the "V.5 pool" (the "v" is short for *vad*, which means "a wager") in which bettors aim to back the winners in five races.

The total turnover for betting on horse races in Sweden in 1962 was the equivalent of about $77,000,000. This money was placed with off-track bookmakers and through totalizators. (On-track bookmaking is not permitted.)

In 1934, a special authority was set up and granted a monopoly for organizing betting on football matches. Now most of the profits go directly into the state treasury. The total turnover of money bet on football matches in 1961 was about $38,400,000. During the winter, betting is on British football matches.

A Swedish national lottery ticket costs $2.80. In 1961, $55,609,000 were spent on lottery tickets.

Switzerland

It is illegal to gamble on horse racing, or to organize a private lottery, or to operate a casino; nor are any gambling machines permitted. Football pools are legal, and lotteries are organized in the various cantons. But they must have government authorization, and all proceeds must go to charity. Lottery winnings are tax free.

Boule was made legal in Switzerland in 1924. Stakes are limited to the equivalent of 46 cents. The federal government takes a quarter of all profits from boule and uses the money to provide help to the victims of national catastrophes (such as floods, fires, or train crashes). Between 1928 and 1954, the government collected about $1,840,000 from boule taxes.

Tanganyika

Nearly all gambles for money are illegal. Raffles and lotteries are permitted, providing the organizers obtain permission from the commissioner of police. Football pools are also legal, but bets must be made through a "licensed agent of the U.K. football pools firms, domiciled in Tanganyika." A pools tax of 10 per cent of the total stake money was instituted in 1961 : It is estimated that the government receives an income of the equivalent of approximately $14,000 yearly from this tax.

Thailand

Gambling is regulated by a gaming act of 1935, which outlawed the organization of any gambling enterprise without a government license. The penalty for violating this law is a fine equaling $100, or one year's imprisonment.

Gambling is permitted on 15 specified games, including cockfighting, fish fighting, horse racing, lotteries, *mah-jongg,* and dominoes. Gambling is not permitted on 41 specified games, among which are slot machines, baccarat, bingo, poker, and games involving cruelty to animals (such as tortoise racing, in which fires are lit on the animals' backs to increase their speed).

Union of Soviet Socialist Republics

By an act of 1928 all private gambling was forbidden in Russia. The state operates a lottery, and organizes public betting through totalizators at horse races. The tote makes an annual profit of the equivalent of about $280,000. Off-track betting is forbidden. All bets are to win only (horses cannot be backed each way) and bets must be made in units of 50 cents, $1, and $2. Tote odds on a winner are usually even money or 2 to 1.

Russian newspapers carry no racing information, and bettors have to be guided by a race card giving the names of the horses (and some information on past performance) and details of the jockeys' abilities.

United Arab Republic

On-track betting on horse racing and betting on pigeon shooting (when these events are held on authorized premises) is permitted in Egypt. Gambling casinos exist, but Arab nationals are not permitted to enter them : Would-be bettors must produce evidence of foreign nationality. Backgammon is played in street cafés, but baccarat, bingo, chemin-de-fer, and canasta are among the games prohibited in clubs and public establishments. Anyone breaking the gambling laws is liable to a heavy fine or to imprisonment for one to three years.

United States of America

Gambling laws in America vary from state to state. In general, though, games of chance for money, gambling establishments, etc., are illegal. But on-track pari-mutuel betting on horse races is legal in most states. And there are exceptions: Practically all forms of gambling are legal in Nevada; New Hampshire established a legal state lottery in April 1963 (to raise money for public schools); bingo and raffles (under strict state control) are legal in New Jersey, New York, Colorado, Nebraska, and Alaska; and most states permit small-scale raffles held for charity, and often carnival games for small stakes.

The exact amount of money spent annually on illegal gambling in the United States is not known. However, it is certain that the American people spend almost as much on gambling as on medical care or education. America's Attorney General Robert Kennedy recently gave as a rock-bottom estimate a gross turnover of $7,000,000,000. Other experts have put the figure as high as $50,000,000,000.

Most of the money is bet on horse racing through illegal bookies. The extent of the crooked bookmaker's business is indicated by an estimate made by the magazine *Nation* in 1959: The annual racing turnover in New York City alone was given as $1,330,000,000. This is five times the sum of money bet *legally* in the same year at all the New York tracks and makes the illicit bookmaking business rank as the largest single industry in New York. It has been estimated that there are about 30,000 bookies in New York.

Police investigations show that illegal bookmaking is big business all over the nation: In Florida bookies handle around $250,000 in bets daily. The records of an Indiana bookmaker (according to Robert Kennedy) showed that he had taken a total of $1,156,000 in bets over a three-day period; a Chicago bookie's records showed that he had taken a total of $6,400,000 in bets in one year; a Tennessee bookie had taken $1,689,000 in five months.

The big illegal gamblers often use their profits to invest in other criminal enterprises such as narcotics, bootlegging, and prostitution, and to keep the law at bay with bribes. In 1951, the Kefauver Senate Committee hearings on crime found that one gambling ring in Philadelphia was paying an annual bribe of $2,000,000 for police protection. (Some gamblers pay up to $3500 to have their police records altered.)

A conservative estimate has placed the illegal policy (or numbers) game in the $1,000,000,000 a year class. (According to Robert Kennedy, one Pennsylvania policy operator collected $587,000 in seven months.) In 1957, nearly 12,000 people were convicted on policy-game charges.

Slot machines are legal in five American states—Nevada, Montana, Washington (in private clubs), Idaho, and Maryland. It is estimated that in 1961 more than 2000 licensed slot machines were operating in more than 200 establishments in Maryland. In Maryland's largest casino, the "Pot of Gold," 233 machines are housed in one building and in Charles County alone, the gross receipts for slot machines (in 1959) totaled $4,544,000.

In 1962, three new gambling laws came into effect : Interstate gambling was made a federal crime, the transmission of bets between states by wire or telephone was made a felony, and the interstate transportation of betting paraphernalia (policy slips, slot machines, and so on) was also made a felony. As a result of these laws, the nation's leading bookies' wire services (which communicated the latest race results and odds to bookmakers all over the country) were forced to close down.

At the time of writing (1963) the New York City authorities are proposing to legalize (and tax) off-track betting on horse races.

West Germany

The state lottery attracts the greatest amount of gambling money. But there is also wide-spread betting on horse races and football pools, as well as in casinos and slot-machine halls. In 1961, state-run and state-authorized gambling enterprises brought in the equivalent of about $425,000,000. This sum (10 times the amount gambled legally in 1950) yielded the government a tax revenue of $71,250,000. Of this $57,500,000 were derived from the lotteries, $6,000,000 from the football pools, $5,000,000 from totalizators, and $2,750,000 from the bookmakers.

There are more than 1000 lottery agencies in West Germany that sell tickets for the two main lotteries, the North West German lottery (with 60 annual drawings) and the South West German lottery (with 84 annual drawings). Only half of the money spent on the lotteries (or on the football pools) is paid out in winnings. Of the remaining half, a third goes to athletic, cultural, and social organizations, a third to state revenue, and a third toward administrative costs. In 1959 the sum of $12,500,000 was given to sports organizations and $6,250,000 to social and cultural enterprises.

By laws of 1922, 1933, and 1944, it is illegal to organize private lotteries. Anyone attempting to do so is liable to two years' imprisonment and the loss of civil rights.

West Germany has more than 13,000 betting shops where bets can be laid on horse races and football matches. (In Bavaria alone, there are 1600 of these shops.) West Germany also has many gambling halls (called *spielhallen*) that contain slot machines, and has many small casinos where some card games can be played. Frankfurt, for example, has seven spielhallen and four small casinos. In Frankfurt there are about 2000 gambling machines, which pay the local government some $250,000 a year in taxes.

Index

Page numbers in *italics* refer to illustrations.

Illustration credits